The Boy from Boskovice

Also by the author

Love and War in the WRNS

The Boy from Boskovice

A Father's Secret Life

Vicky Unwin

unbound

First published in 2021

Unbound
T C Group, Level 1 Devonshire House, One Mayfair Place, London W1J 8AJ
www.unbound.com

Text Design by PDQ Digital Media Solutions Ltd

A CIP record for this book is available from the British Library

ISBN 978-1-78352-906-3 (hardback)
ISBN 978-1-78352-907-0 (ebook)

Photo and text credits
Images and translated text reproduced in this work are the author's copyright except for the following:

Ungar with Pinner and Krojanker © Krojanker estate
Hermann Ungar in 1928 [plate section] © ullsteinbild /TopFoto
Bonnie & me © John Nguyen
Louise © Christopher James

Extract from from A Tourist in Africa by Evelyn Waugh
(Penguin Books 2011) © Evelyn Waugh 1960

Evelyn Waugh letter © Waugh Estate

While every effort has been made to trace owners of copyright material produced herein, the publisher would like to apologise for any omissions and will be pleased to incorporate missing acknowledgements in any further edition.

ISBN 978-1-78352-906-3 (hardback)
ISBN 978-1-78352-907-0 (ebook)

Printed in Great Britain by CPI

1 3 5 7 9 8 6 4 2

Contents

'When he was good he was very, very good, but when he was bad he was horrid'

(with apologies to Henry Wadsworth Longfellow)

'Something to laugh at and something to make you cry … that's what I like best'

Tomy Ungar, aged 5, from *Tomy Helps to Write* by Hermann Ungar

For all my family, dead and alive –
but especially for Louise, Tommy, Sasha and Bonnie:
this is your story

FAMILY TREE OF UNGAR AND STRANSKY FAMILIES*

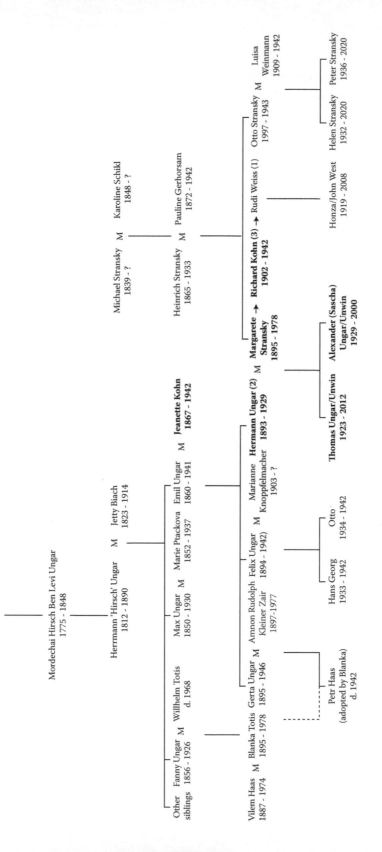

*For reason of space, only those mentioned in this book are included

Names in bold occur on other family trees

UNWIN FAMILY TREE

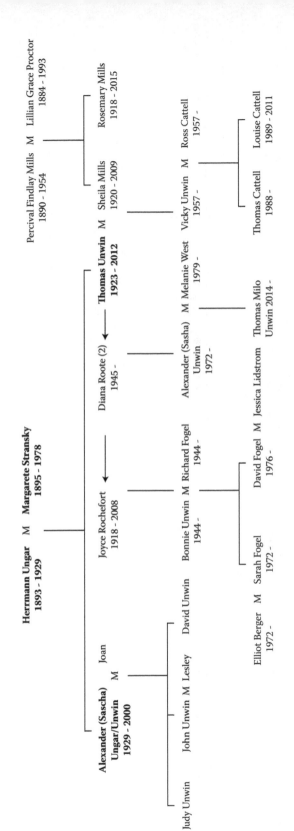

Names in bold occur on other family trees

KOHN FAMILY TREE

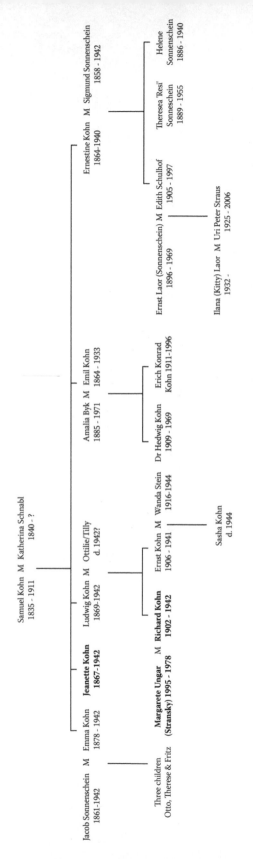

Samuel Kohn M Katherina Schnabl
1835 - 1911   1840 - ?

Jacob Sonnenschein M Emma Kohn   Jeanette Kohn   Ludwig Kohn M Ottilie/Tilly   Amalia Byk M Emil Kohn   Ernestine Kohn M Sigmund Sonnenschein
1861-1942   1878 - 1942   1867-1942   1869-1942   d. 1942?   1885 - 1971   1864 - 1933   1864-1940   1858 - 1940

Three children   Margarete Ungar M Richard Kohn   Ernst Kohn M Wanda Stein   Dr Hedwig Kohn   Erich Konrad   Ernst Laor (Sonnenschein) M Edith Schulhof   Theresea 'Resi'   Helene
Otto, Therese & Fritz   (Stransky) 1995 - 1978   1902 - 1942   1906 - 1941   1916-1944   1909 - 1969   Kohn 1911-1996   1896 - 1969   1905 - 1997   Sonneschein   Sonnenschein
1889 - 1955   1886 - 1940

Sasha Kohn   Ilana (Kitty) Laor M Uri Peter Straus
d. 1944   1932 -   1925 - 2006

Names in bold occur on other family trees

FOREWORD

Dar es Salaam 1963

I was about five or six years old when we met the new Czech Ambassador. 'I'll teach you how to say hello to him in Czech,' said Dad. With great aplomb I marched up to him and said, '*Vilis mi prdel*'. The Ambassador gave a huge guffaw and my father was almost beside himself with glee. 'What's so funny?' I asked. 'Ha-ha-ha,' he chortled, 'you just told the Ambassador to "kiss my arse."'

Who was this man who could play such a childish and cruel joke on his daughter? At that time my father was permanent secretary for foreign affairs in the newly independent Tanganyika. But he was much more than that. I was an only child and 'Daddy's girl' and remember my father as the largest person in my life, dwarfing my mother with his absolute devotion and the way he spoiled me.

He encouraged me to collude with him against her – I was instructed not to 'tell' when he let me drive the car sitting between his knees, or when we made a fire in the middle of the game park and had breakfast surrounded by herds of buffalo, or when we visited my various 'nice aunties' when my mother was sick with TB.

My parents had met in Germany in 1945 at the end of the war; he was attached to Royal Naval Intelligence in Kiel and she was a Wren. They married in Durham in 1946. Dad was an idealist who had become a self-confessed socialist during the war and wanted to make the world a better place. But his public persona was in complete contrast to how he lived his private life and dealt with his family. As I grew older I found it increasingly difficult to understand how this outwardly altruistic character could coexist with a father who was not the man he appeared to be, but was, rather, bad-tempered, cruel and sometimes violent. It was only when he retired from the United Nations Development Programme (UNDP) in 1997 that I began to examine these contradictions.

By then I felt sorry for my father. His days consisted of reading *The Times* and the *Daily Telegraph* and writing letters to the editor, usually about the politics of development or pertinent issues of the day. He relished complaining to phone companies and other service providers, often masquerading as Admiral Unwin – he found that produced results – and enjoyed walking his dogs. After they died it appeared to me that he did nothing but sit in his study in The Fort, his Somerset home; and then in 2001 he developed Parkinson's, his legs black and bloated with cellulitis, his hands and speech shaky.

Long since divorced and remarried, he still visited my mother now and then. She lived in neighbouring Devon and, despite all the lingering acrimony between them, they would reminisce about old times and mutual friends over a good East African fish curry, prepared by my mum. Like me, my mother just could not understand how such an active and intelligent man could sink to such depths of depression and introspection.

By this time it was obvious to me that my father was not the man everyone called 'good old Tom', the perfect Englishman, former colonial officer and UN diplomat, with his pipe, monocle and received pronunciation; the handsome charmer and flatterer who was always the centre of attention at any social gathering, bursting with so much self-confidence and bonhomie that he fooled just about everyone. A man who was simultaneously the adoring father of my childhood and a misogynistic bully of a husband, whose temper and dark side alienated him from my mother, me and, later, his grandchildren. A man who was responsible for the biggest betrayal of all – the betrayal of a child by their father. It was not until I began to delve into his past that the impact of his destructive behaviour and its effect on all of us became clear.

For Tom Unwin was also Tomas Ungar, the boy from Boskovice, a small town in Moravia, a teenager who left Czechoslovakia shortly before the Second World War for a new life and a new identity in England. The young man who became Tom Unwin and achieved a very British respectability by denying his roots and abandoning his family until his past caught up with him.

Part 1

Who was my father?

CHAPTER 1:
NOT REALLY BRITISH
AT ALL

I was born in 1957 in Dar es Salaam, the capital city of what is now Tanzania. When I was five my father took me to an amateur performance of *The Bartered Bride* by Bedřich Smetana, the father of Czech music, at the Oyster Bay Primary School in Dar. It was then that he first told me I was Czech and that our real name was Ungar. I was so taken with the show that I began to call myself Mařenka after the main character and told my father I would change my name back to Ungar when I was 'grown up'.

That was the sum total of my knowledge about my father's origins and it was to take me decades to unravel his history.

Tomas Michal Ungar was born in Prague in 1923, the son of a Czech diplomat and rising author Hermann Ungar, whose family came from Boskovice in Moravia. 'My pride and joy is my son Tomas,' Hermann wrote, and he brings his little boy to life in 1929 in a short story called 'Tomy Helps to Write', first published in 1929 in the *Prager Tageblatt*; this is my father's translation that I discovered among his papers:

Tomas, known as Tomy, five years old, has written a story to help his father. Father complies with Tomy's wish and sends the story to a 'paper for grown-ups.' But one wish of Tomy's Father can't comply with: Tomy asks his father not to say who wrote his story: 'If they know it's written by a little boy, they won't pay as much.'

I make use of the opportunity to tell you something about Tomy just as it comes into my head. Tomy is just like other children of his age who are healthy and normal. ...

So: Tomy is a little numbskull on whom any attempt to bring him up properly is wasted. In any case I have given up trying. I leave it to fate to decide what is to become of him. I admit openly that I envy Tomy his unyielding nature. He is not to be deflected from his aim: there is no bending, no being-got-down, nothing stops him doing what he has made up his mind to [sic]. A little while ago I heard an infernal row coming from the nursery, not the usual daily row, and I knew at once this was something special as I heard the sound of breaking glass. I rushed to help. I saw immediately, without waiting to ask questions, what was up. He was cross at being disciplined by his superiors and so my ever hopeful son smashed the pane of a glass door with a building brick. Without saying a word I put him across the table. I was as furious as only a grown-up can be and beat Tomy accordingly. I only interrupted this educational process to catch my breath and to ask my son, 'Will you do it again?' The little one replied, steadfast to the end, time and time again, 'Yes!' His eyes were full of tears but he suffered the execution without uttering a sound. And as he – rightly I fear – does not take me seriously as an educator he had forgiven me my folly by the time I had finished beating him.

The other traits Hermann alluded to in this story about his young son were his 'love of the female sex' and 'Daddy's typewriter'.

Tomy taught himself how to type and 'wrote daily letters to his grandparents, friends and acquaintances' – a lifelong habit, as shown by the mountains of correspondence to me and my mother.

'Nothing stops him doing what he has made up his mind to,' Hermann wrote prophetically of little Tomy. He is impressed by his young son's wisdom in wanting to write 'something to laugh at and something to make you cry ... that's what I like best'. He 'stops and thinks, just like Daddy,' and then writes his 'big exciting tale ... a short, simple story for us grown-ups':

> *There was wunc a poor widow hoo had a chaild wich ranawy from hoam and stret into the wood in the wood was a bit of the ocean but the I chaild did not see it and fell in this chaild wich was in the forest and fell in the water only looked at clouds and swallows for it was johnny headinair.*

I still have the battered copy of *Struwwelpeter* that he bought me, with its story 'Johnny Head-in-the-Air' that young Tomy referred to. I also have the typewriter.

As a child I knew nothing of Hermann Ungar, my grandfather, except that he had been a neurotic man; so much so, according to my father, that he had died of hypochondria. 'He was like the lad who cried wolf,' he used to say. I knew the story about the shepherd boy who cried wolf once too often and got eaten because in the end no one believed him. It was like this with my grandfather. Hermann was always sickly and complaining about one ailment or another.

But my father never spoke any more about Hermann Ungar or about life in Prague, not even with his widowed mother. Hermann was uncelebrated in our family, so that when I, as a young

German-speaking publisher, grew curious about him and started asking questions, there were no answers. I was not even aware that Hermann's books had been translated into several languages.

All I knew was that in 1939 my grandmother sent my father to London to improve his English and followed soon after with his younger brother. It was only when Dad retired to Somerset in 1997 that his Czech background began to surface. In his dingy, cluttered study, with peeling brown Anaglypta and shabby rickety chairs, among the myriad photographs that shared the walls with his various accolades, two framed pictures of his parents suddenly appeared.

I had never seen them before. 'Where did these come from?' I asked. 'Oh,' he said airily, 'I found them somewhere and had them enlarged.' The black and white portrait of Hermann shows an intelligent-looking man with little round glasses, a high forehead and combed-back dark hair, the epitome, it seemed to me, of a 1920s Jewish intellectual. The more I looked at it, the more certain I became that my father was Jewish. Why else would a Czech family leave Prague in 1939? But my father was evasive when I asked him, and vehemently denied that the family was Jewish. He told me that they had converted to Catholicism 'way back', to avoid the pogroms. He refused to say more.

CHAPTER 2:
A SURPRISE VISITOR

In the summer of 1997 I received a telephone call at my home in Belsize Park, North London. The caller, a woman, sounded American. 'Is that Vicky? I am Helen Stransky, your father's cousin. I am in London for a Kindertransport reunion and would like to come and see you.' I had no idea my father had any cousins, but knew that Stransky was his mother's maiden name, so I invited her over. I didn't even know what Kindertransport was.

A few days later Helen arrived. She was a small woman in her mid-sixties and wore a red beret jauntily on her head. As we sat down to a family tea – I was forty by this time and married with two children, my son and daughter just home from school – she explained how she and her brother Peter, aged four and two respectively, had left Prague on one of the special trains organised by Sir Nicholas Winton, a British humanitarian who organised special trains for Jewish children in 1939 to escape the Nazis. He rescued 669 children from Prague, including Helen and Peter. Her parents, Otto Stransky (my grandmother's brother) and Luisa (née Weinmann), could not get out and, she told me, probably both died in the death camps, along with Pauline, my father's grandmother, for Helen never heard from them again.

She and her brother, Peter, had eventually gone to Canada with her other grandmother and her Uncle Richard, her mother's brother, which was where she grew up. Uncle Richard was, according to Helen, an unpleasant man who put them into care. Her first foster home was loving, but Richard moved them to new families, where the man of the house abused Helen. She now lived in Jerusalem, working as a radiographer, and was desperate to attend the Kindertransport reunion as she, like so many children from that generation, felt she owed Sir Nicholas her life.

The reason Helen said she wanted to see me was because my father refused to have anything to do with her after the war, in case she revealed our Jewish heritage. Later, he also refused to contact her nephew when he was studying in London, despite Helen's entreaties. Undaunted, Helen had found my address in the telephone book. Now, here she was.

Helen and Peter Stransky, my father's cousins who were Kindertransport children

My grandmother, whom I called Nana, had emigrated to Canada after the war with her younger son Sascha, now known as Alec. She had also refused to allow any contact between Alec and the young Helen and Peter in case they told him about their Jewish heritage.

I was appalled by my father's and Nana's callous attitudes towards their closest relatives. How could they – and he in particular – behave with such cruelty? They had been refugees themselves and, in addition, my father worked for the UN, safeguarder of migrants and human rights. It was hard to even begin to understand.

I felt I had to confront him.

Shortly after Helen's visit, my father and I were having one of our rare evenings together in London. We went to Rules in Covent Garden, his favourite restaurant. Dad revelled in the customs and old-fashioned apparel of his adopted homeland – like the pipe and monocle – and Rules, that bastion of Edwardian respectability with its wood panelling, plush banquettes, traditional British menu and frock-coated waiters, fitted the bill perfectly.

The tables were close together, I recall, and Rules seemed more like a trap for American tourists than a quiet place to have dinner and navigate the difficult conversation ahead. We ordered dinner and drinks: wine for me, beer for Dad (he always drank Beck's beer). Then there was nothing for it but to get straight to the point.

'Dad, your cousin Helen Stransky came to see me, she just turned up on my doorstep. She told me that you and Nana both refuse to have anything to do with her and that it's because you are afraid that she will reveal the truth about you being Jewish. And you know I guessed this some time ago, I have been asking questions – but you have never admitted it. You don't have to be a rocket scientist to work out that your flight from Prague was from the Nazis. Why else would anyone leave in 1939? Why have you kept it secret for all this time? I don't understand – it's nothing to be ashamed of – but I simply want to know the truth.'

The twinkle in his eye disappeared and his expression changed to one of great sadness and contemplation. He thought for a long time before speaking, and even then would not look me in the eye. His boyhood stammer returned in moments of great stress, as it did now in his thoughtful reply.

'When Mother arrived in England she told us that being Jewish was the cause of all the pain we had endured, the reason why we had to leave Prague and give up everything – house, money, relatives, status – and become beggars in a strange country, and that our origins were never to be spoken about again. She was worried that if Germany invaded England the same fate would befall the Jews and she was not prepared to risk it. We went along with it, we really had no choice, she was, as you know, not one to be disobeyed. She managed to produce some proof that we were Catholics and even had us christened before we arrived in England. Actually, we thought it was for the best. We had not been brought up in the faith, we were not even circumcised, so there seemed little point in hanging on to it.' The boys were both fair, like their mother, with freckles, so the deception was easy to perpetrate.

I felt no sense of elation that he had confirmed my suspicions, just an overwhelming sadness that his secret had been so carefully suppressed over the years. Dad admitted that he had not told my mother either, but it was extraordinary that she had not guessed. I later discovered some letters they wrote to each other where he was at great pains to joke that his big nose was 'not Jewish.' He felt the more he was able to make fun of the issue, the more he would be believed. He was never one for political correctness and this was often in contrast to his so-called socialist values and denouncing of racism.

Following this showdown at Rules, I repeatedly asked him why he had never revealed his true identity. He never wavered from his belief that anti-Semitism was never far from the surface, always bubbling away beneath it, and it was a gamble he was not prepared to take now that he had found safety, a new identity, and had children to look after.

My father was convinced that his second wife (my stepmother) and their son did not know he was Jewish. He told me that he had a suitcase of my grandfather's books and papers which he had bequeathed to me but I was not allowed to open it until after his death. Only then would I be free to use them as I wished. Until then I was to keep his secret.

Soon after Helen's visit that summer I told my mother I had discovered that Dad was Jewish. She was furious that he had kept this secret from her. 'How could he?' she fumed. 'But I'm not surprised, as he was always such a liar.' She never confronted him about it: she felt doubly betrayed – by the lie itself and by living with that lie for so long.

Several years later my mother asked me if I knew that my grandfather's books had been published in English. She had told one of her Jewish friends about my father's history and the friend had googled 'Hermann Ungar'. I went on Amazon and there he was: two novels in English translation, *The Class* and *The Maimed*, two novellas and a collection of short stories, *Boys and Murderers*, with a preface by Thomas Mann. I ordered them immediately. My father feigned surprise when I showed him the books, but he did at least acknowledge that Thomas Mann had been Hermann's mentor during his Berlin years. He further admitted Mann had been his godfather, and he was named Tomas after the great writer. It was a start.

I began with *Boys and Murderers*. Mann wrote in his Preface:

As I supported his initial novel, Boys and Murderers, *it would be absolutely wrong for me to not to participate in the preparations for the publication of his last, posthumous volume. The spiritual beauty and artistic attraction of this volume appeal to me even more than the properties of the first novel. But at that time Ungar's world was full of hope, aspirations, happiness at the thought of his star rising,*

confidence and conviction ... and today the earth covers his
body, this life that was so full of talent and hope.

I was used to German writers being long-winded, writing sentences with numerous subclauses, so I was amazed by the crisp, clean prose and the simple sentences of my grandfather's writing. But the subject matter was anything but simple: sexually depraved and psychotic characters committing unspeakable acts born from complicated motives, yet all written in this deceptively innocent and spare prose. I was shocked that such things were the products of my grandfather's imagination. It was hard, too, to believe these stories were written in the 1920s.

What made Hermann write such unsettling tales? What had his relationship been with my father and grandmother? What influence did his childhood and family have on his work – and on his son? There was no point in asking my father; he had only been six when Hermann died, although his ignorance was disingenuous. Recently I came across an interview where my father said, 'Is the world really this nightmare that my father portrays? Is life really only about sex and avarice? Is lust really so strong that it inflicts so much pain? How on earth did my father come to describe life in such destructive terms? I can't find anything in his own life that relates to what he describes in his books.' The truth was very different, as I was to discover.

Reading my grandfather's books gave me the jolt I so badly needed to begin researching the family history, spurred on by my teenage daughter's fascination with her heritage – she grabbed the books and devoured them before I had the chance to do so. I began to compile a family tree but was frustrated by the lack of any detailed information regarding the fate of my father's grandparents, aunts and uncles, apart from 'died in Warsaw', which I later learned was a euphemism for Auschwitz. So in 2009 I posted an alert on a Jewish genealogy website asking for help in tracing the Ungar family.

Within hours I had received an email from Israel, telling me that the database in Yad Vashem, the memorial to Holocaust victims in Jerusalem (which I would later visit), had thirteen entries under the name Ungar in Boskovice, submitted by two different people: one a family relative, 'Ilana Strauss née Sonnenschein', living in Israel, the other a friend of the family, living in the US. The writer gave me Ilana's phone number and suggested I call her 'and give her a nice surprise'.

Ilana was indeed very surprised to hear from me. Together we worked out that my great-grandmother and her grandfather were brother and sister. She told me they had emigrated to Tel Aviv from Moravia in 1938 to be near Hermann's sister, who had emigrated in 1926. She promised to send me the work she had been doing on her family tree so that I could expand my own knowledge of my relatives.

By early 2009 my father's health was declining. In May I went down to Somerset to share my discoveries with him and to persuade him to allow me access to the suitcase and to begin recording his memories. To my surprise, he agreed to start telling his story; perhaps he now felt the need to unburden himself as his life was drawing to a close. He also said I could take the suitcase.

It was a battered old thing, kept in a cupboard under the hall stairs, the locks stiff and rusty through lack of use. Inside there were piles of books and papers, all higgledy-piggledy and covered in dust. Slowly, as I rifled through the contents, the suitcase began to reveal its secrets.

And what secrets they were.

There was an impressive 700-page PhD thesis by a German scholar, Dieter Sudhoff, on Hermann, with over 200 pages of family history. The thesis included excerpts from diaries, notebooks and letters written by Hermann and his close friends and fellow members of his literary circles in Prague and Berlin, including Thomas Mann, Bertolt Brecht and the best-selling German-Jewish writer Stefan Zweig.

Buried in the suitcase I also found first editions of Hermann's key works, French and Czech translations of his books, original manuscripts of his plays and two volumes of literary criticism. These latter books contained interviews with my father and photographs supplied by him, yet he had never revealed to his family that he had been in communication with the authors for over twenty years.

I was furious that Dad had kept this cache from me for so long, but also euphoric at finally being allowed to glimpse this secret world. Here were envelopes and albums of old photographs, some of which I recognised – my father, his brother, my grandmother – but the majority were a mystery. Later I would go through the albums with Dad to identify who was who – from the photos of family holidays by the seaside, sad-looking children and young women, a bewhiskered Kaiser Wilhelm lookalike (my great-grandfather) and plump ladies staring out from under parasols or straight into the camera, to his childhood penfriends from England: true to form, Dad remembered the girls well.

It was hard to tell whether he was enjoying this process or simply humouring me, knowing his time was running out. On reflection, I think he found it cathartic to find space in his heart for those he had abandoned when he left for a new life in England. As for me, at last I could go all the way back to the beginning of Tomas Ungar's story to discover how he reinvented himself as Tom Unwin.

CHAPTER 3:
THE SECRETS OF THE
SUITCASE

My grandfather, Hermann Ungar, was born in 1893 in Boskovice, Moravia, in the east of what is now the Czech Republic, but in Hermann's time was part of the Austro-Hungarian Empire. Set amid fertile rolling farmland and forests, Boskovice contained one of the empire's largest Jewish communities in Austria.

The town itself was – and still is – divided into the Christian quarter and the Jewish ghetto, which by the mid-nineteenth century comprised one third of Boskovice. The Jews were confined to the ghetto where they carried out traditional trades – tailor, butcher, sword-maker, tanner, cabinet-maker, barber, carpenter, furrier or farmer. Not all Boskovice's Jews were poor; some of them

The gateway to the Jewish ghetto in the nineteenth century

owned rich land outside the town, while others managed the nearby estates of wealthy Hapsburg landowners, as in the case of Hermann's uncle Ludwig Kohn.

The Ungars were a prime example of how Jews had benefited from the imperial reforms in 1782. In Boskovice, as elsewhere, Jews effectively became equal to all other citizens and were allowed freedom of movement, including the right to attend German schools; previously, the town's strictly orthodox community had spoken only Yiddish and Hebrew and restricted themselves to Jewish names. Hermann grew up speaking German as his first language and counted Schiller and Goethe among his childhood favourites.

Life for the Jews of Boskovice following the imperial reforms was totally transformed: the new culture of assimilation, where local Jews were integrated into German culture, created friction with the town's dominant Czech community. Czech Christians in small towns like Boskovice had only ever spoken Czech, while their Hapsburg masters spoke German. By switching to German as a first language the Jews gained significant commercial advantages; they were already carrying out trades but were now able to break out of the ghetto, exploiting their links with other Jewish businesses across Moravia and further afield.

In the early nineteenth century, Hermann's great-great-grandfather Rabbi Mose ben Hirsch ha-Levi Ungar ('Ungar' meaning 'Hungarian' in German) had been Boskovice's senior rabbi.

Hermann's great-grandfather, also a rabbi, founded the Ungar distillery which over the coming decades became a large and prosperous business for the extended family. Hermann's father personified both sides of the Ungar legacy as an extremely religious, assimilated Jew who was also successful in business and consequently of some social standing.

The family had moved from a small house in Brunnenplatz to a larger residence in the Judengasse, where Hermann's father extended into the neighbouring property, building an upper storey with a roof terrace and an arbour. In an interview with Dieter Sudhoff, my father remembered it well:

Emil [Hermann's father] only had a rooftop garden, which was located above the warehouse – the store – behind the house. All sorts of plants grew there and in the arbour – which we always referred to as the veranda – I used to watch the spiders. I remember my grandparents as very old people and grandmother was, of course, blind, had diabetes and spent her time listening to the radio using headphones. Sometimes she sat and prepared beans on the stairs which led from the house to the arbour.

This, then, was the Kaiser Haus, or Emperor's House, named in gratitude after imperial permission was granted to open the distillery. Today it sits in the centre of the old ghetto, an imposing double-fronted building overlooking a small square. There is a grand main entrance in the centre, to the left of it was the staff door, and to the right the distillery itself, which until very recently served as a bar. As a boy on his frequent visits to his grandparents, my father was fascinated by the pub, as he told Sudhoff:

An old man visited the bar room on a daily basis to drink his koralk *[schnapps]– he called himself 'the Knight of the Mountain' and looked a bit like a dissolute version of my grandfather. I think I must have been slightly afraid of him, for he was mysterious – that is what I thought. I often went into the 'business' and served the customers – I liked taking*

*the money and when I went into the liquor store I always ran
my finger along the taps on the little liquor barrels and then
licked the liquid off my finger.*

The Kaiser Haus in 1964

Tom's grandfather Emil Ungar was destined for the rabbinate
and trained in the Talmud, but he was much more interested in
the secular, read the Bible in French and spent two hours a day
'relaxing' by reading Homer and Shakespeare in their original
languages; when he had finished he would simply start all over
again.

A self-confessed intellectual, Emil reluctantly took over the
family distillery business when his older brother Max left for
Vienna in 1875.* Hermann later caricatured Emil's preening,
dandyish manner through the character of Colbert in his stage play
The Arbour:

---

*   Max Ungar's memoirs *Tradition und Entfremdung: Die Lebenserinnerungen des
jüdischen Privatdozenten Max Ungar* (ed. Mark Hengerer, 2011) are available on
Amazon and in translation to English on www.hermannungar.com.

He [Colbert] dresses with discerning elegance, with French nuances although also lightly provincial. His hair is oiled and combed carefully over a pink-shimmering bald pate. A little, well-trimmed, pointed beard, a moustache just below his nostrils winging outwards and forming twisted peaks. Red cheeks. A beautiful silk handkerchief peeping out of his jacket pocket and white spats. All these give Colbert's appearance something special, which one can only describe as 'soignée' ...

Emil, alias Colbert, 'smiled patronisingly at his fellow citizens' manners and mores and let his superiority show outwardly'.

Emil's wife Jeanette (Tom's grandmother) came from a liberal Jewish family in neighbouring Jemnice. She, too, was bookish and cultured, an avid reader of Goethe and Schiller, and also spoke beautiful French. She made a perfect companion for Emil, whom one friend remembered as somewhat cranky, 'but in the nicest possible way, in a way in which scholars sometimes are'. Following Hermann's birth, Emil and Jeanette had two more children – Felix, born in 1894, and Gertrude (Gerta), born in 1895. Felix was to remain in Boskovice, marrying a local girl, while Gerta trained as a doctor and eventually emigrated to Palestine in 1926 with her husband Rudy Kleiner, who was an ardent Zionist and was

Emil Ungar c.1900

known as Amnon Zair. They had a son, Petr, born in 1920, but they left him with Hermann's cousin and first love, Blanka Totis, in Brno.[*]

Emil decided early on that Hermann, who was evidently clever, should follow an academic and cultural path. At first little Hermann was educated at home, where his father encouraged his precocious son to put on plays, aided by Hermann's younger brother Felix and their cousins, in front of family audiences rounded up by Emil. When he was eight, Hermann made his directorial debut where, as he later recalled, he 'was not only the author, but also the producer and took the main role of the play, so that all the usual conflicts between author, producers and key actors were played out within my own heart'. Hermann's career as a writer was underway.

In 1903, at the age of ten, Hermann was sent off to grammar school in the town of Brno, thirty-five kilometres south of Boskovice, where Felix soon joined him. Here, a less attractive side of Hermann's character emerged. The headmaster recalled that the two boys loved playing somewhat cruel practical jokes.

Hermann's cousin Blanka also remembered how, as a teenager, he especially loved playing pranks on her and her two sisters, and even on his own sister Gerta; it was as if he liked picking on girls. 'For example during dancing classes in Brno it was traditional that the male dancers (and secret admirers) sent flowers to their "beloved" partners. Hermann took great pleasure in ringing the doorbell and then hiding to watch the girls expectantly rushing to answer the door to see who had received flowers and from whom.'

The adolescent Hermann was highly sexed. His schoolfriend Felix Loria recalled that Hermann began an affair with a local

---

[*] This family secret only came to light in 2019. Amnon Zair's story is told in *Vinah Gan Schemu'el* by Dalia Amotz-Weislib (1980, Israel) in Hebrew.

schoolgirl, a relationship 'purely based on sex'; indeed, Hermann blithely told Loria he had no feelings at all for the girl, leading Loria to accuse him of being 'sadistic'. When I came across Loria's reminiscence I was reminded of my father's various so-called 'aunties' in Africa, and of my mother, whom he treated in an equally chilling fashion.

I found many of the descriptions of the young Hermann recounted by Sudhoff uncanny – they could just as easily be describing my father, who similarly revelled in being centre stage, was a sexual predator and also a great joker, often with a streak of *Schadenfreude*.

In Brno, Hermann joined the Zionist organisation Veritas, and in effect became the leader of his Jewish classmates. For Hermann it was a political rather than a religious statement. He had set his heart on emigrating to Palestine and when he left school in 1911 –

Hermann Ungar (bottom right) around 1908 in the Boskovice Jewish sports team Makkabi

passing all his final exams with distinction – he moved to Berlin to study Hebrew, Arabic and Egyptian grammar, to prepare for his new life.

In Berlin he met two men who became his closest lifelong friends: Gustav Krojanker, son of a wealthy shoemaker from Burg, and

Ludwig Pinner, son of a successful Berlin banker and grain merchant. Like Hermann, Krojanker and Pinner were Zionists, and the trio joined Hasmonäa, another Jewish nationalist fraternity.

'One day he appeared in my room,' Krojanker remembered of his first meeting with Hermann. 'His appearance was comic. A blond, rosy-cheeked lad with soft features, dressed in celebratory dark robes with a top hat in his hand ... he seemed half comical, half festive.' In Krojanker's

Krojanker in his fraternity uniform

memory, Hermann 'had hardly sat down in the corner of the sofa' when he 'produced a voluminous manuscript' and confessed to his dream of becoming a writer.

Hermann's father Emil, however, was determined that he should study law. After a year in Berlin, Hermann began his legal studies in Munich; a year later, he moved back to Prague to complete the course on the eve of the First World War.

In 1914, when war broke out, Hermann decided to enlist – in his own recollection this was to try to overcome feelings of inferiority and to prove himself, to become a man and to escape the shackles of his upbringing. Like many Jews, he was also terrified of the

The Ungar family: Emil (front left), Jeanette (front right) with Gerta next to her and, standing behind the two women, Blanka. The other three women are probably nieces, Blanka's sisters, who lived with the Ungars. Hermann stands at the back in uniform

pogroms that might follow a Russian Tsarist victory, so joining up chimed with his burgeoning Zionism. He noted in his diary:

> *I carried out my duties with passionate dedication ... I set*
> *my targets on carrying out the exercises and gymnastics to*
> *compete with the biggest and strongest of my comrades and*
> *would rather have fainted or collapsed than to admit I was*
> *exhausted and tired. It did not require much to exhaust me.*
> *But I clenched my teeth, suffered in silence and just kept*
> *on going.*

In December 1915, Hermann broke his leg after a fall caused by a grenade explosion in an artillery dugout in Königgrätz on the Russian front. Even after his fall he defended his unit's position and was awarded the Silver Medal for Bravery – First Class; the citation described him as an 'industrious, conscientious soldier, and a well-loved comrade'.

Hermann was sent to Brno to recuperate and was nursed there by his beloved cousin and girlfriend of five years' standing, Blanka, and his sister Gerta. But he was never fully to recover from his injury – the leg was badly set – and he walked with a limp for the rest of his life. He was also deemed not fit enough to serve at the front again. As a result, he was able to continue his studies on and off until he graduated in 1918 with a doctorate in law.

The end of the war gave new hope to Hermann, who had shelved his plans to emigrate to Palestine. The Austro-Hungarian Empire was disbanded and Tomáš Masaryk, who was tolerant towards Jews, became state president of the newly formed Republic of Czechoslovakia. In deference to his father's hypocritical wishes that he earn a living rather than follow the life of an intellectual, he trained as a lawyer in the respected chambers of Dr Froeschl in Prague. Despite his sheer boredom with his new job and his dry colleagues – he was later to satirise this period in his short story 'Tulip' – Hermann managed to squeeze in some time for writing.

On Sundays, his only day of respite, he would take a walk across the Karlplatz, along the quays, and then follow the riverbank before going to a café in the Old Town, often the Continental, partaking of two eggs in a glass, reading the newspapers, in those days attached to long sticks and hung on the wall. He would watch the billiard players attentively, never daring to play himself, sipping his coffee, perhaps seeing some of his friends from the Prague literary circle.

The life of a lawyer was not for him, and after a few months he abandoned his secure job and disappeared from view for the best part of a year (May 1919–March 1920). According to Hermann, his heart and mind were in turmoil. He felt stifled, because all he wanted to do was to write. He surfaced in Eger, Sudetenland, now the Czech town of Cheb, where he joined the provincial theatre as a dramatist and actor.

At some stage during 1919 Hermann also completed two novellas, 'Story of a Murder' and 'A Man and a Maid', which his mentor Thomas Mann reviewed enthusiastically when the stories were published

Hermann Ungar in 1919

collectively under the title 'Boys and Murderers'. It was Hermann's first big break as a writer, yet he was so short of money that in September 1920 he returned to Prague and took a lowly clerk's job at the Comptoir d'escompte bank. Hermann was, if anything, even less suited to banking than to law. While working at Comptoir d'escompte, he created the doomed bank clerk Franz Polzer, the protagonist of his first novel *The Maimed*, whose daily routine was clearly modelled on his own: 'I left home at the same time day after day, never a minute earlier or a minute later. When I walked out of the side street in which my home was located, the clock in the tower struck three times.'

Thanks to a chance encounter with a friend of Jan Masary, the Czech Foreign Minister, he was recruited to the Czech Foreign Service and joined the commercial department of the embassy in Berlin as contracts officer in the trade department; in 1922 he was promoted to consulate attaché.

*

Hermann (centre) with Pinner (left) and Krojanker (right) in Berlin

Hermann was to spend the next seven years of his life, on and off, in Berlin working for the Czech Embassy, where he soon had a growing circle of friends to add to Krojanker and Pinner. Hans Gerke, an embassy official, was a native German speaker who rather looked down on older colleagues who only spoke Czech. Hermann had 'an excellent sense of humour', Gerke recalled. 'We were both young at the time and had a lot of fun with the bureaucratic Czech diplomats.' Hermann's other great friend at the embassy was the Jewish poet Camill Hoffmann, who served as the press officer.

Hoffmann introduced Hermann to Berlin's thriving post-war literary circles, where Thomas Mann's favourable review of *Boys and Murderers* was a valuable calling card. Soon, Hermann was a regular among the writers' set who frequented the Café West, or Café Megalomania as it was nicknamed by the Berliners jealous of its rich clientele. Here Hermann met and seduced the actress Olga Vojan, notorious for appearing semi-naked in the playwright Frank Wedekind's domestic melodrama *Franziska*.

Hermann's inner turmoil persisted. Soon after joining the embassy, he was granted extended sick leave in the Bavarian Alps because of some unspecified nervous disorder. By coincidence, his friend Krojanker's future wife, Ella, was staying in the same resort, allowing Hermann (who cannot have been *that* ill) to execute another of his childish pranks. Decades later Ella recalled the incident to a researcher:

> *One night, in the little, highly respectable Hotel where I was staying, I heard someone calling my name from the street ... It was quite late and people up and down the street would have been asleep. Then the bell rang persistently and soon the lady of the house appeared, visibly put out, upstairs in my room. A young man, a Dr Ungar, had come to call to tell me something very important, explained the lady, but she had – at this time of night – sent him away. It must have been a big joke for him, annoying petit bourgeois people, a habit I observed often in subsequent years.*

His position as a diplomat in Berlin demanded Ungar fulfil a range of social obligations. He played a lively part in the social scene and his love of excess and outrageous dancing made him famous in a very short time. In society, during important embassy receptions for example, where all the guests were refined and exceedingly polite, he adopted the role of the *enfant terrible*. Ella remembered how Hermann delighted in publicly humiliating society hostesses at diplomatic soirées in Berlin: 'During these receptions he would greet the lady of the house with a kiss on the hand, while enquiring, "And does your husband satisfy you?"'

Even his boss Camill Hoffmann's mistress, Lela Dangl, had to endure Hermann's crude 'wit'. Lela remembered an evening in an expensive restaurant where she asked the waiter to pack the leftovers for her cat. 'But, Lela, you don't have a cat!' Hermann declaimed, within the hearing of everyone in the room.

Occasionally, Hermann's misogyny was tempered by generosity towards women. He lived near Berlin's red-light district and once, when he was going out with Ella and Krojanker for a meal, they passed a prostitute, 'heavily made-up, neither young nor pretty', crying on the street corner. Hermann went back to find out what was wrong and discovered that all her money had been stolen, so he gave her a huge banknote. 'We didn't speak about it,' Ella remembered, 'we just walked on. As far as he was concerned, it wasn't an act of charity.'

Sometime between 1920 and 1922 Hermann met a young woman in her mid-twenties on a visit to Prague. Margarete Weiss, known as 'Grete', was the daughter of a wealthy Jewish industrialist who owned a factory which manufactured briefcase locks and fastenings; as a sideline, Grete's father also sold icons of the Virgin Mary to his Catholic neighbours, much to the disapproval of the local rabbi. The family was musical and held regular soirées

My grandmother, Grete Weiss, in 1920

(*Hausmusikabend*), with Grete at the grand piano in the drawing room and her father and brother on strings. Family, friends and acquaintances would drop in and be entertained while sipping wine and enjoying snacks.

Hermann's eye may have first alighted on Grete at one of these evenings. She was taller than him, buxom and already a little plump, insisting to anyone who would listen that her legs were too fat to allow her to pursue her dream of becoming an operetta singer. Above all, at this stage in her life Grete was unashamedly sexy, a fact that Hermann's friends later recalled obliquely: she was 'healthy, happy, powerful and earthy', 'richly endowed with female charms', 'a force of nature', with 'a milk and roses complexion' and 'magnificent red-brown hair'.

At this time Grete was married to Rudolf (Rudi) Weiss, a wealthy Prague silk merchant, who may have known Hermann's family and brought him to one of Grete's family concerts. Grete and Rudi had a little boy, Hans, nicknamed Honza, and lived in a mansion with marble pillars near Wenceslas Square, the poshest district in Prague, and drove around town in Rudi's luxury Hispano-Suiza motor car. Somehow Hermann – short of money, consumed by personal failure and with a 'knotty, wrinkled, boyish face', according to one male friend – seduced Grete, prompting Rudi to divorce her while retaining custody of Honza.

According to Grete in an interview years later, Hermann – 'a most amusing and charming person' – was candid about why he married her in November 1922. 'That which you lack in intellect, is compensated by your earthy instinct', he told her. Meanwhile, Hermann told his literary friends that his new wife had 'one virtue – she never reads, for reading ruins the character'.

Hermann and Grete's wedding coincided with the publication of his novel *The Maimed*. Set in Prague, *The Maimed* charts the descent of a paranoid, gauche bank clerk – clearly

Grete, baby Honza and Rudi

modelled on Hermann – who is seduced by his widowed landlady and catastrophically led astray by his best friend, a cripple. The book was greeted with near-universal revulsion. One critic called it a 'sexual chamber of horrors'. Hermann's friend Stefan Zweig described it as 'magnificent and monstrous, alluring and abhorrent, unforgettable although one would like to forget it and escape its abusive oppression. Its sheer unpleasantness comes first.'

Thomas Mann, who had praised Hermann's first book, thought *The Maimed* 'revolting ... sexual hell, full of filth, crime and deepest melancholy – a monstrous aberration'. Hermann could not cope with the reception, especially from Mann, whom he hero-worshipped. He sank into depression, consumed by a sense of personal failure and paralysed by writer's block. Even worse for his new wife, all Hermann's latent misogyny and pleasure in humiliating women was laid bare as he wallowed in his misery.

Hermann's friend Felix Loria remembered going to a cabaret in Berlin with Hermann and Grete, shortly after their marriage:

Hermann was making fun of people who expected their future spouses to be virgins, pointing out to me during the conversation that he himself was far beyond such laughable prejudices, that fidelity as such did not exist for him in his sex life, etc. ... Mrs Ungar was extraordinary, a beauty, possessed huge amounts of sex appeal and Hermann became visibly annoyed when the men around us attempted to flirt with her. He made a scene, she answered back and Hermann fell into a rage. Finally she asked me, mockingly, if I would change places with her so that Hermann could regain his balance.

Grete became pregnant almost immediately after the marriage but, encouraged by Hermann, she remained at home with her parents in Prague. Hermann told his friends that the reason for their separation was the high cost of living in Berlin due to the Weimar Republic's inflation, but he still managed to find the money for another trip to Italy to ease his writer's block without his pregnant wife. Finally, in October 1923, he procured more leave to be present for the birth of his son, my father, Tomas Michal Ungar who was born on the 25th of that month. Shortly afterwards, Hermann decided that Grete and the baby should come to live with him in Berlin, where they stayed until the summer of 1927.

Although Hermann later wrote that little 'Tomy' was his 'pride and joy', my father could not remember much of these early years or indeed of his father. He recalled riding his trike around the apartment, getting his 'arse tanned' for breaking the glass doors, as in the short story 'Tomy Learns to Write', sitting at a white bench in the kitchen with Amy, the nursery maid and being forced to eat his daily ration of spinach (something he also made me do as a child).

During the summer, the family spent their annual holidays back in Moravia, in Brno, Jemnice and Boskovice, staying with relatives.

All this time, Hermann's career at the embassy was advancing. In 1926 he was promoted to legation secretary, but then came a setback, as he suspected he had appendicitis. The doctors examined Hermann and decided not to operate. His friends were familiar with his fretting and fussing about his health and it was to become a family characteristic, with my father also suffering from a 'nervous stomach'. This did not stop Dad from recalling to Sudhoff that 'my father was such a hypochondriac that the doctors never believed him when he said he was ill':

My mother once told me a story about being in a Berlin nightclub with him. Hermann had been eating whipped cream and it stuck in his throat – he almost choked to death.

There was complete silence – Ungar lay in the middle of the dance floor and appeared to be in the throes of death.

Despite his health scares, Hermann had at last recovered his self-confidence in his writing, following the critical mauling of *The Maimed*. In 1926 *Boys and Murderers* was translated into French and in early 1927 he and Grete were invited to Paris for the launch, as guests of PEN International. On his return, Hermann wrote a pompous letter to his publisher, demanding that he should do more in marketing terms for his authors, himself in particular:

> May I finish by saying that I tasted acclaim in Paris, which
> we in Germany are only accorded when it is too late, when
> we are dead. It was delightful to experience lively feedback
> from the readers, to feel that one has achieved a position
> in this world rather than just being the most unimportant
> cog in the machinery, to be asked questions and have one's
> answers acknowledged with thanks. It was an experience
> which gave me encouragement – something we all need if
> we are to work well.

Hermann's immediate concern was his next work, *The Class*, a novel which dealt with his anxieties about love and marriage and which was published in the spring of 1927. To his relief, the book was well reviewed and Hermann felt sufficiently encouraged to send a signed copy to Thomas Mann. And then came a genuine medical emergency.

In the autumn of 1927, shortly after returning to Berlin with Grete and Tomy from his annual summer break, Hermann was run over by a bus which fractured his hip and broke his femur. He spent six weeks in hospital but never fully recovered from this injury.

His nerves were shattered as badly as his leg, and soon the stomach ulcers and grumbling appendix returned – at least in his imagination. He was offered an operation but, according to Ella Krojanker, a palm-reader had told him he would die in surgery, so he refused.

While on a prolonged sick leave, Hermann brooded in a letter to his friend Krojanker in November 1927 on the state of his marriage: 'Please forgive me but I can't write about the things you want to know and about which I should talk. The whole relationship with Grete,

Die Klasse (The Class)

who cannot be shown to be at fault, has broken down badly. I don't know how this will end.'

Hermann seemed oblivious as to why Grete was sick and tired of him. One has to assume that his infidelities and roving eye contributed to the near breakdown of the marriage. His possessive jealousy was laid bare in *The Class* and in his short story 'Little Lies', published at this time. It might also explain the long gaps between the birth of the two boys. Not a fan of the institution of marriage, it had been a career-oriented move as the embassy disapproved of his reputation as a lothario and sexual libertine.

The positive reception of *The Class* had finally given Hermann the confidence to consider leaving the diplomatic service and becoming a full-time writer. But it was not that simple.

Hermann with Hoffmann in Berlin, 1928

Following his promotion to second secretary, the Foreign Ministry posted him back to Prague, where the family returned in the summer of 1928. Hermann promptly took his annual leave, travelling to the Swiss Alps with Grete and Tomy, and his 'wonderful Remington typewriter (marvellous for writers, as it is not just portable, but potentially produces the greatest literature. One only has to hit the write keys. I will do my utmost.)'

It did not seem to occur to Hermann that he appeared to rank Grete and Tomy lower than the Remington in his affections.

After the holidays, Hermann returned to Prague, where he tried to settle into his new office at the Castle. Meanwhile, Grete and Tomy went to stay with Hermann's family in Boskovice. Alone in Prague, Hermann sank into another bout of morose self-pity, blaming Grete for his depression in a letter to Krojanker:

17 July: The disruption to daily life caused by my spouse's absence, with the loss of all the family pleasures and diversions, plus the tropical heat and the oppressive air in this abysmal house which smells of mothballs, have totally robbed me of all incentive to deal with my correspondence.

I write to you today from
my office in the ministry,
where I sit from 9 a.m. to 2
p.m. in complete boredom.
In fact, life is so tedious
that I was hardly able to
make the decision to start
this letter …
Tomorrow Grete and Tomy
will return from Boskovice.
I am so looking forward to
having some order
in my life again. The
bed and breakfast life
is really unpleasant in high summer.

*Hermann sent this view of Prague
Castle to Krojanker, sketched from
his desk*

He was aware of his responsibilities, that he had a 'wife and
child to support', and what would happen if he was to become ill, or
when 'inspiration fails me' or 'success evades me'? He concluded:

These are all very sensible questions you put to me. And
I have no other answer other than the one given by Tomy
after he was lectured for hours upon end using common
sense and threats: 'But I WANT cucumber salad!' And I
feel that I, too, now want my cucumber salad, despite all
the medical warnings and exhortations.

In September 1928 Hermann requested and was granted another six
months' unpaid leave by the indulgent Foreign Ministry. 'Nobody
should hear anything from me during this time,' he wrote in the
introduction to his next work, a play called *The Arbour*. 'Either I

Tomy (left) with Harry Werner, his cousin Hans Georg Ungar as a baby and an aunt on holiday in Boskovice c.1927

will have created something real or I give it all up. Perhaps not life, but art. But without it there is no life for me.'

At the start of his leave, he travelled to Berlin for the première of *The Red General*, a satirical play about a Jewish general based on Trotsky, which he had written the previous year. Despite being well received by theatre audiences, *The Red General* was poorly reviewed, plunging Hermann further into depression. By far the most damaging critique came from one Josef Goebbels, the recently appointed Nazi Gauleiter for Berlin, who accused 'this Jewish drama by Czech author Hermann Ungar' of encouraging 'the thought that the persecution of Christians could break out at any moment ... Oh, they feel incredibly safe these nouveau-riche Jews'. Hermann contemplated suicide and extended his leave for a further six months in March 1929; all the while, he recorded his self-absorbed thoughts about his failures as a writer in diaries and letters which contained no mention of Grete or Tomy.

At the end of the decade he began to have premonitions of his death and wrote a portentous memoir, *Self-Portrait*, published in 1929. In it, Hermann declared:

> *I am thirty-five years old. My pride and joy is my son, Tomas, who is just learning to read. My sorrow is the theatre. I*

consider a critic, when he writes good things about me, to be
a genius – but an idiot if he writes a negative critique. Stated
simply: I am no different from other authors …

Despite the problems with their marriage, Grete was now pregnant again. 'Because of the pregnancy Grete is not well at all,' Hermann complained in another letter to Krojanker. 'She's vomiting all day long. I think she coped much better when we were expecting Tomy.' Their second son Alexander, nicknamed Sascha, was born in March 1929. 'Here there is nothing new to report after the birth of the child,' Hermann wrote matter-of-factly to Krojanker. 'Mother is still in bed, not well.'

For all his many discontents, and frequently declared doubts about his literary talent, Hermann still managed to publish ten short, heavily autobiographical pieces in 1928 and 1929. This burst of activity gave him the final impetus to resign from the diplomatic service, even though he had a wife and two small sons to support. Grete had brought a considerable dowry to the marriage but, to her fury, Hermann had lent the money to his businessman brother Felix. As a result, Hermann was now staking his family's security on his future success as an author. 'Hopefully God won't wreak revenge on my children,' he wrote to Krojanker, 'two minutes' after his resignation in September 1929. 'The last few days have been very exciting, with suspense and panic … It was probably extremely reckless of me, but I couldn't bear it any more, please don't blame me!'

Immediately after resigning, Hermann travelled to Berlin to discuss a production of *The Arbour*, which a theatre owner considered had just the right balance of 'literature and filth' to make a box office hit. Berlin in these years was a hotbed of debauchery, with nightlife offering every sexual fantasy imaginable – this was the city Isherwood wrote of in *Goodbye to Berlin*, and the basis for the film *Cabaret*. It was Hermann's kind of place and he decided he would move back there, to the centre of the German literary world. He then returned to Prague to prepare for the move.

On 21 October, Hermann complained of feeling pains in his stomach, a familiar story to his friends and family. He felt well enough to visit his mother in hospital, where she had recently undergone an unsuccessful cataract operation, but the pains persisted and Hermann went directly from her bedside for a consultation with doctors. They initially failed to make a correct diagnosis, perhaps aware of Hermann's hypochondriac tendencies. It was only after two more days of increasing agony, punctuated by vomiting, that Hermann was admitted to a sanatorium for an exploratory stomach operation. Too late, the surgeon found he had a perforated appendix which had led to peritonitis. 'Ungar's [Hermann's] mother was also in the same clinic suffering from eye trouble,' Thomas Mann wrote later. 'They kept his operation a secret from her, but she dreamt about Hermann's death.'

Hermann came round from the operation and for a couple days seemed in good spirits, and began to make enthusiastic plans for the premiere of *The Arbour*. But septicaemia had set in, and on 27 October his heart began to fail. He sank into delirium and had a vision of his impending death, fulfilling all his earlier anxieties and premonitions.

Mann described the scene, as told to him by Hermann's brother Felix:

A nurse entered the room and he recognised a childhood friend from Boskowitz [Blanka?]. He was horror-struck, as he saw this as an omen. This face from his home country meant that the earth was waiting for him. He was going to die. His last incoherent thoughts centred on the premiere of his drama The Arbour.

Two days later Hermann died, with Grete by his bedside.

'The only thing I have left is my children,' she wrote to Krojanker on 11 November, in reply to his letter of condolence.

The first person I saw dying unfortunately had to be my Schani [Hermann's nickname]. Isn't that cruel? And he could have been alive after all, were it not for 4 idiotic doctors who committed murder through their ignorance, in just under 30 hours ... If only I could wake up from this evil, terrible dream.

A fortnight later, Grete wrote again to Krojanker. *The Arbour* was due to premiere in Berlin – 'a kind of wake' – but the date had not yet been fixed and, besides, Grete was not sure she could go. She continued:

For me it's all destroyed and over ... Who else could ever take the place of a Hermann Ungar? The boys are very dear, especially the little one, who is a big lad, 21 pounds at 8 months. It is a great relief to me that you all loved him [Hermann] so much and are so very kind to me.

    The most heart-felt greetings

    Your Grete Ungar

Despite Hermann's often callous behaviour towards Grete, she really had adored her 'Schani'; all the fault lines in the marriage had been drawn by him. As for Tomy, he knew his father was dead but had little understanding of what it meant, according to Hermann's brother Felix. Tomy scarcely missed his father as he had been absent for much of his young life.

CHAPTER 4:
CZECH CHILDHOOD

After Hermann's death, Grete and the boys moved back to her parents' Prague town house, a grand building with a courtyard round the back, where the factory stood. My father remembered the 'awful noise' of the machinery as it stamped out the silver- and gold-plated zips and locks.

Grete's father, Heinrich Stransky, was a 'good grandfather, a nice man, with a Jesus Christ-like visage and a small beard', my father recalled. He wore a smart suit every day, with a leather clip on the middle button of his waistcoat, where he would hang his hat. At weekends, Heinrich liked to take little Tomy for steamboat rides on the river or walks along its banks.

Grandmother Pauline was a large friendly woman, who loved baking cakes and presided over the kitchen. A woman of 'frugal habits', she liked to wait until midday to pick up cut-price fruit and vegetables from a nearby covered market and was nicknamed 'the midday witch' by the vendors. Poor Pauline suffered from kidney problems and was frequently unwell, which meant Grete took charge in the kitchen. The household was completed by Grete's brother, Otto Stransky, and his young wife, Luisa, whose children Helen and Peter were born in 1932 and 1936.

Heinrich died in 1933 of a lung inflammation, by which time Grete and her two boys had moved into an elegant art deco

Tomy with his baby brother Sascha and half-brother Honza in 1930

apartment in a mansion block directly opposite the National Theatre. It was a grand building, its stucco facade embellished with ornate flowers and nymphs gracefully intertwined, mosaic floor tiles in the hallway, coloured glass inserted into metal fretwork on the stairwell and little brass bobbles on the bannisters as if to prevent naughty boys like Tomy and Sascha from sliding down them.

Grete, now somewhat impoverished but with an entrepreneurial bent, launched a successful lingerie business from the apartment, selling delicate silk brassieres and panties to her girlfriends. The silk was provided by her former husband, Rudi, sewn by village women, with the finished products displayed in a large glass cabinet in Grete's bedroom; the two boys shared the other bedroom. From the apartment, the sociable Grete resumed the family tradition of musical soirées, providing ham sandwiches with

My great-grandparents, Heinrich and Pauline Stransky

pickled cucumbers – the young Tomy was frequently sent to the corner shop to pick them up – and wine and beer.

Grete was only thirty-four when Hermann died, and was still attractive and alluring; quite the merry widow of her operetta repertoire. It was not long before she had a string of lovers and several offers of marriage, although she declined them all. Hermann's old friend Krojanker disapproved of her relationships with other men, something he made clear after a visit to see Grete and Tomy, in his words 'a charming, lively and lovable boy'. Krojanker recalled how Grete told him she now had a 'second' male friend, but 'according to Felix [Hermann's brother] she should have said the 102nd. I personally feel that Felix's figures are more reliable, minus a small discount!'

At about this time, in 1933, Grete considered sending Tomy to Palestine to be with his Aunt Gerta, Hermann's sister. Krojanker felt Grete's motives were driven by embarrassment at her 'horizontal sport', as he crudely described her sex life, rather than any Zionist idealism. My father, then ten, recalled going to Boskovice to be measured up for a leather coat to take with him for his intended emigration. Meanwhile, Krojanker remembered Tomy taking an instant dislike to Gerta on one of her rare trips back home: 'Tomy told me time and time again what a revolting impression she had made on him, with her advancing decrepitude, and that this impression had coloured his thoughts about everything and everyone over there [in Palestine].'

In old age, my father did not pull his punches either, recalling: 'My memories of Aunt Gerta were those of a skinny, scruffy woman, who smoked continuously and sat on a bed with me somewhere, going through my stamp album. Spectacles and messy hair.'

In many ways it was not surprising that my father had no wish to go to Palestine; after all, he had not been brought up in the Jewish faith by Grete (those ham sandwiches were a bit of a giveaway!) and had hardly ever visited a synagogue. There were no bar mitzvahs, they did not keep kosher, say grace, keep or light a menorah (the traditional Jewish seven-pronged candle) or observe the restrictions of the Sabbath. Despite his rabbinical ancestry on Hermann's side of the family, Dad's childhood was entirely secular. Hermann had not been a practising Jew himself; his Zionism was political rather than religious, a protest against his strict upbringing perhaps. Grete would have gone along with her husband's wishes.

Dad's memory of these Prague years was sketchy. He remembered going to primary school, close to the entrance of the Charles Bridge, the Old Town side, where his form teacher's party piece was spitting on the floor and making a sort of 'porridge' out of the gob with his foot, much to the boys' amusement. Later Tomy attended the Prague English Grammar School, close to Grete's apartment, to learn 'English as she is spoke', as all the teachers were British. He recalled a bad-tempered Scottish teacher named Weir, who would, as was the wont of so many teachers, throw the blackboard duster at him whenever he was naughty.

Most of his classmates were Christian and one of his earliest memories was when the boys were made to stand in rows

Sascha (left) and Tomy (right) with their cousin Harry Werner on the Vltava River

according to religion. Tom hated this casual segregation; as far as he was concerned religion played no part in his life, and he saw no difference between himself and his Christian friends. It was while at grammar school, in his early teens, that he 'fell for one or two girls', including the daughter of a British Embassy passport official whom Tom later said was a spy. I found her photograph, inscribed on the back, buried deep inside Tom's suitcase of souvenirs.

There were boats for hire near Grete's apartment, and Tom would go rowing on the river with his younger brother, his cousin Harry Werner from Boskovice, or his best friend, the son of a Czarist family who had fled Russia during the revolution.

After school, friends would come round to the apartment, where Grete would provide them with delicious cakes and snacks. The boys loved going with Grete or schoolmates to matinees in the nearby cinema, where there was still a pianist; there were frequent outings with the Stransky grandparents, and summers in Boskovice with the Ungar grandparents and cousins. And in the winter, there was skiing in the Tatra Mountains in Slovakia. The boys would strap on their wooden skis, affix sealskins for traction and plod up the mountainside before enjoying the thrill of whooshing downhill.

Most memorable of all was a trip to Yugoslavia in 1936 or 1937 to visit Grete's Aunt Edith, who had married a Croatian-Jewish doctor, and Edith's daughter, Hetty. For this holiday, Grete was accompanied by her latest lover, a retired German-speaking colonel who had settled in Bratislava after the First World War. According to Dad, Colonel Janisch was a 'very civilised man',

Sascha, Tomy and Harry Werner in Rab, Yugoslavia

but even though Grete was 'very fond of him', he had promised his late wife before she died that he would never remarry. Their cousin Harry completed the party.

Holiday snaps of Grete and the boys show them swimming and sunbathing on the Adriatic coast – Grete statuesque in her bathing suit, Tomy on the cusp of adolescence, Sascha still a sweet little boy, Harry grinning for the camera. They look happy, oblivious to the horror that was about to envelop Czechoslovakia's Jews as Hitler's anti-Jewish rhetoric rose and his military designs on his neighbours became increasingly vocal.

All through the 1930s Grete stayed in touch – and perhaps rather more – with her first husband, Rudi Weiss, who had never remarried and still had custody of their son, Honza. Dad recalled regular visits to Rudi's palatial Prague town house, which was now run by an elderly aunt. It seems possible that Rudi provided Grete with financial assistance, since Hermann's foreign ministry pension was small and she had been unable to recover Hermann's 'loan' of her substantial dowry from his brother, Felix. At the

Grete, Sascha and Tomy in Rab

same time, Rudi allowed her full access to Honza, and there are quite a few photos of the three boys with Grete in the 1930s. Despite living apart, Honza, Tomy and Sascha grew up together.

Their biggest thrill was being driven around Prague by Rudi in his Hispano-Suiza motor car, the height of ostentation and luxury. My father remembered Rudi as 'a clever, nice man, kind to us boys', and indeed every time he saw Tomy and Sascha he gave them each a Marie Theresa Thaler, or silver dollar, a significant sum of money.

By the mid-1930s Grete was weighing up her options with other men, since Colonel Janisch was out of the running, for marriage at least. Hermann's favourite first cousin, Richard Kohn, was a frequent visitor to Grete's apartment, and together they were hatching plans to emigrate to Canada, where the government was advertising for experienced farmers. She also accompanied Rudi on a silk-selling expedition to the French city of Lyon in the Hispano-Suiza, leaving the boys behind with their grandparents.

The worldly, well-travelled Rudi was no fool and was monitoring events in Germany as National Socialism took hold. Shortly after the Munich Agreement in September 1938, which paved the way for Hitler to annex the Sudetenland from Czechoslovakia, Rudi and Honza departed for London. The Kristallnacht pogrom in early

Glamorous Grete (centre) in Prague with her girlfriends shortly before she left for London

November, where Jewish shops and synagogues in Berlin were destroyed while the German authorities looked on, forced Grete's decision that sixteen-year-old Tomy should follow them. Later, she and my father explained that it chimed with Hermann's wishes for the boys to learn a useful language; there was no reference to anti-Semitism being a factor in his flight.

While it is natural that Grete shared Rudi's concerns about the gathering threat to Czechoslovakia's Jews from the Nazis, her decision to remain in Prague with Sascha was probably governed by the commonly held notion that they would be safe as assimilated Jews who weren't even observant. She also had the protection of her Colonel Janisch. With Rudi in London, Grete may also have sensed an opportunity for Tomy to pave the way for their arrival – just in case things went wrong – and perfect his already excellent English.

Much later, I tried to prise out of my father the truth about why Grete had sent him to England. He claimed to remember nothing about his arrival in London – not even the exact date – nor the real reasons for his departure from Prague. He stayed with Rudi and Honza, now known as 'John'. Ella Krojanker, now divorced from Gustav, had escaped to London and described Tomy in an undated letter as:

> … working and earning money, unfortunately he was not able to finish his A Levels – that will become a big hindrance if he wants to improve his lot in the world. He is supposed to be very interested in social and religious issues (the family have been christened) – so he is less average than one is made to believe and than his rosy-cheeked pretty face indicates. No idea what will happen to the little child – he learns well, is highly strung and a hypochondriac, he is sturdy but slightly pale.

He also took a secretarial course at Pitman's and, perhaps under Rudi's influence, began to make vague plans to move to Canada. According to my father, he had always wanted to be a forester, and was looking at various courses in agriculture as part of the Canada scheme when all Rudi's prescient fears about the vulnerability of Czechoslovakia's Jews were suddenly vindicated.

In March 1939 Hitler invaded and annexed the rest of Czechoslovakia, renaming Germany's new vassal state the 'Protectorate of Bohemia and Moravia'. Dad later claimed to me that, as a sixteen-year-old, he had alerted his mother to the necessity of flight, spinning me a tale about shoving his last pennies into a London phone box while he urged Grete to get out of Prague with Sascha immediately. Yet it is clear that wily

Grete had been preparing her escape for some time. She had already obtained forged christening certificates, and now used the most effective weapon at her disposal: her body. Her lover, Colonel Janisch, was now a high-ranking Czech government official, and my father acknowledged that he managed to arrange the paperwork that enabled Grete and Sascha to flee Prague. They moved fast.

Grete and Sascha arrived in Dover on 29 March 1939, exactly fourteen days after the German invasion. My father remembered going down to meet them off the boat – Grete in a suede overcoat and matching hat, her jewellery sewn into the coat's lining, clutching young Sascha in one hand and her suitcase in the other. Grete's social standing may have plummeted but at least she was still alive. All her hopes for a better life in this strange new country now rested with Rudi and Tomy.

CHAPTER 5:
THE METAMORPHOSIS
OF TOMAS UNGAR

Grete's Certificate of Registration, issued on 29 June 1939, allowed her to stay in Britain for three months on the condition that she did not 'establish himself [*sic*] or seek any employment'. She rapidly agreed with Tomy that they should emigrate to Canada, where Rudi and Honza – now very firmly John – were also planning to go as soon as it could be arranged. Meanwhile, she rented a cheap flat on Fairfax Road near Swiss Cottage in north-west London, close to where I now live, from a couple whom Grete recalled had 'dirty feet' and 'didn't wash their clothes enough'.

During these last summer months of peace, there were other Jewish refugees from Czechoslovakia passing through Swiss Cottage and neighbouring districts, almost all in the same precarious situation as Grete, Tom and Sascha. Tom remembered how they would get together in each other's dingy lodgings and seek solace in their music, just as in Prague. At these impromptu *Hausmusikabends*, Grete would play the piano (if one was available) and sing German operetta and lieder, while new-found friends performed chamber music on the violins and other instruments they had managed to bring with them as they fled the Nazis.

Everyone was acutely aware of all the family and friends they had left behind. Grete's brother and elderly mother were still in Prague, now hard up and in fear for their future. Somehow, Grete was at this stage in communication with them. She had also kept up with Hermann's friend Gustav Krojanker, who had emigrated to Palestine, and she was delighted to resume her friendship with Ella, who was now in London.

Grete had a specific reason for making urgent contact with Krojanker as she prepared to depart for Canada. She hoped Krojanker might still have some leverage over Hermann's brother, Felix, regarding his failure to repay her dowry, which Hermann had 'lent' him. '... My noble brother-in-law, Felix, has unfortunately defrauded his nephews Tom and Sascha, whom he loves so much, of a quarter of a million Czech Koruna, a sum which would come in very handy nowadays,' Grete wrote sarcastically to Krojanker on 13 July. She continued:

I showed Ella the respective letter by Felix, which was addressed to Hermann, and in which he confirmed that the money, my dowry, was lent to him by Hermann for his various [business] branches in Berlin, I believe there were nine. In the beginning he did pay the interest, but then he declared that these were joint business ventures with Hermann.

I am telling you all of this for the simple reason that I have heard that I have been roundly condemned over there, because I broke it off with the Ungar family. I was just too well-mannered to go to court at the right time and get the money for my children. But this money will not turn out to be a blessing for the Ungars. Please forgive me for bothering you with this sordid tale, but I don't want,

in addition to the serious loss which my children had to
suffer, to appear in a bad light.

Unknown to Grete, before war broke out Felix had been granted
a travel certificate to leave Czechoslovakia for Palestine; his sister,
Gerta, settled in Tel Aviv, had even transferred the equivalent
of £1,000 to pay for Felix's departure. Fatefully, Felix delayed,
unwilling to leave his elderly, frail mother, Jeanette. When war
broke out in September 1939 and Germany invaded Poland, it
became much more difficult for Jews trying to leave Europe. Felix's
travel certificates were rescinded on 10 January 1940. Felix, his
wife, his mother and his two sons were rounded up in 1942 and
sent to Terezín.

Terezín, or Theresienstadt as the Germans called it, was a
concentration camp on the border with Germany. It had two
purposes, first to serve as departure point for Jews being deported
to the camps in Germany such as Auschwitz, Treblinka and
Buchenwald, where members of my family were murdered, and
second, to serve as propaganda to showcase the Nazis' sympathetic
treatment of older Jews, who lived there in 'retirement settlements',
to try and deceive people about the Final Solution. However,
the conditions of these 'retirement settlements' did nothing but
precipitate their deaths – 33,000 in all, while more than 88,000
were transited through Terezín to labour and death camps in the
east.

In the same letter to Krojanker, Grete also revealed that she
had married Hermann's farmer cousin Richard Kohn by proxy,
'for purely practical reasons'. By implication, Grete was not in love
with Kohn, but the pair must have felt they had a better chance of
being permitted to settle in Canada as a married couple. 'I am now
waiting for my husband to come here in order to quickly leave for

Richard Kohn (left) on his winter sled

Canada,' she told Krojanker. 'But from what I hear from home it won't be easy to get out.'

Grete waited in vain for Kohn who, like Felix, had missed the narrow window of opportunity to leave Czechoslovakia. Meanwhile, Rudi and John had already departed for Toronto. Grete, Tomy and Sascha were stranded in London with Grete's three-month permit due, as things stood before the outbreak of war, to expire at the end of September.

In August 1939, Grete decided it was time to flee again, perhaps all too aware that war was about to break out. According to my father, the family stuck a pin in a map and alighted at random on the quiet cathedral and market town of Wells in Somerset. Once there, they lived first as paying guests at a farm just outside Wells, then lodged at a vicarage and finally moved to small house on Chamberlain Street near the town centre, which Grete rented in October 1940.

Grete found a job as a cook on the night shift at the Scophony factory outside Wells, which produced radar components for the RAF. By now inclined to plumpness, she teetered around the country lanes every day on her bicycle, the 'lady who lunched' in Prague off to serve goulash and other Austro-Hungarian recipes in a British works canteen.

As soon as he arrived in Wells, my father anglicised his name. Tomas became Tom and he signed up for an agricultural course at a local institute. Meanwhile, Grete somehow got twelve-year-old Sascha, now called Alec, a scholarship to Bembridge, a public school on the easternmost tip of the Isle of Wight which, at the start of the war, was evacuated from its rather vulnerable location to Coniston in the Lake District. This was too far away, so eventually she managed to get him a place at the prestigious Millfield School, close to their new home in Wells.

Tom received a first-class diploma at the end of his short agricultural course and then found a job at Scophony testing electrical parts for the radar. Eager to do his bit for the war, he also joined the Home Guard, for at seventeen he was still too young to join up. Tom wore his new-found 'British' fighting spirit proudly on his khaki sleeve; 'cowardly' was how he described two young friends in Wells – one a local lad, the other a Russian émigré workmate at Scophony – who initially agreed to join the Home Guard with him and then opted for the Fire Service.

I later came across photographs of Tom, larking around in his Home Guard uniform with his fake gun at the ready (at the start of the war there were not enough weapons to distribute to the volunteers).

What was real, however, was Tom's love of the Home Guard. In his fond memory, it epitomised the coming together of 'normal patriotic citizens – people from all walks of life, from the squire and the bank manager, to the butcher and grocer – to deal with the enemy, who they were expecting to drop from the sky, or land from the sea, in the only way they could. They put aside their bowlers and put on tin hats.'

In Wells, the Home Guard manned underground concrete shelters, with slits for shooting at the enemy. At night they patrolled the streets and watched the skies for any sign of enemy action; then they went to sleep on gym mats in the town

Tom, in the Home Guard, Wells

hall or school, not bothering about changes of clothes, and woke each other up with cups of tea when it was time to swap watch. It is unsurprising that *Dad's Army* later became one of Tom's favourite television programmes.

And then he met Joyce.

Sometime in 1943 my father became friends with twenty-five-year-old Joyce Rochefort, another employee at Scophony who sat on the adjacent bench. 'Seeing Tom in the distance for the first time, I was strangely convinced that I knew him and had always known him,' Joyce recalled. 'He came charging along and opened up [the door to] the office for me.'

The twenty-year-old Tom she saw was handsome in a baby-faced way, spoke good English and seemed charming and well brought-up, apart from a taste for practical jokes and pranks. Once he got to know Joyce better, he delighted in sneaking up on her unannounced; soon he graduated to tweaking her nose.

Originally from Derbyshire, Joyce had trod a miserable road before ending up in Wells. Her parents were travelling repertory actors who had left Joyce and her little brother in the care of their adoring grandmother. When she died, Joyce had been sent to an orphanage, where she contracted meningitis. She was tiny, perhaps due to her orphanage upbringing, and was mentally and emotionally fragile. At the age of sixteen she was sent to live with her mother, now divorced, who remained completely indifferent to her.

Joyce won a scholarship to the local art college in Wells but could not afford to take up the subsidised place. Instead she had got a job as live-in parlour maid and when she was seventeen, pretty and naïve, fell for a local boy called Eddy Farrell, who had a fine voice and dreams of making it in London. A year later they were married.

Eddy the aspiring tenor turned out to be a violent drunk. According to Joyce, he regularly beat her after one too many at the pub, where he repaired nightly after work as a farm labourer. They moved to a small cottage where the young couple soon had two small daughters; while they gave Joyce some comfort, Eddy's beatings continued until war broke out and, to her relief, he was called up.

Joyce's brother was killed at Dunkirk in 1940 and by the time she got to know Tom, three years later, Eddy was missing in action, presumed dead. Soon Tom was running errands for Joyce and carrying her shopping home, close to Grete's rented house on Chamberlain Street.

The two women bonded, despite the age difference. They would go foraging for food, make clothes and share the rigours of rationed wartime together. 'I was always made to feel welcome in Grete's house, as were the children ... sometimes I was invited round to a musical evening with people like her, usually war-time refugees who brought their instruments ... sometimes I just went to her house and chatted while we knitted.'

In Joyce's version of events, as told to her daughter, Bonnie, years later, it was *ITMA* (*It's That Man Again*), the popular wartime comedy show with Tommy Handley, that was the cause of all her problems with Tom. They were talking about it at work, and Joyce complained that her radio was not working. Tom gallantly offered to come and fix it that evening.

According to Joyce, once he had got the radio working, 'he was kissing me – and very much meaning it ... we just talked, very happily, sitting on my sofa'. For a while 'there was nothing other than holding him ... and he would tell me he loved me ... and I him. Somehow it was all very innocent and totally pure. I adored him; no one could ever have cared more. Some weeks later, it *did* happen and a few times maybe after that.'

Joyce said that the relationship changed when Tom began to talk of getting a better job. Grete and Tom had begun talking again about emigrating to Canada after the war, to join Rudi and John, for now Grete knew that her third husband, Richard Kohn, had been arrested in Prague. At one point, Joyce recalled that this family debate even led to a suggestion that Joyce might perhaps join them in Canada as well.

Joyce's happiness was not to last. One night, she was woken by a crashing noise downstairs. She found her husband, Eddy, blind drunk, with a bottle in one hand and a bayonet in the other. He beat Joyce again and again and then stumbled out of the house. Joyce rushed to Tom's house, expecting comfort and a refuge for her and her little daughters, only to be told she should go back home, 'although he was still as loving towards me'.

Soon afterwards, Joyce discovered she was pregnant, a fact she did not disguise from Grete or Tom. Now it was Grete's turn to shun her. 'One day I went to [Grete's] house with some finished sewing, to find for the first time a locked door,' Joyce remembered. 'Later there was a note pushed through my door saying, "I know you have been having a relationship with my son."'

Grete clearly knew that Joyce was carrying Tom's baby. Yet however far Grete had fallen, she could not tolerate her eldest son moving in with a country girl who was still married and had two children to support.

Nor could Tom; he had applied to work at the BBC Monitoring Service at Caversham, near Reading, and had just learned that his interview had been successful. Soon Tom would be quitting his mundane factory job for the glamour of Caversham Park, monitoring Nazi and Axis broadcasts for the War Office. As for Joyce, with Grete's connivance she would be conveniently erased from his past.

It was not hard for Grete to persuade Tom that he could not possibly be the father of Joyce's unborn child. Grete reminded Tom of Eddy's one-night reappearance when clearly, she insinuated, Eddy had got Joyce pregnant before beating her up. On his side, Tom persuaded himself that he had always taken 'precautions' with Joyce. To complete Joyce's misery, once Tom had left for

Grete in Wells

Caversham, Grete started to spread rumours around the factory and town that Joyce had taken many other lovers.

Yet Tom did not abandon Joyce entirely. He would come back to Wells from Caversham for the odd weekend when he would drop in on Joyce after seeing his mother. He was not completely heartless despite Grete's machinations.

Part 2

Becoming Tom Unwin

CHAPTER 6:
A BRITISH OFFICER
AND GENTLEMAN

Tom spent a year at Caversham where his fluency in German and English was invaluable for monitoring enemy signals. His days involved listening in on enemy frequencies and supplying simultaneous translations which were then passed on to intelligence for assessment. Tom learned his radio skills here, which were to be the stepping stones for his future career in the Royal Navy.

He would have been a good catch for the BBC. It was a huge step up for a twenty-year-old Czech refugee, but Tom was demonstrating the first sign of his obsession with upward mobility, with becoming a naturalised Briton and serving his new country. Here he began to mix with a more sophisticated crowd for the first time: officer-class British men and women and other émigrés such as himself who had fled the war in Europe. He remembered going on long paddle-boat trips down the Thames with Russian countesses and fellow refugees, and generally enjoying himself, despite living in rather ordinary digs away from his mother's cooking.

We know from Joyce's accounts of the young Tom that he was handsome, humorous and gallant. His European manners must have been quite something in sleepy Wells and then in Caversham. Thanks to his time at the British School in Prague, then his studies in London, his fluent and unaccented English allowed him to gradually leave his Czech roots behind and adopt a new rather British persona, Tom Unwin Esq., so that by the time he joined the Royal Navy Volunteer Force (RNVR) in 1943, he was every inch the dashing young English naval officer. He always claimed to have plucked his new name from a telephone directory on the basis of the respective similarity between the first two letters.

Decades later he recalled, 'I thought more and more the war was being fought for people like me and I should take an active hand in it, and the Navy said they could make good use of me in intelligence'. He had heard via Grete, who was in touch with people from home, about the transportation of his remaining family to concentration camps, although probably not of their final fate, and he claimed his conscience compelled him to do something altruistic, as one of the lucky ones to escape. He did not want to be a bystander to the horrific events that were unfolding in Europe.

Was it a coincidence that his joining the Navy was simultaneous with Joyce's pregnancy? His mother was aghast. 'What a foolish thing to do, you got a safe job, why you want to risk your neck?' She spoke English with a heavy Czech accent, which she never lost, and although the conversation was probably in Czech this is how Tom remembered it. He said his jobs at the factory and the BBC were both considered important war work and would have exempted him from being called up, nevertheless his altruism won. Grete was conflicted over the safety of her son versus the danger of being ensnared by Joyce, for Bonnie was born in January 1944, just after he joined up.

The RNVR was an offshoot of the more established Royal Naval Reserve (RNR), founded to provide a volunteer force to supplement the Royal Navy. During the Second World War, the RNVR provided experienced volunteer officers in all fields, ranging from commanders to specialist navigation officers and radio operators like Tom, working for Special Branch. They were nicknamed the 'Wavy Navy' as their stripes differed from the straight ones sported by regular officers.

New recruits undertook some fast-tracked training, usually no more than three months, to get them in action as soon as possible. Tom was sent to a converted telephone exchange in Southfields, near Wimbledon, where he practised intercepting messages before eventually moving on to his official enrolment centre, HMS *Royal Arthur*. This was not a ship at all but, somewhat unglamorously, a converted Butlin's holiday camp in Skegness, where they slept in the wooden chalets. Tom recalled that 'one or two chaps froze to death because we didn't have enough blankets'.

In early 1944 Tom's first job as a radio operator was intercepting messages from German naval vessels on HMS *Pytchley*, a small 900-ton Hunt-Class destroyer. She was an agile vessel, ideal for her

HMS **Royal Arthur** *intake, Tom is in the back row, far left*

Outside the Butlin's huts at Skegness;
Tom on the left, already smoking a pipe

role, trying to protect the Atlantic convoys from the German E-boats which were mining the English Channel. Small and extremely fast, E-boats were responsible during the war for sinking more than a hundred merchant ships, twelve destroyers, eleven mine-sweepers, eight landing craft, and even a submarine. By the winter of 1943–44, the threat from the E-boats was at its peak.

Tom changed ships with remarkable frequency throughout the war as the Special Branch radio operators were highly valued for their sophisticated equipment. They always worked alongside the commanding officers of the escort ships, as the admiral wanted the latest information in order to avoid attack. His next posting in late 1944 was to Scapa Flow, in the Orkneys, where he was attached to the commander-in-chief of the home fleet. The Scapa Flow ships were at anchor, waiting for news that German battleships like the *Tirpitz*, hiding in the Norwegian fjords, were on the move and about to attack the convoys.

Tom wrote frequently to his mother, but only a couple of letters survive, as she sent most of them on to Alec who was still at school. In November 1944 Tom described Lyness, the naval base in the Orkneys, as 'rather wet and cold, but we keep a good fire going … I share a cabin i.e. a little room in a hut and it is quite homely'. In another letter he sent a sketch of the view from his bed entitled 'Siesta', showing his feet, his washing on a makeshift line behind the free-standing Rayburn, a stew bubbling on top. He reported he now had 'sufficient blankets, but if, and only if you have sufficient blankets, you may send me a normal one – not a double (I have to get it into my hammock)'. He also suffered from seasickness, which must have been difficult in the rough North Sea.

Tom had his closest brush with death in Scapa Flow, en route for an Arctic convoy. Imagine a whole British fleet of over 100 ships lying at anchor and the radio operators being summoned for duty and setting out in small drifters – converted herring boats – over a dark and misty loch at the start of a mission, a mix of fear and adrenalin coursing through their veins. It might take two hours to finally locate the admiral's battleship in the dark – which flashed little lamps to guide them – towering above the tiny boat 'like Buckingham Palace'. A small swell for the capital ship was equivalent to a massive twenty- to thirty-foot wave for the drifter, and the trick was to judge when to jump from the drifter on to the battleship's gangplank, laden down with kitbag and an enormous, valuable Hallicrafter American radio complete with huge aerials. As he told me decades later:

> There I was standing with this radio in my arms, waiting to jump, with two or three chaps standing by with boat-hooks waiting to see if you made it. And this time I didn't make it! I jumped, and I thought to myself, 'My God even if I come up out of this, I have to come up between my tiny little ship and the big ship and, even if I come up, I might get rubbed a little on the way.' As I sunk deeper holding the radio, I said to myself, 'Tom old boy if you don't drop that bloody radio you will go to your grave on it'. So, I did drop it and immediately

returned to my old fear of coming up with my head between
these two ships. Anyway all went well and I got to the top and
I was pulled ashore by a sturdy boatman with a boathook,
was taken ashore and before the Chief of Intelligence Staff,
who said, 'Well now, have a cup of tea, we'll give you a change
of underwear, go back and get a spare radio and come back
in a couple of hours' time.'

Scotland was also the starting point for the Navy to join some of the Arctic convoys bound for the ports of Murmansk and Archangel, laden with military supplies for the Soviet Union following the German invasion in June 1941. The Arctic route, dubbed by Churchill 'the worst journey in the world', took about ten days. All in all, there were seventy-eight convoys during the Second World War, comprising over 1,400 merchant ships. They left every ten days or so and transported over 4 million tons of equipment. A typical convoy was made up of between 100 and 200 ships, ten abreast, but each as much as a mile apart. The merchant ships were encircled, at close quarters, by smaller warships and destroyers, while a couple of cruisers kept a wider berth, along with some subs. In this way they hoped to be able to avert the worst of any attack.

They were sitting ducks for the Luftwaffe and the U-boats which would line up waiting to torpedo them just off the Norwegian coast. There were heavy losses, especially in the Merchant Navy, which lost eighty-five ships and up to 3,000 lives, for the loss of only sixteen Royal Navy vessels. The Merchant navy mariners were brave men, sailors who had not signed up to fight a war and were ill equipped for the Arctic conditions, where ice threatened to sink the ships and foul up the winches.

The call from the flagship would come at about 2 a.m. and the radio operators would set out to arrive for 4 a.m., when the whole fleet would be lit up and ready to move. The admirals valued these 'funny little men' as Tom described them, who spoke several languages and understood the quick-fire colloquial German used by the enemy. The escort commanders wanted them close at hand so that they could change the direction of the fleet immediately in response to updates on the U-boat positions.

Tom was proud of his service on the convoys and his memory of this time remained clear, in contrast to his selective amnesia over his childhood.

I would make my way to the Admiral's sea cabin, a special cabin on the bridge where the captain, who was on duty 24 hours, could take a nap every now and again, and we were amply provided with naval cocoa, but we had to stay awake all night and all day sometimes for days on end to keep on 'watching out' on frequencies on which the Germans were known to broadcast. Sometimes it was successful and sometimes we lost a lot of ships. All the things that were said about it are not exaggerated: [but] in books like The Cruel Sea *you get all the action concentrated into one ship, one sea and one voyage. The voyages weren't fun.*

There were some advantages to being on the admiral's flagship, according to Tom; they went to the 'best jetties' in Archangel and Murmansk, and had 'the best food and entertainment', Russian singing and dancing. 'When we went ashore all the Russians wanted to do was trade – our chocolate and cigarettes in exchange for steel-bladed knives with brightly coloured plastic handles, which were considered a desirable item. But there was no real friendship,' Tom remembered, although his Russian (not difficult to pick up as it is similar to Czech) must have been useful in the bartering.

Larking about (right) as a new recruit with a rating

'Through the porthole we saw hundreds of POWs, who had been drafted in as labour to unload the ships, and you saw they had no boots, just sacks tied over their bare feet, it was snowy of course. It was not difficult to deduce they were political prisoners.'

It was bitterly cold in the Arctic Circle – the thermometer often as low as −30°C – and it was difficult, 'coming from England, with all its freedoms', for Tom to feel any empathy for the Russian allies, just pity for the prisoners. Coming ashore was 'nothing very grand' although there was plenty of vodka, 'some of it was very good, some quite bad'; but there was no personal hospitality: 'we were never asked to people's houses, probably due to instructions from the NKVD against fraternising with foreigners. I would rather be put ashore in Alexandria, Suez or even Germany than Russia.'

Nevertheless, some British officers were intellectually attracted to communism, despite the obvious lack of freedoms. One winter's morning in Murmansk, Tom was woken up by one of his great friends, who summoned him to the upper deck of their aircraft carrier. There he stood with his kitbag, tin hat tied on to the top. Tom recalled the event as if it was last week:

'What are you doing?' I asked. 'I'm going ashore, Tom. I'm leaving the Royal Navy and I'm going to hand myself over

*to the Russians as I believe their social system is fairer than
ours.' He was an enthusiastic young socialist as we all were to
different degrees. I said, 'Don't be so silly; you can't just walk
out of the Royal Navy and expect the Russians to welcome
you with open arms. They'll think you're a bloody spy.' After a
long, long argument I said, 'Now come down below and I will
buy you a bottle of beer from the canteen.'*

The Russian convoys were extremely hazardous; the fighter
pilots knew that if they miscalculated and missed the deck of
the aircraft carrier, which was continuously see-sawing as much
as fifteen to twenty feet, they would ditch into the sea where
they wouldn't survive for more than a minute or two. The same
went for any ships that were torpedoed; despite rescue destroyers
being on hand, no sailor who went into the sea stood a chance.
Hence the fearsome reputation of these convoys and the very
belated recognition of the bravery of those who sailed on them.
Tom received his Arctic Star posthumously, seventy years later,
in a plastic box with a mass-produced citation and only after a
protracted application to the MOD which I completed after his
death. It was poor reward for all those who served in those convoys
and who showed such courage.

Tom also participated in the preparations for the June 1944 D-Day
landings on HMS *Hart*, under Commander Martyn Sherwood.
They were escorting half a dozen destroyers, four or five frigates
and other smaller vessels, which were bringing troops, food,
mechanical equipment and even harbours from the south coast to
the Normandy beachheads in advance of the invasion of Europe.
Sherwood valued the radio operators highly, as the success of the
mission depended entirely on the accuracy of the smallest detail

of intelligence; there were meetings every three to four hours to update him on the status quo.

Tom missed D-Day itself and never spoke about it, as he was posted back to patrolling duties in the Norwegian fjords, under Nazi control, which were used by the German navy to deliver supplies to their troops. These patrols were at constant risk and Tom remembered many near misses as the German U-boats would line up to torpedo the ships, and nights on end 'watching out' on German frequencies for enemy activity: 'Sometimes we were successful, sometimes not.'

In December 1945, in between missions, Tom was called to London for his commission – he was being promoted to acting sub-lieutenant. Even though the war had ended, interpreters such as Tom were needed for the denazification programme. The

Tom (centre) in a relaxed moment between missions. Note the wavy stripes on their sleeves

meeting took place in a former residential house in Queen Anne's Gate, just off St James's Park, where there was a row of admirals waiting to interview him. He was sitting on the edge of a converted bath, now part of the waiting room, when a blue-eyed admiral gave him a withering glance and asked him if he got ashore a lot. 'Not enough, sir, not enough,' he replied, 'we don't get ashore much.' 'Well,' barked the old boy, 'do you get any fun?' To which Tom replied in all sincerity, 'No, sir, that's what I mean, we don't get much fun as we don't get ashore much.' The admiral was enraged: 'No, not that sort of fun! I mean, action, boy, action!'

Luckily Tom's small faux pas did not cost him his stripe, but he rather rued his levity while recognising it as something inherited, thinking 'this little boy followed in his mother's footsteps and preferred the other kind of fun to the action kind of fun. Really the British are a rather strange people.' This impertinent attitude to authority and inability to judge a situation – a weird kind of bravado, showing off, even, just like his father – would continue to get him into trouble all his life.

On 3 July 1945, after the end of the war in Europe, Tom was posted to the 30 Assault Unit, a special commando force set up by the director of naval intelligence in 1942 and made up of troops from the Royal Marines, the Army, the RAF and the Royal Navy. One of its key figures was Ian Fleming, creator of James Bond. Their task, as the British and Americans advanced through Germany, was to scoop up German academics and rescue valuable equipment, both likely to be destroyed or taken away by the Russians, who were by now regarded with suspicion, owing to their occupation of Eastern Europe once hostilities had ceased; Churchill remarked that it was if 'an iron curtain has descended across the continent.' Their work was top secret.

Tom was stationed at Kiel, situated in the northernmost tip of Germany, on the Baltic, one of its most strategic ports and naval bases. The Allies had bombed Kiel heavily, and more than 80 per cent of the old town and the majority of the central residential and industrial areas were destroyed. It was snatched on 5 May 1945 from the teeth of the advancing Russians by T-Force, the joint US–British operation of which the 30 Assault Unit was a part.

Kiel housed the programme known as Walter-Werke under the leadership of the Nazi scientist Hellmuth Walter* who was decorated in early 1945 with Germany's highest medal, a Knight's Cross encrusted with gold and diamonds. Walter had devised a prototype submarine which could travel underwater at a speed twice that of any other submarine, powered by hydrogen peroxide. This technology was intended for a new missile, Germany's next devastating secret weapon after the doodlebug or V-1 flying bomb.

Tom was working under Commander Jan Aylen at Kiel, investigating the Walter-Werke factory and research centre, much of which was submerged in the form of a prototype submarine in the Kiel Canal, while another was in Cuxhaven. Having captured the subs, 30 Assault Unit's aim was to entice Walter and his gang to come to the West instead of to Russia. Tom was part of a small team whose main role was to liaise with Walter, 'a swine or a genius scientist, a Nazi through and through', who liked and trusted this witty twenty-two-year-old German-speaker: 'I spent many days and nights talking to him, we could exchange opinions freely without fear of persecution.' It might seem extraordinary that such responsibility was given to one so young, but Tom had been recruited for his fluency in both English and German, a rare

---

*   Fleming, probably as an inside joke, named one of his German spy characters Dr Walter in *Moonraker.*

commodity; as he said, 'my job was part interpretation, part getting on with people, they tended to trust me, and it was very successful'. His German and Czech upbringing gave him a real inside track in this sensitive work. Like his father, he had a natural bonhomie, especially when speaking German. He had a knack throughout his life of charming the most unlikely people.

After long negotiations, the prototypes were loaded on to a freighter and, together with the scientists and their families, ended up at Vickers Shipbuilding and Engineering in Barrow-in-Furness.

Tom was also involved in the handing over of the defeated German navy or Kriegsmarine – 500–600 ships, from large motorboats to battleships – to the Russians. This was unpopular with the German navy because, despite being enemies, Tom said there was a 'bond of respect between the German and British navies' due to their shared suspicion of the Russians.

In early January 1946, the British German-speakers were commanded to gather at Wilhelmshaven, ready for a two-week trip, where they were ferried out to the German admiral's vessel and the other bigger ships. 'At 2 a.m. the commanding officers of various vessels were to be rudely shaken from their slumbers to prevent any scuttling of the fleet', as had happened in Scapa Flow in the First World War. 'We broke into some unsuspecting destroyer captain's quarters and kicked him out politely, told him to get his stuff out in 30 minutes and get the crew lined up.' The German sailors were then commanded to sail the ships from Wilhelmshaven to Libau (now Liepāja), near St Petersburg.

Tom found himself in command of one of the largest former submarine escort ships, the *Otto Wünsche*, with a squad of 'regimental lieutenants and five soldiers, some Russian liaison staff and a crew of German sailors'. The soldiers were there to guarantee

Tom dressing up in German uniform as a joke

the Germans' safe return. With such a mixed bunch on board, the Russians, Germans and British had 'great fun as each night the cooks provided their own national dishes, and much vodka and pickled herring was consumed'. Many years later Tom was to send parcels of old clothes to one of these German companions, who had found himself destitute at the end of the war. I found photographs of these naval chums of his among his personal effects, one inscribed fondly, '*mit herzlichen Gruss, Dein alter August-Willhelm Hönck*'. As ever, Tom was able to show empathy to those less fortunate than him – despite having just abandoned Joyce and his baby daughter.

The trip was not without drama, Tom remembered, as the vessels 'were not new and kept breaking down'. Just outside Lübeck the Russian admiral signalled an immediate halt as the fleet was 'in the middle of a minefield'. All motors were shut down immediately and frantic messages sent to the Admiralty. Thanks to the ingenuity of a German cartographer on Tom's ship, who worked out that there had been mistake in the encryption of the original signal, the armada was able to set sail again, albeit in single file, so that only one ship would be blown up if it hit a mine. Tom, as the senior Allied officer on board, was in charge and ordered that the entire crew don life jackets 'just in case'.

When they finally reached Libau, the Russians refused to allow the German sailors to return. 'One of the reasons for the British riflemen was to give the Germans the necessary guarantee that they would be allowed to come back ... Various negotiations started buzzing and I spent 3 days in some prison which they called a "hostel" while discussions continued.' In the end they were allowed to set sail, although some of the sailors did, in fact, elect to stay in Russia, preferring the ideals of the communist state.

OLD HEIDELBERG 1945

Paper silhouette of Tom done in Heidelberg in 1945

CHAPTER 7:
SHEILA

My mother, Sheila Mills, arrived in Kiel in late May 1945. She was born in Scotland in September 1920 to Captain Percival Findlay Mills and his domineering wife, Grace. Findlay had won a Military Cross during the First World War, but had been gassed, causing him to be invalided out of the army when peace came. Sadly, his gassing meant that he was never able to work properly again –

Grace with Sheila (left) and Rosemary c.1921;
Capt. Findlay Mills (right)

and he only held such jobs as selling encyclopaedias and vacuum cleaners, which appalled Grace, who was an inveterate snob despite her farming background. Sheila's sister, Rosemary, said shortly before she died, 'Daddy was never brought up to earn money.'

Grace was one of ten children, from Norfolk farming stock. She had been a governess to a family in Appleby and, on one of their summer holidays to Scotland, she met Findlay, who was several years younger than her. They married and soon two girls were born, Rosemary and then Sheila, two years apart.

Sheila's childhood was unhappy; she was unwanted and unloved by her mother. Luckily, her cousins lived nearby, the children of Grace's sister, Dorothy, who had married well. Throughout her life, Sheila remained close to the youngest, Hazel, who remembered Grace's 'terrible temper' and how she used to hit Sheila, but never Rosemary.

In 1939, as soon as she was able to escape her social-climbing mother, Sheila went to London, to St James's Secretarial College, where she topped the class in shorthand and typing – she was a clever girl, despite her rural schooling in Hunstanton. She worked for a few months as a secretary to a law firm, Currey & Co., and in September 1940, when she was twenty, she joined the WRNS (Women's Royal Naval Service, known as the Wrens). She spent about eighteen months training in Rosyth in Scotland as a cipher officer and in March 1942 was posted to the Egyptian port of Alexandria to work in the office of the Commander-in-Chief Mediterranean.

Her job was to monitor the signals of enemy ships as well as the Royal Naval fleet that was standing by to support the Allied army in El Alamein. The second battle between October and November 1942 was the turning point of the war in North Africa. In July 1943 she moved to Cairo as part of Admiral Ramsay's small team that planned the invasion of Sicily in Operation Husky. She had been promoted to second officer by then as a reward for her hard work.

Her letters home from this period paint a portrait of an ambitious, intelligent woman, who loved having a good time in between the gruelling shifts, and who took intrepid holidays to Palestine and the Middle East. She had no problem finding boyfriends for she was gregarious and attractive. She had been engaged once, while in Egypt, to John Pritty, a captain in the 8th Army, the Scottish brother of one of her Wren friends from Rosyth, whom she had jilted because of his controlling and jealous temperament, and she was considering another suitor when she returned to Europe in 1945.[*]

Finding an officer to marry was a primary objective for many of the girls serving abroad who, like Sheila, came from modest backgrounds. She arrived in Kiel in May 1945 as a cipher officer, just as the war in Europe ended and the programme of denazification began in Germany and Austria. She continued to write her weekly letter home to her mother, more out of a sense of duty than love, and also as a record of her extraordinary transformation. She frequently reminded her mother to keep her letters to await her return after the war.

Soon, the naturally sociable Sheila was getting out and about in Kiel. She first met Tom on 23 June 1945 at the Yacht Club with her fellow Wren Betty Mackenzie. She appears to have been underwhelmed at first, for all she told her mother was that she 'went out sailing all the afternoon with Tom Unwin – he has had some frightful rash and hasn't been able to shave for about a week – looks quite fierce!'

Sheila had developed from a rather shy country girl into a woman of the world. She described Kiel as 'in the most terrible state –

---

[*]   My mother's war is recorded in my book *Love and War in the WRNS* (History Press, 2015).

sunken ships, twisted steel, salved boats lying high and dry on the quay, and hardly a building left standing'. Yet her frequent letters also describe another Kiel, a 'very gay' city, whose social life centred round the various officers' messes and the Yacht Club, 'a beautiful place. It was the Kaiser's own yacht club, and the equivalent of Cowes in England'; they enjoyed horse riding, went to concerts and sailed. The occupying forces seem to have enjoyed sumptuous parties and dancing until 4 a.m.; 'It was such fun, all on Champagne too ... wonderful food and drink', while the locals starved.

Both Tom and Sheila were ambivalent about their situation: the lavish parties, with free-flowing champagne, caviar, fine wines and nightly dancing. Sheila wrote in October 1945 that her driver survived on 'four bits of bread a day', which he gave to his children. She was shocked that, on one occasion, after a party the band was arrested for smuggling out leftover food in their music cases, and that the German cook in their mess was imprisoned for six months for stealing scraps. Sheila's letters constantly reference her disquiet about the situation: 'I can't bear to see them all so hungry, with so much food that we leave over, just being thrown away.'

As part of the denazification programme, they fraternised with the remaining German nobility:

> Princesses, counts, countesses, generals ... all charming, well-mannered and cultured. Interesting and amusing to think that their sons had all been arrant young Nazi officers ... they all have a very narrow outlook ... of course all denounce the Nazis madly, but would have been among the first to acknowledge them had they succeeded. All spoke English well, and most had been to England.

Tom and Sheila did not meet again for another year. During this time, Tom was posted to HMS *Royal Albert* in Cuxhaven and Hamburg from July to September 1945 (for Walter-Werke). From the end of 1945 to April 1946 (after his promotion in December 1945), he was stationed on HMS *Royal Caroline* as harbour master in Travemünde, the port for Lübeck. Tom felt sorry for and fraternised freely with the German citizens, many of whom were hungry and had lost everything – too freely for the naval officer-in-charge who forbade him from teaching some local children English in a little informal school he set up there in 1945, under the name of Uncle Tom.

Only two of Tom's letters survive from this period, both of which suggest that he was worrying about the state of the world and what his future role might be. His desire to work for the United Nations reflected his high opinion of himself, and his newly discovered socialism: 'There is a great deal for the UNO to do if only they grab the chance and bring peoples of the world closer together. The best way to do it, or one of them, is to give me a job there.'

On 11 March 1946, he tried to reassure his mother that, despite being a vegetarian, he was 'quite alright, very fit, eat plenty of vegetables and cheese. I really find something rather repulsive about meat – I don't like the idea of eating things that have been killed ... all this business of eating meat is terribly primitive and belongs in a bygone age, together with war, slaughter and cruelty of any kind.' His vegetarianism did not survive the war.

Later that month, he wrote of his work with 'my Russians' who were 'amazing ... they are real Slavs, rather peculiarly dressed, one is very proletarian and wears a pink silk handkerchief in his breast pocket. They are good-hearted people if they see you are honest with them and don't laugh at them.' He was horrified by the lies they have been told: 'they said, quite innocently that Finland attacked Russia (in 1938) and that the Persian Prime Minister had reached agreement with Stalin before leaving Moscow. Just imagine! Well, no wonder international relations are what they are.'

Tom's sketch of his supervision of the spoils of war

He sent a drawing of himself with 'Vassili', a Russian sailor, on one side and 'Jerry' kowtowing on the other, to illustrate 'loading some Russian ships with war materials (booty) for the USSR ... we spend the day clearing up muddles between Russians, Germans and British'.

Tom made a better impression when he and Sheila met again on 10 June 1946. He had left Lübeck and was now attached to HMS *Royal Harold* back in Kiel. As Sheila wrote home, 'On Victory Day, I took half the morning off and went riding – in the afternoon I went out sailing with an awfully nice young Sub. [Lt] here – Tom Unwin – we had such fun.' In the evening they went aboard the destroyer HMS *Zenith*, and then on to a film. 'I reckon I had as good a day of Victory as anyone.'

Sheila was determined to come home with a husband. She had another tempestuous on–off relationship with a captain from the Tanks who was desperate to marry her but, like John Pritty, was prone to fits of jealous rage. She had set her sights on an old boyfriend from Egypt, Major Bruce Booth-Mason, who was proving hard to pin down. As a fall back she was in constant touch

Sheila in Germany

with another old flame, Robin Chater, and was seeing a couple of other officers in Germany.

In mid-June Sheila wrote, 'I have got Tom Unwin coming to tea – he is very bashful because he has produced some frightful spots on his neck and has taken some persuasion to come.' He must have been somewhat in awe of this older, sophisticated and higher-ranking officer – he was only twenty-two, she was twenty-five – although his work gave him an authority way beyond his rank of sub lieutenant, equivalent to third officer. It gave him the self-belief that was to drive his ambition for the rest of his life.

Suddenly Sheila's letters home were full of Tom, although she was worried about the age difference: 'He really is the sweetest person – but 3 years younger than I am!' They went riding together, for walks in the woods; he was even tasked with buying cheese for Sheila's mother in Durham; and they planned to go away together for her birthday in September. Within a few weeks the romance was serious, although one incident was to niggle Sheila for the rest of her life.

Tom was taking Sheila for a drive one afternoon 'and suddenly we were sitting in a tree!' Tom always maintained it 'wasn't really my fault at all as we were going uphill … The police said there was something wrong with the wheels and were concerned someone had sabotaged the car … poor Sheila had a couple of teeth knocked out and a big bump on her head'. He took her to a German naval hospital 'with her bag of teeth' and they patched her up. 'She was incredibly brave, no anaesthetic'. Tom was eternally grateful to the doctor and sent food parcels to him.

Sheila never really forgave Tom, as she was scarred horribly. Whenever she complained, Tom would reply callously, 'I did marry you, you know.' She felt the loss of her pretty face and had to wear a dental plate for the rest of her life. When she was feeling particularly annoyed with my father, she would refer to this incident with a hollow laugh.

Tom showed her a different side of life due to his understanding of German culture. In July 1946 they visited some White Russian relations of Tom's old friend from Wells. They had lost everything in Berlin and were now stateless but 'still in hope that something would turn up'. Tom and Sheila spent a most amusing evening dancing and talking to the Russians – 'Tom is a very good linguist and the nice Lithuanian Colonel thought him marvellous'.

They were planning to spend their July leave in England together, but Tom's work intervened. He added in a letter to her, in a rather offhand way, 'do you know I miss you rather a lot. Sounds silly, doesn't it? I didn't think I would!'

The romance continued on Sheila's return from leave in early August 1946. Her letters home were now full of the fun times with Tom – dining, swimming, picnicking, visiting Lübeck, driving through the country. They had an adventure while out riding when they were attacked by a stallion which took a fancy to Sheila's horse and Tom, 'frightfully brave', had to fend it off; they spent a 'marvellous afternoon' at Schleswig cathedral; and then Tom went on leave to see his mother 'for a whole fortnight – Awful!'

A typical poem plus sketch

While away he wrote a series of tortured love letters and poems to Sheila. She kept them all. Sheila, meanwhile, was keeping her options open and still seeing one of her other officers; I wonder to what extent his inherited jealous streak spurred Tom's new romanticism.

The first anguished letter was from the cabin on the boat taking him home: 'Spare a thought for me on the first stage of my journey ... send me a written thought now and again, please' and ends 'I love you very much, darling. You mean a lot to me but it all sounds like drivel at this time of night ...'

Several poems followed, on naval message paper, unashamedly romantic: 'It may just be a reverie, Of a Sub [Lt] on morning watch: But that's how you appear to me, At times when I am took with fright, I'd love to have you near to me, My light'; and 'Forgive these lines, Writ down in haste, For beauty they have none, All they really show to me, Is the damage, You have done!' adorned with a carefully etched bleeding heart.

He wrote the following letter on Salvation Army paper, while waiting for his train to take him on leave to England.

Railway Stn
Bad Oeynhausen
15.8

Madam

May we interest you in corresponding with a lonely
young man who is off on leave to England today?

He is a young naval officer – his plane didn't fly owing
to the weather and so train is the answer. He is rather
unhappy at the thought of going home and so, knowing
you, we hope you will not mind the Xian [Christian] deed
involved in writing to him.

He was rather bashful of writing to you himself but
appears to be very fond of you. In fact, he forgot to take
his change of [unreadable] and when asked why, said 'these
bloody women, always on your mind' from which remark
you will readily deduce the depth of his love.

In the hope, dear madam, that we have not offended
you by our forthright request and wishing you the happiest
possible of correspondences.
We sign ourselves
   Respectfully
   Josiah H Turmoil
   Stn. Welfare Officer
   NB the young man's address – his name is I believe
known to you – is 17, Chamberlain St, Wells, Somerset.

Just as Sheila wanted a husband, I often wonder if Tom was also
seeking respectability through a British wife?

CHAPTER 8:
COURTSHIP AND
MARRIAGE

On arrival in London in August 1946, Tom stayed at the RNVR Club where he wrote:

> Darling Sheila, I only have to go away to realise how awfully I have fallen. It sounds daft ... but the truth cannot be denied. No doubt if I stayed away from you long enough it would all cool down, but at the moment I am dying to share that sofa with you again, not only because of your comforting physical features ... we do understand each other, don't we darling?

He was lonely in London and full of self-pity:

> I walked back to the Club, feeling rather low – longing for your hand in mine, for your pleasant sweet face to look at, to talk to you, to go somewhere with you ... you make all the difference to me. Perhaps one day if it all goes right, there will be no need to part any more, but that is very distant, very ideal and does not depend on me (and you) alone. Excuse my innate pessimism, darling.

His burgeoning socialism, brought on by the horror of his wartime experiences, especially on the convoys and in starving post-war Germany, was awakened in London, which he found 'depressing and seeing the revoltingly wealthy people' made him 'quite angry ... as they look so smooth and smug'. He was strangely cheered up by the Hare's Foot pub, 'full of very poor strange people, a typical Soho lot, the usual mixture of queer and normal and eccentric, but with a good, warm-hearted atmosphere of common misery'.

His brother Alec joined him in London for a few days. Tom was debating whether Alec should continue studying, but there were now few university places left, or whether he and their mother should go to Canada, Tom's preference. He took Alec to *Die Fledermaus*, 'lousy performance, cheapened by a music-hall atmosphere', and to Hampton Court. He found Alec 'annoying' and admitted he was 'not kind to the little devil', although he had been looking forward to seeing him.

Tom was on the point of being demobbed, so he was job-hunting, but this did not go well either. His frustration gave rise to feelings of anxiety which were recorded in the rambling handwritten letters of this period. He acknowledged that he was a 'soft and semi-mad creature' who wrote 'drivel ... Damn and blast it, how am I to tell all these thick-skulled employers that I am a jolly good worker, reliable, good organiser, etc'. Despite his high opinion of himself, he recognised that 'influence' was required and rued that he had been 'silly enough to hob-nob not with those at the top but with those at the bottom. It's all rather galling'. He wanted a job that earned good money, and 'something that squares with my ideals'. This inability to relate to his superiors was to be a lifelong problem for him.

The Colonial Office was swamped with applications, but he thought the BBC was 'bound to give me a job'. He was very aware that without a job he could not 'keep a wife at a reasonable level of comfort'. His application to the UNO to be a 'liaison man, a missionary of peace, the UNO is bound to require people of my kind' was full of self-belief: 'I am intelligent, an excellent organiser and a good administrator. I have had the opportunity of testing these attributes in Germany since V-Day.'

Acknowledging his new-found zeal, he continued that his main qualification was his 'burning desire to further the cause of peace' and described himself as a 'militant-pacifist … an idealist and intend to remain one'. He always had a tendency to pomposity when orating or writing, as I discovered when interviewing him, and he continued in his letter:

> I have been greatly cheered by the brave words of Churchill in Belgium and of Mr. Bevan and Mr. Eden in the Commons. I believe in the possibility of achieving a peaceful future. It is the most important, the one vital thing, in the world today. I beg you not to deny me the chance of doing my very best to help with this great work.

He did not get the job.

Despondent, all he wanted to do was 'bury my nose in your smelly hair, feel your scented skin and your hand in mine. I wish I could listen to Chopin with you and kiss you, hold you because then I would, for a time, forget all these little worries and realise that I am really very happy because I love you and because I think that my feelings are not entirely unreturned'.

On 19 August 1946 he came clean:

> I've got something on my mind – a confession in fact. I don't tell everyone because it only leads to millions of questions I have answered before: I am not really British, I

am Czech by birth and my naturalisation is only just under way. Admiralty have just lost the forms (!).

I had to keep all this quiet during war-time otherwise it would have been very dangerous in case I got captured. I didn't tell you from the first because I thought you might not 'go much on it'. Sorry if I underestimated you. Very few people at Kiel know as it is – it saves so many silly questions and is very much easier all round, but I do think you ought to know, if anyone.

Look Darling, if you think I am a cad for not saying so at once, you can say so. These things are easier written than said, and that is partly the reason I'm writing. I left Prague in 39 to finish off my education in UK and got caught. Mummy came over later. And now the beastly situation has changed again making a return difficult.

Well, we'll talk more about it when I get back. Hope it isn't too much of a shock for you. At least you have time to think about it. Be quite candid darling, please, I much prefer it.

Job-hunt still pretty lousy. Difficulties everywhere and Admiralty have lost my wretched papers.

Damnation!

All my love, darling

Tom

As ever, Tom evaded the whole truth – no mention of being Jewish. His confession was forced out because Sheila was bound to question why he was finding it so difficult to get a job; he wanted to be on the front foot on the issue of his Czech nationality. His lack of courage on personal matters was in contrast to his war record, and it was something that never changed.

*

Tom arrived in Wells in late August 1946 to see Grete. At last he had some good news, which he imparted to Sheila, the letter adorned by a cupid with bow. He was to join the International Federation of Agricultural Producers (IFAP), an offshoot of the National Farmers Union (NFU), to organise a conference to discuss post-war cooperation among eighteen of the world's largest agricultural producers. It was 'just the sort of thing I want, my chance to improve international relations and to provide food'. The salary would be £600 p.a., on a par with that of an MP. But he was plagued by doubts as he had not told them about the problem with his naturalisation and prayed that it would be 'through' by his demob date in October: 'unfortunately absolute honesty is not always the best policy ...' he wrote, 'I am most uncomfortable ... but then people of my kind are in so unusual and strange a position that it is impossible to say what is right'. (In the event he didn't receive his naturalisation papers until the end of January 1947.)

As a PS to this letter, he added, 'Do you believe in engagements? I don't! Engagements are only for people of strong character'. Marriage, now he had a job, was uppermost in his mind.

He was frustrated at home, which was rather 'cramped', and Grete was getting a 'little oldish in her outlook and losing a little of her "class". Is this the woman who had dined with Presidents?' While wishing he could spend his leave with Sheila, he admitted the 'temptation' to have sex would be 'too great ... self-denial is alright but inwardly I ha'e me doots ... that anticipation is better than realisation'.

For Sheila, despite all her boyfriends, was still a virgin and several of Tom's letters reflect his obsession with sex – or lack of it – hence the desire to get married as soon as possible. On 30 October, he told her he had consulted books and written to various

Harley Street doctors for advice on the best way of losing her virginity painlessly, and of preventing pregnancy. He went into great detail describing 'sheaths', 'pessaries' and the pros and cons of condom use in married life – 'it's essentially an unmarried sinner's method ... and is unsatisfactory as you don't get the right "contact"'. He even made her an appointment with a specialist and frequently referred to the 'problem', exhorting her to visit the doctor who can 'fit you up with a device ... the best and most civilised thing to do ... A lot of people just muddle along in a terribly primitive way because they are too silly or shy to ask ... there is no room in the world today for these remnants of Jane Austen or Victorian puritanism ... How wonderful it is we can talk and correspond about these things without embarrassment'. We will never know if Sheila agreed but it smacks of what we would now recognise as coercive control, something that would only get worse.

He had already decided that Sheila, 'a not unattractive camel-shaped young woman', should be his secretary at IFAP, uniting them in their vision of utopia, with 'no prospect of war at all, and we would discuss music, the best way of bringing up children ... consider buying a little house which we shall call Shangri-La ... a new world of happiness would open and we would live in peace and happiness til death us do part'. He tempered this 'rose-tinted view' with his resurgent worries over 'trifling things' like his 'opinions and nationality, that material facts may mar a permanent union', that 'war may return, and we cannot stop ourselves hastening our own suicide as a species. Is it really too late to stop the rot? Can nothing really be done?'

He ended this *cri de cœur* with the words, 'let us hope that we, perhaps, shall achieve our Shangri-La. If there is a God – and I don't think there is – he certainly should favour us. We have both deserved peace of mind and body'. Alongside, he sketched their Shangri-La cottage, emblazoned by a smiling, pipe-smoking sun. These letters combine an odd mix of romanticism and sentimentality with a chilling subscript of misogyny.

This was his last letter before he returned to Germany after his leave. In the few weeks they had left together, they went sailing, to concerts, to the opera *Falstaff* and to Bad Harzburg for Sheila's birthday weekend. Before he left for his demobbing in London on 15 October, Sheila wrote that he gave a 'bumper party in his office for all his employees, both English and German and what a collection appeared – the 3 officers themselves, 2 marine drivers, German drivers, German friends and so on – It really went off very well. It is strange for me to be here without Tom as we have done everything together for the past 3 months.'

Sheila was also set to leave the WRNS but not until late November. She occupied herself by going on a domestic science course, for by now they were informally engaged, although Sheila did not tell her mother until 30 October. Blinded by love, desperate to marry, this is how she described her future husband:

I think you will like your future son-in-law, tho' you may find him a trifle unorthodox – He is 3 years younger than I am – tall, fair, grey-eyed and well built. He is Czech by birth and lived in Prague till 1939 when he came to England to study – now being naturalised. Subsequently, his mother and young brother, Alec, came over and settled in Wells, Somerset. His mother is a widow, her husband having been in the Czech Diplomatic Service, I think and who died of appendicitis when Tom was 9 [in fact he was six] – Of course, they have lost almost everything. They have much property in Czechoslovakia, but that is all Russian now.

As for Tom – he is an extremely clever linguist – and no one could tell he wasn't English, as he gabbles away faster than we normally talk. His German is the same – He is far-seeing politically, and deeply interested in world affairs, and – a Socialist!! A terrific peace-lover – almost to being a conscientious objector! He is brilliant and almost fanatical in his views and ideals, and everyone who knows him well says they think he will go far. I hope he will. He loves music and the country and has had to do everything for his mother and brother since they came over here …

I'm sure you will find him most loveable and easy to get on with – he's sweet with children … is temperamental and often gets fits of depression regarding the state of the world – But not the sort of temperament that flings frying pans about!

Tom, meanwhile, had returned to London and his new job, and began swamping her with daily love letters, which simultaneously reflected his deep anxieties, although he was looking forward to 'D-Day' – their wedding. He moved into digs in Russell Square where he planned to stay until they were married, despite the fact there was no heating in his room.

Tom was finally demobbed on 18 October, a 'simple, short ritual taking ½ hour, after which I was a civvy'. His naval record described him as:

… a keen, industrious and efficient young officer who should go far. An outstanding linguist who speaks fluent German and French above average. Though of Czech nationality he has lived in UK since 1939 and speaks word-perfect English. He can also fill a gap as a Russian interpreter. Completely

reliable and a pleasant personality. Intellectual rather than sporting type. Well above average intelligence.

He celebrated by buying a suit, for the 'frightful price' of twenty guineas, and a few shirts. The Navy also gave him a demob suit, 'a dark brown thing with a fairly unostentatious chalk stripe which will do for work', plus a shirt, a tie – 'oh what a tie!' – and some shoes.

He went off to Wells to see Grete. Her transformation from high society lady to impoverished housewife was now complete, and Tom was 'horribly depressed ... mummy annoys me so much with her petty little swindles'. His major worry at this point was where they were to live, and the letters up until Sheila's return reflect his dithering over this. 'It worries me very much and I wish I had you here to tell me what to do.' He missed her hugely, he longed 'to kiss you, and live with you ... I'm positive we shall be very happy and never regret having married'.

At this time Tom began to exhibit great neuroses, mirroring his father Hermann's introspective self-pity. He was 'so much in love, miserable, depressed and unhappy ... all I want to do is cry. But that is pure nerves and high tension. I was so done in this afternoon I thought I would scream'. His need to be in control was in evidence on day one of his job with IFAP which was 'sheer agony when you don't know what's going on and have to grope in the dark'. He took against his assistant, the 'uninspiring' Miss Fagg, simply because she had been there longer, was a woman, older, more experienced than him and did not want 'to work under me'. She 'has the advantage over me as I can't really boss her about – I like to be an absolute dictator in the office'. Most galling of all, the unfortunate Miss Fagg stood in the way of his getting Sheila a job there.

His letter of 24 October was no happier. Although he had only been in the job a few days, he was 'at sixes and sevens', disorganised and unwell, a 'physical reaction to a mental state'. No doubt he had real symptoms, like his father, but they were as a result of a similar obsessional anxiety. He was living off sandwiches and worrying about how expensive everything was, to the point where he told Sheila, 'we shall have to content ourselves with ourselves and your radio.'

He had moved to a new room in Leinster Square, W2, with a 'double bed!' but no washbasin, for £3/10 a week – he included a sketch to show the positioning of all the furniture – where the landlady provided 'breakfast and dinner, fish or chops, or bacon and omelet [*sic*] – almost as good as Kiel, no joking'. He remained 'still full of uncertainties and fears about not making enough money and doing the wrong thing in getting married ... but I do love you very, very much and I *must* have you and because I love you, I feel perhaps I am not being fair to you to offer you marriage on a shaky foundation'. He suggested she still had a 'good chance of gracefully declining and I should understand your motive'. The only 'shaky foundation' was Tom himself.

This anxiety was to surface again when he wrote on his birthday, 25 October, that he was feeling the 'change of life from the Navy ... all this scrounging, cheap existence in an unfriendly room and so dear ... and [I] suffer from tonsillitis and sleep badly at night. Don't I feel sorry for myself?' He still felt that he 'ought not to marry ... if you marry me you are marrying a madman – I may be quite clever but make no mistake about it, I am also mad.'

He continued in this vein in the next letter, telling her his father was 'mad too, mad and genial ... I fear you will find me a difficult man to live with even as mother found father. The trouble is I am too highly strung ... always dissatisfied, always dripping ...' A few weeks before their marriage he wrote, 'it isn't too late for you to realise you are marrying a soft fool, a dithering and undetermined semi-lunatic ... when I say I'm mad I am quite serious about it. Perhaps you could reduce my madness to something more human'.

Meanwhile, he reported that Grete was trying to cheer him up, telling him he was a 'silly blighter ... that I am very lucky indeed'. However, both work and the tonsillitis were still bothering him. He wrapped his neck in a moist handkerchief, sealed with cellophane, with a scarf on the outside 'as the doctor made me do as a kid'; he was getting 'no sleep', was 'delirious, having phantastic thoughts, worrying about things and unable to get up in the morning ... I even thought of suicide because life just doesn't seem worth living, and had it not been for Ma, Alec and you, well ... I know now what they mean by balance of mind disturbed'.

He was certain there was an impending war – he was haunted by Hiroshima and Nagasaki, and suspicious of both the Americans and the Russians. His solution was to escape to New Zealand where he could become a schoolmaster, 'teaching farmers' children the elementary truths and the decencies of life ... we'd live in a lovely little house in a beautiful climate, have all the things we want and be happy', or he could teach 'Negros in Kenya', living a life 'of absolute goodness and of gentleness and non-violence and understanding others, of easy, peaceful leisure and contentment. I do so passionately desire to be a pacifist and a vegetarian ... will you come?'

His next worry was the wedding. He shared his father's attitude to marriage as a middle-class institution and was dead against a church wedding: 'do you see how horribly complicated it would be ... I'm so confused ... I feel like committing suicide sometimes'. Hardly encouraging words for his future bride especially as he continued to have doubts, 'My love for you has become a deep and lasting affection – as it is not the wild passion of fiery youth – not entirely anyway. And that is why I still feel, sometimes, that I may be doing the wrong thing in marrying in these circumstances of uncertainty.'

Sheila's bourgeois mother insisted on a church wedding, but Tom remained adamant that there should be no fuss, 'I presume that it will NOT be a pukkha [*sic*] wedding where I would have to wear tails or something? Please darling, anything but that.' When he discovered it was to be formally announced, he exploded:

> Now why the hell do your people want to put it in the paper? I am very much against it. There can be no practical argument for it apart that we shall have a lot of mail to answer, and it's just middle-class pomposity and you can tell them I said so, or I'll tell them myself. NO, I am ABSOLUTELY against it.

He had to have his way, dictated the wedding notice and instructed her to keep the parents' names out of it – he did not want the Ungar name mentioned; he was still not naturalised and wished to keep a low profile. He added, 'No flowers or letters, by request' and a saucy 'RIP' to Sheila to indicate the matter was dead.

In a later letter he complained further: 'Oh you wretch, so we are going to have to be terribly suburban and have cards and cake ...' Signs of his meanness resurfaced with the guest list when he said, 'shall we just confine it to your friends?' and only reluctantly agreed that spare invitations could be sent to his German colleagues at Barrow-in-Furness, and notices to his friends in Germany – 'but no cake, it would be like a mockery', given the food shortages.

Other aspects of marriage and domesticity began to get him

down. The letters become hectoring in their tone: 'For goodness sake don't buy too much bric-a-brac in the form of glasses and things. Much more useful if you buy sheets and pillow cases'; as for wedding presents, they must be 'useful ... an iron; anything from carpet to lavatory brushes'. Even the honeymoon was to be short – he supposed he 'could wangle a few days off ... the brevity and austerity of it all will make it all the nicer'. Poor Sheila.

Despite Sheila's domestic science course, he held out little hope for her culinary prowess. He urged her to learn how to cook 'meat – not stews except Irish stew, how to roast; omelets [*sic*] and pancakes, custard and pastry; not vegetables the English way, awful'. He said Grete should come up and teach her 'how to cook and other housewifely achievements' because 'mummy is an excellent housewife, much better than yours probably'. He thought English standards were 'shamefully inadequate. Polish the brasses, sweep the shit under the carpet and "Oh where's the tin opener, dear?"' In fact, Grace was an excellent cook and housekeeper, far less slovenly than Grete, who had never had to lift a finger before the war, although she was an accomplished cook.

This controlling, bossy tone increased as the date of Sheila's return from Germany and the wedding drew nearer. He was enraged that 'this is the second consecutive day with no letter from you ... I suppose this is more of Robin what-not's [old boyfriend] doing. You wait – I'll get my own back for all the humiliation and sorrow you inflict on me'. Similarly, on house-hunting, he ordered her, 'For goodness sake write to your cousin in Royston. Don't wait for *me* to have to tell you – where's your personality?' And when she muddled the date of his birthday, Sheila got both barrels: 'You silly old witch – you big bosomed elephant – you shunt-arsed camel – you bullying hippopotamus – you trestle-necked giraffe. Darling, don't take any of the above to 'eart, I still loves yer, yer sour faced old xxxx [illegible].' Like his father, he thought his cruel sense of humour was amusing to others.

He was determined that Sheila should get a job as soon as she arrived. Indecisive, he wavered over her working with him at IFAP, but when his bosses started discussing sacking Miss Fagg, his conscience got the better of him, and he felt like a 'cad'. He came to the conclusion that it would be 'just as well if we didn't work together – we'll be fresh and new to each other every evening'. He hoped that once she had 'a home to run', she would be 'very busy' and 'if not, you can always do a part-time job'. He even sent her some job advertisements cut out from *The Times*.

Sheila returned from Germany at the end of November. What little time she spent with Tom was miserable as he was 'rather bad company' and admitted he had 'some sort of cloud on my horizon'. He reassured her he still loved her and gained 'great comfort and strength from you' and apologised for being a 'despicably weak character'.

They stole a quick weekend in Wells to meet Grete, who later said in a letter to her son:

> Sheila is such a good girl, and I am sure you will be very happy. I am so glad to see how completely devoted you are to each other and Sheila is so sensible ... And I am proud of you, having been through the war ... God bless you ...

Waiting for Sheila to arrive ...

Don't worry about anything, all will come in good time ...
you know my children's happiness is all that matters to me.

She also advised the couple not to do too much 'sightseeing'
as she euphemistically put it, as 'love is like a new suit which gets
shabby with too much wear'.

From there, Sheila decamped to Durham to arrange the
wedding. Characteristically, Tom was pulling the strings from afar.
On 30 November he sent her this list:

Book accommodation
Find a best or second-best man [he was too mean to pay his
closest friend to come up from Wells]
Write off lots of applications for jobs
Fix a date to see Griffith [the gynaecologist]
Do any other things you can think of

Tom joined her for a weekend to meet Grace and Findlay where,
on best behaviour, he charmed them both. He was desperate to
sleep with Sheila and he told her he had a 'great fear of a strange
bed, and therefore I insist'. A strange request from a naval officer
who must have slept all over the place. Unsurprisingly, this was not
going to happen in my grandparents' very middle-class household.
Nevertheless, he 'rather liked your folks. Don't put their backs up
the last week you are with them'.

Sheila was finding her mother trying in the run-up to the
wedding, attempting to square Tom's desire for a low-key event
with her mother's conventionality. Tom took Sheila's side but his
enquiries about 'the battle on the home front' were rather snide
and two-faced, setting the precedent for the future:

Ho, ho what fun you must be having you poor dear. Please try to stick to our 'no fuss policy'. Don't let the buggers get you down, it's our wedding, our life. So even if they have their own way a little, well, Maleesh [never mind], sweetheart. One we are out of that kirk, it's just you and me ever after and damn the last man.

Nearly all the letters reflect his love for Sheila but also reveal the extent to which he remained tortured about his perceived inner turmoil. It seems extraordinary that he was preparing to wed the love of his life, as he continually told her, yet was unable to send her a letter without rambling about his depression, frustration at work, the everyday worries of life, with an extra lashing of bossiness.

He was also increasingly fed up with IFAP, despite the success of his conference in mid-November, and a 'pat on the back' from the secretary general. 'I still don't know if there is a future for the job. I don't know whether there is a future in anything. Honestly the world today is the most depressing place ... I will NOT work for an organisation whose aims run counter to the general prospects of mankind.'

He was never satisfied, 'always dripping', as he wrote on 30 November:

I suppose I can keep this job as long as I like ... but Lord, I do wish for something else. I don't know quite what though. Really, I don't know what is the matter with me ... perhaps I have been too much of an idealist in the past and I now feel life has very few ideals ... it's a stupid uneasy sort of feeling which depresses me. I think I should get away from it by being very far from all this mess.

Presciently, in one of his final letters, he says, 'I feel most unworthy of all the praise you heap upon me and one day you will see me for what I am. However, until then you might as well delude yourself.'

Despite Tom's professed misgivings, the wedding day arrived, and my parents were finally married in St Oswald's Church in Durham on 23 December 1946. It is an austere, grey building, with a square steeple, dating from the twelfth century, set atop a hill in Durham's North End, where Grace and Findlay lived. Several of Tom's German colleagues came from Barrow-in-Furness, despite his hopes that 'none of these people you send invites to turn up as we should be faced with the problem of accommodation'. He even sent an invitation on Sheila's behalf to her best friend Betty 'with strict instruction not to dream of coming'. There is no record of how these Germans were received by the bourgeois Durham friends and Norfolk relatives, nor of how many of those invited attended.

Extraordinarily, Grete was not at the wedding. Tom supposed 'she didn't feel up to it' but I suspect the cost and transport difficulties put her off. It is also quite possible that Tom dissuaded her, embarrassed she would show him up, with her heavy accent and secondhand clothes. Alec came in the end, although Tom's meanness about paying for his accommodation had almost extended to denying his brother an invitation. Sheila took pity on him and arranged for him to stay with her parents. The only mementos of their wedding that I found are the wedding photograph, an invitation in silver print on card for 'Mrs Ungar and Alec', and a small box of cake crumbs.

They then went on a short honeymoon to the Lake District, staying at the Sun Inn in Coniston, before returning to their new digs in Leinster Square. Pointedly, Sheila always said that Tom changed on the day they got married – from the romantic suitor into a domineering and undermining husband.

When she married Tom, Sheila knew only what he had told her in his letters; she had been distanced from his mood swings. She had fallen for the handsome officer, three years her junior, whose idealism, charm and irreverent humour had proved seductive, despite all the early warnings of Tom's darker nature. She dreaded her mother's disapproval if she returned home a single woman, so went ahead with the marriage, despite the signs of Tom's depression, misogyny and controlling nature. And she really did love him at that point – her letters to her mother anticipated the loyalty she displayed during their twenty years of marriage, despite all the difficulties he threw in her path.

CHAPTER 9:
THE GROUNDNUT
SCHEME

As preparations for the wedding came and went, Tom had been casting around for a job he felt to be more in tune with his idealism. He had heard of the Groundnut Scheme from a fellow Officer in the RNVR. As he told me much later, it chimed with his 'desire to help the poor nations of Africa to make food for the world, to do something constructive'.

Labour under Clement Attlee had won a landslide victory in 1945, ousting Churchill and his National Coalition, and this fed Tom's altruism. The new Labour government had commissioned the Wakefield Report to explore the possibilities of growing peanuts in Africa to supplement the post-war British diet. It proposed that millions of acres be cleared, mostly in Tanganyika, with the aim of producing 800,000 tons by the early 1950s. It glossed over the finer detail of the *how* – preferring to simply state that 'highly mechanised forms of agriculture' be used; 25,000 Africans would be required as labour, along with 500 Europeans, rising to 750. The capital cost was to be £24 million – and this did not include the running costs.

Such was the speed, lack of clarity and planning accompanying this new Scramble for Africa that the advance party was arriving in Tanganyika as early as January 1947. Tom always said that he was seduced by the notion of 'turning swords into ploughshares' and jumped at the chance to join the Groundnut Scheme as a field assistant in July (although he had to take a salary cut to £550 p.a.), courtesy of his naval record and his agricultural diploma from Somerset. He was excited by the prospect of working with Africans for the greater good and the thrill of the adventure that beckoned.

Grete and Alec had finally emigrated to Canada in May 1947, helped by her ex Rudi Weiss, shortly before Tom left for Africa in advance of Sheila. 'You are off now and we shall not see each other for three years at least,' Tom wrote in his farewell letter to them. 'We have been terribly lucky ... Blood is thicker, much thicker than water, and I shall never forget the debt of gratitude I owe both of you for all the love and care which has sustained me so far and will, I trust, continue to do so until I am no more.' His emotion reflects the strong bond between mother and son.

The physical distance from Grete might explain why he felt such an attachment to Sheila's mother, Grace. In this rare letter, the first from Africa in July 1947, he wrote to Grace about Grete, who 'was not having much fun as she doesn't like [my older brother] John's wife', so much so that they moved from Toronto to Vancouver, where Alec got a place at the university, Grete got a job and eventually bought a house and rented rooms to students. 'As for Sheila,' he adds 'you can't believe how much I am looking forward to having her here with me. Don't you worry, I'll look after her – and we'll see you in 3 years' time in UK! With a right royal JAMBO, I am your ever-faithful son, TOM'.

What records we have of Tom and Sheila's married life in Africa come from the huge collection of letters she left behind; Tom himself had little time to write, apart from an occasional PS. His job was to supervise the scrub clearing, working with local tractor drivers. All this was back-breaking work in high temperatures and long hours in the bush, often 6 a.m. to 8 p.m., with few days off. In the rainy season he would be in charge of planting the peanuts.

Sheila's letters are peppered with anecdotes about day-to-day living – difficulties with housing, food, servants and fellow Groundnutters. Careful reading gives insights into their marriage and to Tom's character traits, many of which were in their infancy at this stage, but would become more pronounced as he grew older.

Wives were not encouraged to join their Groundnut husbands in the early days, but Sheila's formidable secretarial skills and war experience made her welcome, and she worked first for David Martin and then John Mellor, the joint general managers of the Scheme. She arrived in August 1947 by flying boat, a journey that took two days and nights to reach Dar es Salaam, the capital of Tanganyika Territory, one of Britain's African colonies. Tom was in Dar to meet Sheila, and after a couple of days' acclimatisation they made the long journey up to their new home by train, with the last leg by station wagon.

The centre of the Groundnut Scheme was a dry and dusty place called Kongwa, several hundred miles due west of Dar, which was on the notorious slave-trading route travelled by both David Livingstone and Henry Morton Stanley, described by the latter as 'a droughty wilderness … an interminable jungle of thorn bushes'. A Boer farmer put it more succinctly: 'Mile after mile of damn all.'

The experts mistakenly thought that the bush could be cleared easily, based on soil samples taken after the decision to go ahead with clearance had already been made. There was no way of measuring rainfall, nor any reliable records; they turned a blind eye to the fact that the plains were devoid of any African cultivation, populated by wildlife and occasional herds of cattle. They were sure that mechanised production would turn the dust into gold. In their enthusiasm they even failed to notice that there was no access to spring or river water and initially no railway.

There were already 250 Europeans living in Kongwa when Tom and Sheila arrived, but it was a frontier town in all other respects, albeit one resembling an army camp with its serried rows of tents and mess buildings – unsurprising, as most of the Groundnutters were recruited from the forces. In her first letter home Sheila described their new living conditions:

GROUNDNUT SCHEME, KONGWA

A Groundnut Scheme map, drawn by Sheila, showing the locations of the units

What roads! Sandy + incredibly bumpy + dust, dust, dust. It is now the dry season here + the wind blows + loads of thick red dust envelops everything ... The camp here is situated in the scrub with most picturesque hills all round covered in trees ... Tom + I have a large tent between us, with a concrete floor – complete with 2 beds, wardrobes, 1 dressing table + long glass + easy chairs, + 4 folding chairs, 2 bedside tables, bath and washstand, to say nothing of mats on the floor. The tent has little windows which fold open or closed and we have a primus lamp to light up at night. Electricity will come soon, we hope ... Lavatories are holes in the ground tactfully disguised in little thatched huts.

In the early days they had to share lavatories – with a separate ladies and gents (Tom and Sheila were not to get their own until May 1948), and meals were taken in the mess, cooked by servants. It was a tough life, even for people who had experienced the privations of war – the officer class was not used to cooking or washing-up and the irony of being waited on by servants was lost on the 'socialist' Tom and Sheila, although Tom's thick skin meant that he was equally as capable of deceiving himself as others. Trouble with the 'boys' or servants was a constant theme in Sheila's letters and reflects the double standards common at the time.

Living in a tent in the African bush would have tested any couple's relationship. The challenges were exacerbated by not having a kitchen, the dullness of mess food, the lack of many everyday items and the health risks. Tom was stricken by frequent bouts of what he called tonsillitis and by a chronic stomach upset: 'He complains of funny feelings in his tummy but has never had a temperature and the doctor can't find anything wrong with him'. He suffered from what he called a 'nervous stomach' all his life, heavy bouts of diarrhoea, especially before he went on safari (he would prepare 'for days beforehand, as fussy as an old maid'), on holiday or changed jobs. Sheila found Tom's illnesses perplexing, with no diagnosable causes – an unconscious echo of his father's hypochondria.

In contrast to Tom's psychosomatic maladies, Sheila had a couple of bouts of serious illness shortly after she arrived – jaundice and pneumonia – requiring several weeks of

Sheila leaving the thatched lavatory hut

sick leave, which she bore stoically. Following one hospital stay (there was a rudimentary hospital in Kongwa), Tom added a note on her weekly letter, 'After Sheila's interesting screed I feel loth to add my share – However, I don't often write, and I feel rather ashamed. It is good to have S. back + see her looking much better, she really works rather hard.' Apart from the extra cash, it was good for her – and

Their first tent in Kongwa

Tom's – self-esteem to be working for the most senior people in Kongwa, first for the joint general managers, and later for Robin Johnstone, the district commissioner.

When she gave up work in June 1948 after a long spell in hospital, Sheila wrote home, 'I just love doing "nothing" which means slaving hard all day, sewing and mending, tidying, doing the garden, taking the dog for walks, trips to Kongwa and generally not having a moment to read or knit or sit down and do nothing', but said that Tom was 'most wrathful' that she was 'too tired to mend his socks'. He began to carp about her 'absent-mindedness' which made it 'worse than ever' and her purported 'inefficiency' – a complaint he made 'at least seven times a week, but which of course is quite untrue'. As early as 1948 he revealed his cruel streak in this PS to her parents, superficially in jest: 'The husband, too, sends his respectful good wishes to ma + pa + hopes that they are as well as he is. The daughter, too, is behaving quite well + is being kept under control.'

Despite the remoteness of Kongwa, there were Indian trade stores not far away, and the occasional visit to Dar es Salaam enabled the Groundnutters to furnish their tents with colourful curtains and bedspreads and replenish supplies with luxury imported items. Trips to the island of Zanzibar opposite Dar es Salaam, via the company's small plane, produced Persian carpets and copper coffee pots, while one couple had their dinner service, family portraits and silver sent out from England, much to local amusement.

Sheila delighted in gardening and wherever they set up home she soon had glorious flowerbeds which they both watered and tended lovingly. Tom's main contribution was to dig the irrigation channels required to marshal the scarce water supply, for he had very little leisure time. Their tent was completed by a Dalmatian, Nelson, and a succession of African wildcats, which were useful rat-catchers.

Despite all the privations they were happy enough in Kongwa; Tom loved his work despite the chaos, muddle and long hours and, on the whole, Sheila appeared to enjoy her new life. 'You would have laughed if you could have seen him this afternoon sitting under a tree with a sheet round him having his hair cut', she wrote to Grace. There are several photographs of those early days: Tom in his baggy colonial shorts – in the field, with colleagues and with Sheila in front of their various tents; Sheila in one of her many home-made skirts, sitting in the sun on the step, cat on lap, dog at her feet, surrounded by her zinnias and nasturtiums. They liked to catch the dying rays of the sun, Sheila with a book, Tom 'sitting in his singlet in a deck chair by the door of the tent darning his socks', smoking his beloved pipe.

Later in 1948 there was more evidence of Tom's controlling nature: in one letter Sheila pleaded with her mother to make a bank transfer of some money from her account to the joint account 'else Tom will tear the hide off me'; compounded by the occasional aside in his rare letters to his in-laws, 'I try to keep S. out of mischief as much as I can' and again, 'we are both very fit apart from the occasional

Tom having his monthly haircut

row occasioned by living in such close quarters – the foundations of the marriage are still very firm.'

It was a shared adventure whose memory gave them a close bond which, notwithstanding all the ructions to come, they never lost.

The units were all in the middle of plains teeming with wild animals. It was not unknown to wake and find the daily barrel of water being sucked dry by an elephant in the more remote camps, and the bush-clearers often came across herds of elephants and the odd rhino. Oryx, hartebeest, gazelle and giraffe were everywhere. They spent weekends walking, picnicking and tracking game, or visiting friends in outlying units or in the small towns.

Once Tom was supervising some clearing with two tractor drivers. The drivers parted the bush to see two lions lying there. Terrified, they both ran back to the tractor, shouting, 'Oh Sir, we have seen such a frightful sight – lion ... It was terrible sir!' and refused to carry on working. Eventually Tom persuaded them to return, telling them to jump on the tractor next time instead of running away: 'Lions won't touch you, they are merely curious and there is plenty of game for them to eat.'

Aside from the challenge of clearing the scrub for planting, the biggest headache was lack of rain, which was disastrous for the groundnuts. When the rains did come they fell only for a short few weeks and were extremely heavy. Tom and the other field assistants were often out all-night planting but then were frequently washed out, as were the tents, which flooded easily.

The original surveyors had taken no account of the vagaries of the African climate; Hugh Bunting, the scientific adviser, admitted that 'actual rainfall figures for the area are entirely lacking'. As it turned out, 1947, the year he took his samples, had seen a good rainy season. Tom always used to say, with his characteristic touch of vulgarity, that Bunting had tested an area where someone had just peed and pronounced it entirely suitable as a result.

Tom had been promised rapid promotion from field assistant to unit manager and was frustrated by the lack of career progression. Due to the failure of the experts, 'who should have known better', as he put it, 'there was not enough water and we should not have tried to outwit generations of African cattle herders – if the land was known for cattle it was because it was not good enough for agriculture: the soil was wrong, rainfall was wrong'. In vain, Tom and his colleagues attacked the bush trying to hit the ridiculous targets that had been promised to the British government. For an idealistic and impatient man, this was infuriating. As he scribbled on the bottom of one of Sheila's letters in October 1947, 'Groundnuts all day & all night is the main topic of everyone's conversation here –

what a bore. And we aren't growing any more to show for it.'

As a result, by 1948 he was already looking for new jobs in the region. He had a pay rise to £600, which levelled his salary with that of IFAP, but it was galling to see new-comers with no experience coming in on higher sal-aries and getting better houses and jobs. He was good at his job – a 'better worker, more intelligent,

Tom clearing the bush

more conscientious etc. than some who have received promotion', according to Sheila – and the youngest field assistant 'bar one'. He also spoke excellent Swahili – he was fluent by the time Sheila joined him and passed his written and oral exams, earning him a bonus, in 1948. Most of all he was a good manager of the African staff. He had the support of Mellor, Sheila's boss and one of the general managers of the Scheme. But he still had a knack for offending people – for instance Mrs Mellor who, like him, 'always had to have her way ... needless to say Tom was always managing to get her back up with his forthrightness'.

In later years Tom sentimentally recalled his early idealism of 'turning swords into ploughshares'. He never lost his sense of fair play at work, despite the frustrations of living in tents, eating in the mess, seeing the same people day in and day out, and an increasing realisation that the Scheme was doomed. This egalitarianism did not extend to his wife or servants, his so-called socialist principles sublimated by the colonial way of life, his public and private persona at odds. Many of the British who came out were just the sort of people he loathed: small-minded racists who were only interested in what he considered the bourgeois trappings of life – money, status and class. Nowhere was this more apparent than in the heated debate over the membership of the Kongwa Club.

In February 1948 there was a vote to decide whether Italians should be admitted as members. There were about 140 working on the Scheme, remnants of the Italian POWs, who made a great contribution to the smooth running of the project. It was decided that only people of British descent were eligible for membership – which immediately disenfranchised all the Irish, South Africans of Dutch descent, Italians and Jews. Tom and several others resigned in protest, and Sheila gave up her music recitals at the club, where she had played her favourite records on her gramophone. They were both 'sick to death' of the heated arguments, and it only added to Tom's anxieties, very real at the end of the 1940s, that another world war was imminent. It is unlikely his colleagues knew he was Czech by birth and no one had any inkling of his Jewish ancestry. The vote was eventually overturned – several of the big wigs like General Manager Professor Philipps and some unit managers were South African – and social life returned to normal.

The Club was the central meeting place for this small community and provided much-needed refuge from the rigours of day-to-day living. It was the scene of the Christmas and New Year fancy-dress parties; the first year Tom went as the absent-minded professor (an amicable joke at Professor Phillips's expense) in a red pyjama jacket, belt as a tie, beard, moustache and eyebrows of cotton wool, glasses and a mortarboard which Sheila made from crepe paper. The outfit was set off by some books under his arm and a huge handkerchief trailing from his pocket. Despite almost refusing to go as he felt such a fool, he won first prize. For the Valentine's Day Dance, Tom dressed as a baby, in a white servant's robe, a little Muslim prayer cap tied on with a blue ribbon, a dummy and a painted rattle; while Sheila was got up, at Tom's suggestion, as a Tyrolean girl in lederhosen with climbing ropes and pickaxe slung over her shoulder: her turn to win first prize.

It was also the venue for the annual pantomimes where the Groundnutters could let their hair down and poke fun at their bosses with no recriminations, as they did in the notorious *Cinderella* production in January 1949, which Sheila reported as 'most amusing take-offs of all the high-ups, racketeers, glamorous lazy secretaries, copy typists etc.' She particularly enjoyed the ditty:

We're secretaries, not typists, Oh we're very very smug
You can find us any morning, having coffee at the Club
If we're asked to do copy-typing we merely give a shrug,
We only work for Departmental Heads.

Tom would have recognised himself in verses such as this:

See the suffering Field Assistant
Way down on the housing list
See them in the HQ Office
They don't know that I exist.

I came out to the Groundnuts
Nearly eighteen months ago
But with all this blinking admin
This is all I've got to show ... [one groundnut in a pot]

Still I go on madly toiling
From early morn till dewy eve
For a very meagre pittance
Can't afford to go on leave.

There were jokes around the tough meat, the 'lack of real coordinates', 'nothing in the store, it's always on the water' and that the only things they had were 'left-overs from the war'.

Tom remained worried about the international situation, convinced that war was looming. He would have been particularly concerned by the communist takeover in Czechoslovakia in January 1948 and the dubious 'suicide' of diplomat and politician Jan Masaryk, who had been a friend of his father. Despite calling himself a socialist, he was no communist, having witnessed Russian behaviour first-hand. It is telling that several of Sheila's letters – she as the official mouthpiece for their political views – at this time reflect their joint concerns, as here in October 1948, 'Yes the international situation looks bad and we are wondering what will happen … and imagine we shall be back in Navy blue ere long. Tom has never been "discharged" – only "released", and is therefore due to go back if required.'

He had tempered his political views somewhat, Sheila reported, 'As you know Tom has always had "conchie" views but I was surprised to hear him say that he thought perhaps it was silly to immure oneself in prison because of ideals when so many went through hell.' He felt bad about some of his German friends and requested that Grace continue to send clothes parcels to the former officer he had met 'ferrying German ships to Russia', who was now destitute with two or three children.

In January 1949 Tom was promoted to senior field assistant on £750 p.a. He was promised a unit of his own before the end of the year and a further increase to £900 p.a., and was excited. They moved to the remote Kongwa Unit III where their tent was set into the side of a hill and had glorious views and sunsets – but still no kitchen.

Life without a kitchen was hard, and food supplies were difficult depending on the seasons and where you were living. It became a habit for meals to be transported in finest tableware from the mess to the tents and huts. In February 1949, Sheila volunteered to take over the mess, providing food for thirty-four people, 'an uphill job', for three weeks while the caterer was on leave. She had never really cooked in her life, apart from on her domestic science course; after their marriage, their landlady had provided meals in their digs in Leinster Square. As she wrote home, one day she 'had neither bread nor potatoes, sugar, butter, rice and flour are also rationed … the meat never came till 6.30 pm, after I'd got some people to go out to shoot some birds + at this time of the year it is impossible to get eggs as the locals keep them all for hatching … I really wonder anyone gets any food at all!'

Sheila and Nelson looking out of the hut at Kibumbuni, Unit III

Tom referred to this at the end of one of his only surviving full-length letters to Grace on 8 February. He seems intent on currying favour with his mother-in-law while doing her daughter down, as he knew he had a sympathetic ear.

> Just now I am having rather a quiet time while Sheila is the busy one! She is a most talented lass, really. The incessant rain has made the ground so wet that we cannot get on with anything, so I spend most of my time fiddling about with odd jobs … Sheila is rather tired by her job, but only a few more days and she will be able to leave it. The experience is most valuable, I am sure. At least she has learnt to boil spuds now!

Tom felt justified in his snide remarks because he was rather a dab hand in the kitchen, as Sheila reported when she was ill. 'Tom has blossomed into an expert cook and has just produced a thick tomato soup (from real tomatoes, milk, spaghetti, puree, onion), poached egg in spinach and rhubarb and cream (tinned!)'.

There were signs that all was not well in the marriage, but Sheila could not admit it to her mother. They always slept in single beds, hardly romantic given Tom's earlier obsession with getting a double bed for his London digs. I later discovered that Tom was vehement about not bringing children into such a wicked world, but it is equally likely that Sheila was already fed up with his roving eye. In 1949 Sheila reported to her mother that she had been extremely rude to a 'most attractive loose girl I did know by repute!!! … who stops at nothing and vamps every man, married or single … Tom was horrified at me'. Tom must have been flirting with her – or worse – as this incident took place after Sheila's sick leave in Nairobi following her jaundice.

In February 1949 Tom was offered another job as assistant to Professor Phillips. Despite the promise that he would be given his own unit, there would not be a new unit at Kongwa III for some time, and he was tempted by the offer. Just when their new place 'was looking really lovely', they grudgingly moved back to Kongwa and Sheila got a part-time job with District Commissioner Robin Johnstone, at the new Boma (government headquarters).

Things were coming to a head in London over the mismanagement of the Groundnut Scheme. There was a power struggle between the unpopular head of the Scheme, Leslie Plummer, who was misrepresenting the real state of affairs, and John Strachey, the Labour Food Minister, who visited Tanganyika in December 1949, ostensibly to sort it out. Tom accompanied Phillips and Strachey to Urambo in the Southern Province. Sheila proudly reported, 'Tom has done his little bit within his most limited range, not being an executive, his voice isn't considered very important … I hope he will manage to have a word with [Strachey] over the weekend.'

Phillips, who Tom described as a 'wonderful, charming, knowledgeable and extremely well-thinking man', spoke frankly with Strachey on this trip, telling him the truth about the disaster on their hands. He was infuriated that Strachey was misleading Parliament to protect his reputation and that of the Labour Party in the impending 1950 general election. Both Plummer and Strachey were subsequently removed from their respective positions, their careers in ruins, but Labour narrowly squeaked back into power.

After three years Tom and Sheila went on home leave in March 1950 for several months. Tom was determined to go to Canada to see his mother and Alec, but it was 'too dear' for Sheila to go too. Alec, much to Tom's annoyance, had given up forestry for an Arts degree but was not doing well. Sheila had noticed a dearth of news from Canada and confronted Tom, who admitted he had withheld letters from her. She wrote home:

> As you know [Alec] can do no wrong in Tom's eyes and knowing that I rather disapprove ... he purposefully didn't tell me ... His mother says that he is lazy ... Tom is far too tolerant of him, always taking into account that he's had rather a disturbing earlier life, having to leave his native country ...

Alec inspired contradictory feelings in Tom: although he felt sympathetic towards him, he found his spoiled younger brother irritating. As with me later on, Tom blew hot and cold.

In an affectionate letter to Grace from Canada on 3 April 1950, he asked what he could bring from 'this land of plenty'. His first stop was Windsor, Ontario, to see his big brother John: 'His people are very well but I was disturbed to see how badly he gets on with his wife – not just the occasional storm in a teacup, like Sheila and I, but fundamentally bad relations. And they row in front of their little boy.'

Tom had another reason to be anxious as Grete had not been well, hospitalised with pleurisy and pneumonia. In Vancouver he found Grete 'well on her way to recovery' although Canada was 'overheated and sweatingly hot. And the highlight of transatlantic civilisation are [sic] their lavatories. They are simply magnificently clean, deodorised and what have you. One's daily round becomes a real pleasure'. As an afterthought he added, 'Being away from Sheila is having its usual effect on me: I realise again what a wonderful girl she is – with all her faults – and how fond I am of her. She may not be the world's most beautiful woman, but she is certainly one of the best and most loyal'. This was not fair or kind as Sheila was very attractive, despite the scar on her face from the car accident with Tom, just as Tom was a handsome man. They were a striking couple.

Sheila spent the time in England catching up with her parents and her older sister, Rosemary, who had joined the WRAF (Women's Royal Air Force) after the war. She had just returned from Egypt and Sheila was looking forward to getting news of her wartime friends from Alexandria and Cairo. She and Rosemary, though not close, corresponded and there are frequent mentions of Rosemary's love life in Sheila's letters – poor Rosemary had no luck with men and only married when she was sixty.

While on leave, they bought a car, which accompanied them on the ship back to Tanganyika. They drove down from Kongwa to Nachingwea in the Southern Province where Tom was sent in September 1950, to take over a unit. Sheila had not wanted to leave Kongwa, which she was now enjoying, but £900 p.a. and a kitchen were not to be sneezed at. Tom was thrilled – but then furious when, after a long wait, they gave it to another senior field assistant who was junior to him. Sheila reported that the other man was deemed more appropriate, as Tom's bosses thought he had difficulty in dealing with 'a certain type of bolshie, common mechanic'. They felt that with his egalitarian tendencies he was too lenient on them. Sheila was convinced his fate was sealed by the incumbent, 'a pompous little pig', who wanted to 'get his own back' for a previous slight. Tom 'blew up in smoke and said that this job wouldn't keep him occupied fully and that if he didn't get what was promised him, he'd resign'.

Additionally, he was 'fed up with the new S African contingent now here, who are frightfully optimistic and won't listen to the voice of experience'. Not unnaturally he felt that his three years' experience with the Scheme should have carried more weight than recent know-it-all incomers. As Sheila said a couple of weeks later, 'Tom is working extremely hard and in consequence gets very bad-tempered!! He is having trouble with the S. Africans, all of whom seem to think we look down on them!' – which was true as Tom despised the Afrikaners' racist views. In November 1950 Tom's impatience and frustration boiled over when he had a row with a visiting dignitary from Durham of all places, which ended up with Tom being told off for discussing politics at a party.

Meanwhile, life in Nachingwea was expensive and Tom loved dishing out largesse, inviting guests with 'offers of beers all round', much to Sheila's annoyance. 'The cost of living here is ruinous – suffice to say that we spent more than we earned last month! We really must cut down guests. Tom has absolutely no idea that they put up your cost of living so much.' Despite the lusher surroundings and heavier rainfall, meat, fresh vegetables and potatoes were difficult to obtain, and Tom and Sheila resorted to growing their own and keeping chickens.

Throughout his life Tom was a workaholic. This was evident during his time on the Groundnuts when he was hardly ever at home. Although he threatened to resign when he was passed over in Nachingwea, in order to do so he needed a job to go back to. Quitting would have meant giving up pension rights, repaying the car loan and probably finding their own fares back to England. According to Sheila, he was understandably despondent from such 'loss of face' – his reputation was always important to him – and also bad-tempered, giving the gardener 'a heavy clout over the ear'. Sheila was shocked, 'this is absolutely against the law. You're not allowed to touch an African'. Despite his declared socialist principles he tended to treat his staff as he would his family, losing his uncontrollable temper in private rather than public.

Thanks to Sheila's friendship with her former boss, Robin

Johnstone, the Kongwa District Commissioner, recommended Tom for a job in the Colonial Service. Sheila noted that while there were no queries about Tom's Czech origins, which he had to reveal on his application form, the chief secretary was 'rather intrigued as to his looks and speech, which everyone thinks are typically English'. Tom was relieved that he had succeeded in hiding his Jewish heritage.

He was given a temporary contract as district officer in Mikindani, on the south coast of Tanganyika, a place they had both visited and loved, with its Arab influences and German colonial architecture. During Tom's probation his detractors tried their best to get him sacked for his 'Communist' treatment of Africans as equal to Europeans, an unfashionable attitude in colonial Africa. Special Branch was called in to investigate this naturalised Czech because he had been visited by politicised 'Communist youths', union activists who organised the many strikes on the Scheme – unavoidable in the early days when workers' rights were contentious. The British were sensitive, as murmurings for self-rule were rising, and Tom as a fluent Swahili speaker, sympathetic to Africans,

The Boma at Mikindani

was a natural port of call for local agitators. Sheila rescued Tom by vouching for him, something he found galling, especially as Sheila subsequently claimed he owed his career to her.

By 1951 the strain of living in the bush for three and a half years was taking its toll. Tom was always exhausted and tetchy, at times possibly violent – as he would be later in the marriage. Sheila's stoicism annoyed him further, and he was jealous of the ease with which she mingled with the 'high-ups' and the colonial set, while his peevish and brittle attitude to authority undermined his career prospects. He hoped his new, more senior position with the administration would restore his self-esteem.

CHAPTER 10:
ASPIRING COLONIAL,
IMPERFECT HUSBAND

Tom and Sheila moved around southern Tanganyika for the next six years until I was born in 1957. It was a lonely existence, with only a handful of Europeans for company, and Tom's job, being both administrator and magistrate, was varied – one day as judge for a series of cases ranging from petty theft and murder to witchcraft, and the next going on a week-long safari to visit the outlying villages, planning famine relief when the rains failed, overseeing development projects and collecting taxes. These safaris were usually on foot, Tom in his khakis, a team of porters to carry his tent, bedding and food, and a servant to cook and look after him, as well as one or two other members of the District Office. Tom saw no contradiction between what he considered his socialist principles – as a pacifist and a believer in the equality of men – and his new colonial lifestyle, which he saw as a benevolent dictatorship. One can cut him some slack as in the 1950s there was a different mindset, but it underscores how he had no self-awareness about anything contradictory in his personal life

As he wrote in July 1951 in one of his rare letters to Sheila's father:

I am settling rather slowly into my new responsibilities ...
very much to do and it is rather difficult if one has to look
everything up before one does it ... this applies especially
to the Law ... the other day made a real hash of a case and
rewrote it all according to the book ... this one came back
[from the High Court] with the comment 'the learned
magistrate has tried this case exceedingly well'. Amazing
what you can make people believe ... The car and Sheila
are both behaving themselves ... S has been very busy
with the puppies for the last few weeks, but I have reason
to believe she will find a little time for me soon. I am not
exactly a neglected husband ...

*On safari – Rajabu Saidi: 'He steals the
odd drink of gin but otherwise is ok.'*

All of Tom's biggest
failings in one – false
modesty, condescension,
self-pity and the desire to
impress.

Sheila continued to
write weekly letters to her
parents, describing their
daily life. Conditions had
not eased since joining
the Colonial Service – the
salary was lower than with
the Groundnuts; their first
post, Mikindani, had no
electricity; and she was
lonely as 'there is no one
here I really warm to'. Soon
after their arrival, both

Dalmatians died of sleeping sickness, although several of their puppies survived. Ill health was a worry for them both; as she wrote in early 1951 just before they moved, 'My houseboy has had VD, bilharzia and hookworm, the cook has had a tooth out and the dhobie [laundry-man] has been cured of hookworm – dreadful isn't it? The puppy has worms, I am wondering what we shall get now!'

Sheila was on the whole tight-lipped about their marriage, and only when I read their divorce letters did details of its turbulence come out. Tom, however, wrote the odd disparaging note to his in-laws, as here in October 1951:

> I must say I continue to be satisfied with my purchase of some many years ago – or so it seems. 'Never a day too long' (much!). I am delighted she likes Mikindani as much as she does. She really is enjoying her sojourn here, though not as much as she would, did the financial position allow her to live an entire life of ease and leisure.

Tom's caption on the right-hand photo reads: 'Our poor dead dogs and a very live Sheila.'

For Sheila, always hardworking despite Tom's assertion to the contrary, was now supplementing their meagre colonial pay as a secretary at the District Office and was involved in local activities like the Red Cross committee and teaching women in hospital to sew.

As if to assert his moral superiority, in the next sentence Tom says,

> I am writing this at 6 am on a Sunday. For some reason, on the only day I can sleep, I don't. I always feel ready to get up, and there is always some pretext. Either the dog to be taken down, or some report from the gaol or elsewhere in my domain. There is never much peace. I usually get up at 5.30 or whenever it begins to get light, because the early morning is the best time to see what goes on.

There were nevertheless amusing distractions. In 1951 they had befriended a retired agricultural officer, Leslie Latham Moore, whom they met after he had written furious letters to the DC. He had declared independence – and even ordered a crown from London – over the small island he inhabited, complete with local wife and, as Sheila wrote in June 1952, 'new silver and linen bought in 1938 and not yet used ... He is quite fanatical, runs around in a loin cloth, has a beard as well as a weak heart and is almost Somerset Maugham-ish. His estate has a glorious beach quite deserted and we bathed among porpoises diving in and out.'

Being so remote, they mixed freely with the Indian and African populations, often sharing curries with the former in their homes – on one occasion leaving Sheila 'hors de combat' after eating three in a day – and receiving gifts of 'chocolates, bottles of whisky and brandy, cakes and biscuits'. Later in Mwanza, on the shores of Lake Victoria, they held an interracial gambling night, much frowned on as it was not 'done' to 'socialise' with Asians in the evenings. There were also Greek traders and businessmen and missionaries of all persuasions, plus an endless stream of official visitors and old Groundnutters.

The Africans, some of whom professed Christianity, nevertheless believed in witchcraft and there was the occasional lurid case of child sacrifice. The office messenger was convinced he was under a spell and insisted on having a witch doctor remove it, while the cook's wife who suffered from headaches travelled 1,000 miles back to her village to sacrifice a cow and a goat for an exorcism.

The arrival of a new DC in Mikindani in January 1952 bucked Sheila up no end. Alan and Jeannine Scott were a 'breath of spring, all so gay and natural'. They brought a friend of Jeannine's with them, 'a most charming girl ... Tom has taken quite a fancy to her and has taken her out on safari once and is going to go again next week ... I rather gather she would like to come and stay with us rather than go home.' Sheila seemed quite relaxed, plain naïve, or perhaps she was too fed up to care.

Tom with the office messenger

She complained about Tom's love of hard work to her mother in January 1952: 'Tom is always so busy ... he is much keener on his work, which he loves, than anything else – home, house, family, everything'. She was particularly annoyed by his diligence as Alan Scott's charm masked his flaws; he was 'sozzled' at times and rarely worked at weekends. He and Jeannine were to part in 1954.

Sheila was irritated by Tom's absences throughout 1952, often occasioned by Alan Scott's laziness, as she describes in this letter of 16 September:

> ... charming as he is, [he] is extremely selfish, and thinks only of feathering his own nest and doing only what he wants to do ... Tom away all last week ... off again on Sunday for the day, rather to my annoyance as we haven't had a decent Sunday for weeks owing to Red Cross and his beastly work. Alan never works a minute overtime, and I get rather fed up with Tom putting in two Sundays running. Tomorrow he is off on safari again ...

Tom with Alan and Jeannine Scott

These safaris were physically challenging. In December 1952 Sheila reported that on one safari Tom 'walked 17 and 20 miles respectively in 2 days and found it very tiring, but he seemed in good spirits'. They had run out of water and were drinking it unboiled, giving Sheila concerns about typhoid, 'one of our Boma messengers in Mikindani just died of it, poor little fellow'. Tom did have something to prove, however, as his appointment was still probationary and was not due to be confirmed until he appeared before a board on their next leave in early 1953.

The stress of it all got to him, and although Sheila made light of it in a letter to her mother in March 1952, the temper that was always simmering beneath the surface exploded at moments of tension at work, as here:

> Tom and I are having such a laugh over a letter by one
> of our African clerks ... entitled in capital letters 'A
> Complimentary Letter' and goes on to say how wonderful
> Tom is. It starts off 'as a bird flies to its nest after a live
> long day of hard work, so you go to your leave' ... We
> can't imagine what urged him to fly into prose in Tom's
> honour. Especially today which has been a bad day ...
> A man accused him to the Police of assaulting him (the
> office messengers were marvellous and stood up for Tom
> who had been very angry and hadn't remembered what
> happened) and the manager of the sisal estate came down
> and made a big row about a letter Tom had written him.

Tom's violent outbursts demonstrate that he was a complex man; in public he almost lived up to being the perfect colonial but was quite capable of losing his temper and meting out violence to his subordinates. Similarly, in private he was not all bad: he sent regular food parcels to his German friends, he was generous to his mother and brother, and to Sheila when he was in a good frame of mind. He liked to think of himself as a caring and good person but perhaps the clerk and messengers had other motives for flattering and supporting their boss. Tom was blind to how he fell short of his ideals.

In early 1953 Sheila reported with some glee that he had left all his shirts and shorts behind when departing on safari: 'I couldn't imagine Tom leaving such essentials behind. According to him I am the only careless person in this house. They have been sent to him on the back of a bicycle, a distance of some 60 miles.' Stress found the chinks in his armour.

In late 1952 Tom's hard work was rewarded by a move to neighbouring Mtwara as an independent district officer, reporting back to Alan Scott in Mikindani. Sheila, who was still working in Mikindani at the Boma part-time, was put out as she had to commute the ten kilometres separating the two towns, hitching a ride with the local policeman.

Despite this they liked their 'little house ... thatched and looks out on to a sea of sisal.' In a letter home Sheila described it:

> Far over to the left we can see the blue thread of Mtwara
> harbour ... we have quite a tidy little garden into the front,
> screened from the road by a thorn hedge, scarlet cannas
> and a few shrubs – frangipanis and passion fruit ... Tom
> seems to enjoy his work ... I think so long as he had plenty
> of food, warmth and a roof over his head he wouldn't mind
> living on top of Mt Everest!

In January 1953, just as they were about to go on home leave, Sheila had a miscarriage:

> I had previously not been feeling too well, as it seems I
> have had some sort of miscarriage but wasn't incapacitated
> for long and didn't suffer any great pain or have to stay

in bed or anything. It was rather a disappointment and
depressed me no end but anyway, it would have been most
inconvenient whilst we were home on leave, so one must
count one's blessings, and hope for better luck next time …

She must have been devastated, though it is hard to tell from
her understated tone. It was to be another four years before she
was to conceive again.

Reading the divorce letters, it is clear that their physical
relationship was almost non-existent, each blaming the other for
its failure. Tom claimed that her aloofness and lack of tenderness
was the main barrier, while Sheila maintained that his cruelty, both
mental and physical, his constant belittling and criticisms of her,
his flirtations and, later on, his affairs, combined with his sexual
gaucheness and 'fumbling', made it almost impossible for intimacy
to exist. She always alluded that he was hopeless in the bedroom,
although she also admitted that there had been several miscarriages
earlier in their marriage, and that my eventual birth was a surprise
as they had more or less stopped having sex. Nevertheless, there
was an element of a deal with the devil: a longed-for baby was
Sheila's bargaining chip for not divorcing him.

Tom did admit later that his feelings of sexual inadequacy had
been a barrier, and in 1964, just before they separated, he sought
treatment in London. Perhaps he felt Sheila knew too much about
his foibles and character for him to feel masterful and in control; he
needed his ego bolstered to compensate for his insecurity, feelings
that only Sheila was party to, and she was unable to give him the
unconditional adoration that he craved.

As part of their leave they went by boat to Yugoslavia where
they hired a Morris Minor and toured around, visiting the Croatian
island of Rab. Tom never mentioned that he had been there as

a child on holiday. When they arrived back in London for Tom's meeting with the board – which was apparently successful – Sheila found her father in poor health; he had never recovered from being gassed in the First World War and had developed cancer as a result. He had moved to a convalescent home, and was to die in early 1954, shortly after they returned to Tanganyika and a new posting in Mwanza, on the shores of Lake Victoria.

Capt. John Pritty

While on leave, in early 1953, Sheila met up with her wartime fiancé, John Pritty. He was still a bachelor, living and working in Leicester as co-owner of a yarn merchant. He had adored her, but was too possessive; perhaps she should have taken note because he and Tom seem, on the face of it, quite similar characters. She seemed to have a knack of falling for difficult men; the only one who didn't fall into this category was Bruce Booth-Mason and he jilted her.

Looking for photographs for this book, I casually opened an old brown envelope and found a cache of letters between John and Sheila. Characteristically she had kept copies of her own letters, including one to him in May 1951, where she recalled a meeting in 1945 in Glasgow on one of her leaves from Germany. Now, spurred on by her miserable marriage to Tom, she wrote:

> My conscience won't let me forget how heartless I was
> … you meant far more to me than I ever imagined … I

hope time has glossed over how unkind I was, and you
remember the good things ... I look upon the time in
Egypt as one of great happiness ... People would have been
surprised to discover I was not a scheming witch but a
stupid undecided little girl.

She did not mention unhappiness specifically but said Tom was
'tolerant of my rather unusual introspective ways and thinks I am
very silly ... Now I have lived a little longer I am intensely aware of
the quality of love which you had for me. It is a rare thing. Thank
you John.'

They met up in London in March 1953. John wrote after the
meeting, 'since I have got back I have thought a great deal ...
tremendous to see you again ... far from being strangers even
after 8 years ... just like old times ... your eyes are still blue, your
smile the same, [but] your spirit of old seems subdued'. They made
arrangements for Sheila to travel to Leicester for the weekend,
where he lived in a modern flat and said all he needed now was 'a
wife'.

They rekindled their romance. He wrote again to her on 1 April:

... how complicated it is ... for me it is all so simple, one
does, or one doesn't [love]. I do – so that is an end as far
as I am concerned. You are putting me in an Alexandrian
situation ... perhaps yes, perhaps no, you seem to say. You
write of patience – is that months or an eternity? Darling
I am not being harsh but frankly and boldly it boils down
to this – will you ever know your own mind! I will clear off
... wait until I hear from you, see you now – any of these
things ... but PLEASE tell me what I am to do. If things
are so awry between you action must be taken now ... my

dearest don't think me a tyrant or dominating because
really, I am only wanting to help you ... my heart has
always been yours – tell me soon what we are to do.

Sheila was unable to make up her mind. It is not clear at what
stage she had told Tom she intended to leave him, but he was
prepared to use every trick in the book to make her stay and it
affected her judgement. John meanwhile was 'demented' with
anxiety waiting for her to phone, 'so much to discuss, cannot wait
to see you again'. After a brief holiday in France he wrote on 1 May,
'I am very impatient as there is only one solution to our problem as
time runs out so quickly'. Tom was due to return to Africa in late
May, leaving Sheila in England until July. It was the first time John
had found such 'calm tranquil happiness – Sheila it is love, just love
... I do know we can be happy in every way ... we know each other
so well ... my darling I do hate to think of you being unhappy'.

But Sheila, alternately sweet-talked and bullied by Tom, was
torn with indecision, and wanted to wait three months to clear her
head. John did not 'honestly think it sensible ... like you of me I
think of you constantly, [which] makes it all the more difficult to
keep a level keel. God bless you and keep you always, with all my
love, ever your loving John'.

By 21 May John was beginning to doubt that 'you really love me
and am sure you are still very fond of Tom who by his telegram to
me [of the same day] seems nearly demented. Whatever I feel has
no bearing in morality and I am sure that it is better to stay outside
and not interfere in your lives'. In the last letter he wrote two days
later, John was curt and to the point: 'Sheila I wish you would not
continue trying to contact me because the sooner you return to
your normal way of life the quicker you will be settled and happy I
am quite sure – and I don't want to see you again. Good luck'.

The final letter from Sheila, dated 12 July, just before she was due to return to Africa, was tucked in among these papers, one a rough copy, much struck through and scribbled over, plus a clean copy. She had realised her terrible mistake in prevaricating, and that John could not bear to be treated thus a second time as 'opportunity does not knock two or even three times'.

> … my darling I love you more than anything in the world
> and all I want to do is make you happy – to look after you,
> mend and sew for you, cook (not that I can but I'd try),
> keep house for you entertain your friends and last but not
> least, bear and bring up your children … I know you said
> you didn't want to see me again, but you never said you
> didn't love me and that is the reason I am so brazen as to
> write to you now – because I can't bear to see our mutual
> love being wasted through pride.

In desperation, she had dropped in on him in Leicester but he was out of the country, and planned to come and see him the next Saturday:

> … we must get this finally settled, sweetheart … it is really
> funny I should be pleading with you after all these years
> … PS I know you may feel you ought to say go to hell but
> don't … please write to say you expect me on Saturday –
> for having written this I can never attempt to approach you
> again.

It is hard to tell whether she sent this letter or not. The clean copy suggests that she bottled it, believing Tom's undertakings to reform and afraid of the consequences of leaving him. She returned to Africa heartbroken. During the divorce he threw the affair with John in her face, accusing her of hypocrisy, although he admitted he had persuaded her to stay through lots of 'false promises'. She responded tartly, 'If you hadn't made such a fuss in 1953 I would have married John Pritty then and there. Yet within a year you were behaving in the same old way.' Who was the real hypocrite?

In 1966 during the divorce discussions, Tom acknowledged this: 'I am also remembering 1953 – I am reluctant to make any promises for the future, which with the best will in the world, I may be unable to keep.' A year later, in 1967, Tom was convinced he was being generous in allowing Sheila to sue him as he claimed she had committed adultery with Pritty. Although this was true, Sheila had been driven into the arms of her former fiancé by Tom's cruelty and constant bullying.

Why she was persuaded that Tom would change is hard to understand – he even spied on her by opening her letters, including one from John Pritty, just so he could be in control. I suspect that she was her mother's daughter and simply could not face the ignominy of divorce in the 1950s; until 1973 the only grounds for divorce were adultery and cruelty, and women got a raw deal if they could prove neither. She knew her mother would never forgive her if she was to leave Tom and, indeed, Grace later took Tom's side in the divorce. Above all, Sheila knew how venal, mean with money and nasty Tom could be and, when the divorce negotiations finally came about in the late 1960s, her fears were justified. Sheila always regretted not leaving Tom for John Pritty, even though she would temper it by saying to me, 'But then of course I wouldn't have had you.'

Life trundled on after this drama. Tom's world consisted mainly of safaris in the 1950s; sometimes Sheila would go with him, especially to the remoter regions where Europeans had seldom been seen before, remarking in 1956, after shaking the hands of 'every single old crone in the village', that she 'furtively went down to the dispensary afterwards. One might perhaps get ringworm or leprosy at worst!' There were advantages to his constant absences as she enjoyed being alone when he was away and having time to herself: 'Tom is away on safari ... it is heavenly being on my own ... no chasing or chivvying ... Tom returns tomorrow, and I shall have to be on my toes again!'

Tom disappears from view in these years, a reflection of her underlying misery. Sheila rarely wrote of him except in passing – her letters are full of their social life, her job, servants, her attempts at cooking, gardening, pets and their various moves, which took up a lot of time and effort. He popped up from time to time as here in Mwanza in 1954, in a passing reference to his irrepressible nature:

> Told you we are now Yacht club members ... Tom much to his delight came in first ... He was frightfully bucked but bade me not to announce the fact as he thought it appeared 'bad form'. Perhaps he is learning at last!! I fear, though, nothing will kerb [sic] his tongue or his behaviour if he decided to react in a special way to any odd circumstance.

Again, in Geita, a sub-district of Mwanza in north-western Tanganyika, where they moved in late 1954, she was 'ready for the lunatic asylum ... I am truly very cross with Tom – our house is nothing but a hotel and I as well as the servants are sick of it'.

Her work was important to both of them, not least for the extra cash it provided. In June 1954 Sheila was justifiably proud that she was 'Clerk to the County Council, the first in Tanganyika!' Tom had a pay review and a rise of £100 plus back pay for time served in Africa, 'quite a sum'. In a typical grand gesture, he bought Sheila a new dress; although he could be penny-pinching he also loved spending money when he had it.

Apart from being magistrate and keeper of the peace, the colonial officer also had to ensure that the great British traditions were upheld. Empire Day was always the most important date in the calendar, and in May 1955 in Geita, 'Tom inspected a Guard of Honour of Police in full uniform and then took the salute and the march past. He delivered a speech in Swahili.' Sheila, as DC's wife (Tom was acting DC), was the hostess for these occasions, as at the Queen's birthday celebrations in June 1955:

> Tom had arranged that a platoon of police should come from Mwanza ... A large number of people gathered at the Boma to watch, Tom and Tom Moon [his acting deputy] were in their uniforms and it was all very smart and well done, complete with bugles, three cheers for the queen. Afterwards we had over 100 people to our house in the garden, to drink the Queen's health – and we had some tribal dances and drums.

Tom's infrequent letters to his in-laws to thank them for Christmas or birthday presents, barely mentioned Sheila but were always affectionate and solicitous, calling Grace 'Dearest Mummy' or 'Ma' and signing them 'your devoted son-in-law' or 'your loving son'. As Grace had mixed feelings – pride blended with resentment towards her clever and successful daughter, his casual references demeaned her in her mother's eyes. It was as if he and Grace saw Sheila through the same lens; it reflected a shared life but not a loving marriage.

In this letter written in November 1955, he thanked Grace for her 'kind wishes for my birthday and for renewing *The Countryman* ... It is very good of you indeed'. He complained that 'my young scoundrel of a brother' Alec forgot, which he ascribed to Alec's recent marriage. Alec had apparently 'fallen madly in love with a very attractive and wealthy girl ... but I think he is too young, and penniless, to get married yet'. Typically, there was no mention in this letter of Sheila, who only featured in Tom's correspondence with Grace when she showed him in a good light.

The Queen's birthday in Geita 1955

In his annual letter of 1955, he thanked Grace for hankies – 'nothing more useful or more welcome' – and boasted of his thoughtfulness and generosity towards Sheila, 'I have got S quite a number of presents: 2 books, a filled sewing basket and some nice talcum powder. I hope she likes them all, she usually does'. He hoped that on their leave 'next summer you will be able to meet my ma' whom he planned to get 'out here'.

This was not to happen as Sheila had discovered a letter from Grete with 'lots of nasty remarks about me in it – a very mean trick but only what one can expect from such a person'. Sheila always claimed that Grete, like Tom, had changed the day they got married. She was increasingly alone in the marriage, with Tom buttering up her parents, playing the loving son-in-law and siding with his mother against her. It was Machiavellian in the extreme, part of his increasingly controlling behaviour.

Part 3

Father & diplomat

CHAPTER 11:
FATHERHOOD

In September 1955 Tom was finally promoted to be a district commissioner and he and Sheila moved to Tukuyu, a small, wet town on the northern shores of Lake Nyasa that was home to only twenty Europeans. Their main preoccupations there, in between official duties, entertaining VIP visitors and hosting Empire Day again, were a series of burglaries and extended servant trouble which Sheila recounted with gusto.

In 1956 they went on home leave, via Egypt, where they were on the anniversary of the invasion of Sicily, which Sheila had helped plan, then to Istanbul and Athens. Grete was waiting for them in London – luckily for Sheila she had '12 invitations' so they did not need to share a flat with her. The relationship between Grete and Sheila reached an all-time low on that leave as she told Grace months later:

> I don't know where Tom's mother is ... I feel I never want
> to see her or hear of her again, so please don't mention
> her in future, if you don't mind! Tom still stands up for her
> manfully, which hurts very much. We never talk about her
> if possible as it only leads to quarrelling.

On their return Tom was put in charge of Kilwa District, halfway between Mtwara and Dar es Salaam, and they moved there in January 1957, the year I was born. Kilwa was an old German town by the sea and they loved it from the outset. Their house was on a slight bluff overlooking the bay, where the bathing was superb. As Sheila wrote, they had 'no servants ... no meat, no fresh vegetables – nothing but fish twice a day helped out with coconuts, limes, mangoes and milk'. They hoped to get meat from the weekly SS *Mombasa* and sometimes by air from Dar. There were only ten Europeans in the town, including wives and Plymouth Brethren missionaries, and she didn't think they would have 'a very exciting social life but never mind. There is so much to see and do here ...'

They soon settled in, Tom to his duties and Sheila to homemaking, charitable works and entertaining. In March Sheila recounted Tom's dramas as DC, including presiding over a lurid 'murder of a small child found with its throat cut ... turns out the stepfather had killed him as the mother was giving all the food to this child and not to him and his son ... We hope he will get off with a few years in gaol as the provocation seems very great and in African cases this is very much taken into account'; meanwhile 'last weekend the African cashier was put inside as it appears he has made off with several hundreds of pounds! Tom was most upset; he liked the man who is within 2 years of retiring on pension. The trouble is he is keeping a concubine as well as a wife – she has been excessively demanding.'

Despite his new responsibilities, Tom's bad temper got the better of him on occasion. He had a serious falling out with a Greek sisal estate owner which almost ended in 'fisticuffs'. He also had big rows with two sets of local Englishmen, though Sheila defended him in the first instance as 'they are great social climbers and scroungers ... I get so angry and Tom isn't very brave I'm afraid ...' The other row was over a neighbour keeping a ferocious dog unchained. Tom called the man 'a liar' to which he retorted that Tom was a 'bloody dictator'.

The first hint of Sheila's pregnancy was via a throwaway remark to her mother that she had an appointment in Dar – an expensive air journey – in April 1957. In May she felt confident enough to confirm it:

> We have good news for you for I am hoping to have a baby
> at the end of October so that will be something to look
> forward to. I didn't tell you before as with a past history
> of various troubles [her miscarriages] I wanted to be quite
> sure this time. I have had to be very careful and take pills,
> rest and even go to bed once every month until now, but so
> far so good. I have made arrangements to go to Dar where
> there is a very good hospital.

Sheila had told John Pritty in 1953 that Tom had agreed reluctantly to having a baby. He feared it would deflect Sheila's attention from him, so I was born with his 'consent for Sheila's old age' as he told one of their friends. When questioned about his attitude to my impending arrival, Sheila presciently noted,

> I think he is really quite thrilled, though he seems adamant
> he wants a boy! Anyway, I think once it is here, he will be
> quite the model father, if his treatment of Ajax [the dog]
> is anything to go by! As you know he is the world's worst
> old fusspot, and I can see I shall have quite a bad time if he
> thinks I am not doing my stuff properly.

By June Sheila's excitement was palpable: 'I am getting so plump, quite apart from a very minor bulge – it's awful!' She began to send long shopping lists to her mother, as here, in June: '2 doz Harrington napkins, 2 doz towelling napkins, packets of curved safety pins, cot blankets, rubber sheeting for cot and pram, feather pillow, 4 soft bath towels, 2 smaller ones, 3–4 pillow slips ... I hope for a girl, but bet I get landed with a nice tough little boy for my "maiden" effort.' She was determined to make all her maternity and baby clothes herself, as it was 'much cheaper', and complained about the 'incorrigible' Grete sending 'some very second-hand stuff ... incredible marks and worn patches'.

Sheila's pregnancy went smoothly despite the distance from a hospital. She declared she was 'busy charging about as usual and feel fine. I have 2 hrs on my bed every afternoon and thanks to practising relaxation find myself asleep in no time. Consequently, I can cope very well with the visitors and can stay up till quite late hours without feeling tired at all.' She managed to fit in safaris, entertaining, sewing classes between her own dressmaking and preparations for my arrival. She drew the line at having a home birth or local delivery, given her great age of thirty-seven, and went to Dar es Salaam three weeks before her due date.

Tom drove up at the end of October, 'a bad trip as after a fair amount of rain the road was horrible, and he had to use chains'. On 3 November I arrived, 7 lb 7 oz. 'We are thrilled with our daughter', Sheila wrote to her mother. They decided on Victoria as it abbreviated 'prettily' to Vicky, although my mother always told me she chose the name to celebrate her victory. Tom 'forgot' to add my middle name 'Mary' when he registered the birth, much to Sheila's annoyance. He described their 'gruelling trip' back to Kilwa in his celebratory letter to Grace, with a typically cruel reference to Sheila:

> ... absolutely wonderful – just like an old milch cow going
> off to her favourite corner of her favourite field for her

fourteenth calving down … She loves her little Vicky – naturally – although the poor girl seems to look more like me than S and has a monstrous nose – which considering Sheila's and mine is not really surprising. Sheila has already started wondering how many Jews I have in my ancestry. I must start making enquiries!

Even Sheila was to remark the following year that 'everyone says the baby is like Tom, but I can't see it except the nose'. Tom took pride in his daughter, nose notwithstanding, as he smugly informed Grace on my first birthday, 'Vicky is a sweet little child … fortunately she takes after me more than after Sheila.' He extended the distasteful simile when I had my own first child in 1988, when he reported to a friend that 'Vicky is about to calve'.

In the long term, Sheila's fears about Tom's obsessive parenting were justified. Yet in the begin-ning, she was grateful to Tom as a very active, though interfering, father and my arrival brought them closer together for a time. Sheila had problems

The proud parents

feeding and reported that 'Tom is a great help mixing feeds and sterilising bottles etc. I don't know what I shall do when he goes on safari!' He was 'so funny … exclaiming at her beauty (she really is a most pretty baby) and fussing over her generally. I cannot convince him that the most glorious smiles to which we are treated are naught but wind.' The letters home are full of how I was always smiling, 'everything is a great joke – having her face washed, hair combed, everything is treated with beaming smiles ... too sweet'.

Grete caused a major disagreement by taking an 'egotistical' interest in her grandchild and threatened to come to England on their next leave, something Sheila 'simply couldn't bear' and 'talked seriously to Tom ... she is an old b... and completely self-centred ... I loathe her'. This was to be a constant refrain until the leave itself as Tom refused to 'ration' time spent with his mother; Sheila wished 'she wouldn't come at all, she is so selfish and self-willed'.

In March 1958 a young archaeologist, Neville Chittick, arrived to excavate the Arab fort on Kilwa Kisiwani. He was 'full of fun' and 'breaks the monotony', according to Sheila, for Tom was, as ever, often on safari and she was left to her own devices. Her letters were now peppered with news of Neville's visits and their trips over to Kisiwani with me in tow, sometimes accompanied by Tom, to visit the dig. Neville had recently married a young Englishwoman called Helen, who joined him in Kilwa occasionally, when they would stay with Tom and Sheila.

With the arrival of Neville and all the archaeological team, Sheila did not mind Tom's long absences, the lack of interesting company or that their only friends were the bachelor district officer, evangelical missionaries, sisal farmers, the Seychellois Public Works Department (PWD) man and his wife, Indian *duka wallahs* (shopkeepers) and some Capuchin monks. Influenced by Neville she developed her lifelong interest in archaeology and became involved in the excavations.

By August 1958, Sheila's old irritations over Tom's largesse had resurfaced, compounded by having a nine-month-old baby:

Tom seems to think we are a hotel and invites absolutely everyone. We never pass a day without someone in for a meal – and I haven't had a piece of meat in the house for over a week … and to crown it all he is going on safari tomorrow for 5 days plus the new cadet and I have to provide food for both of them.

His double standards continued – in February Tom 'went on safari with the car keys! He was most sheepish, always being so critical when I am forgetting things!'

When Tom was around he enjoyed 'dandling' me on his knee but declared that 'thank heavens' I was a 'good baby'. In a letter to Grace for Easter 1958, he refers to me as 'our latest toy' and 'the sweetest thing' and asserts no one had such a 'grand baby'. Always the martyr he continued, 'I say this as I have just finished clearing up her dirty nappies – that's my job every morning', as well as preparing my breakfast. Luckily, the cook's wife Maria was on hand to take the pressure off Sheila, who was suffering from a bad back and a painful fungus on her hand.

They had to entertain numerous VIP visitors: the governor general (Tom had to translate all his speeches into Swahili), bishops from all denominations, the chief of police, members of government, 'big wigs' from England and one Julius Nyerere, the young

Mum with me aged six months or so

leader of the TANU (Tanganyika African National Union) Party, approved by the administration to lead the country into a new African majority government in 1961. According to Sheila he was 'a moderate, intelligent person, most interesting to talk to ... quiet and not a bit flamboyant'.

The novelist Evelyn Waugh also visited Kilwa and stayed with Tom and Sheila as part of his Africa journey in 1959, recounted in *A Tourist in Africa*.

> *Here I was met by the District Commissioner and his wife. His isolated position gives him a larger measure of freedom from bureaucratic interference than is enjoyed by many of his colleagues in Tanganyika. With the help of two young district officers he governs 5000 [corrected by Tom to 6,000 in his copy of the book] miles of territory. Inland it is said, there are more elephants than tax-payers; the few villages are visited on foot in the old colonial style ... The DC himself is one of the few benefits of that [Groundnut] scheme; the 'groundnutters' have a low reputation, largely I gather deserved, but there was among them an appreciable number of zealous and efficient officers ... the first to realise that the scheme was fatuous; some returned to England, others, of whom my host was one, remained in Tanganyika to do valuable work in other services. His wife and he are an exhilarating couple, both devoted to their large and lonely territory, without any regrets for the social amenities of the towns.*

Much to their surprise, Waugh was a perfect guest, for his irascible reputation had come before him and they were dreading the visit. He bought with him a huge frozen leg of lamb, which was most welcome. As Sheila wrote to her mother, he was 'portly, pink and Churchillian – most affable and pleasant. He is a man of few words but does talk agreeably when manners demand. He is not at all boorish as I had been told – rather a gourmet who doesn't eat much but will take second helpings if he likes anything (gratifying for the harassed Kilwa cook) and he doesn't drink much.' I found his thank you letter among my mother's most treasured possessions; he wrote, charmingly, 'I enjoyed my visit enormously and shall long remember it. It was most exhilarating to find a man so keen on his job and so good at it. I hope you don't get moved away from the place where you are both doing so much.'

Waugh wrote 'the DC and his wife knew everyone in the place and were welcome at every door'. I believe this to be true, judging from the letters. The negative observations about the private Tom stem from his own and Sheila's pens, and from his inability to get on with other Europeans, especially ones he considered nouveau riche and bourgeois. On the other hand, the public Tom generally got on well with people of all races who were lower in rank than him. His good points were his support of those not so lucky as himself – the 'quiet word' for the Goan doctor who despite being due first-class tickets for leave was only allocated deck class, and the 'very badly paid, new working-class PWD chap', whom Tom was helping as he had been 'under a cloud' and asked to resign.

In 1959 Tom was 'unanimously elected' as chairman of the District Council, a rare achievement for a white man, confirming his popularity among the Africans; for instance, in 1958 there was a terrible famine which would have been 'much worse had Tom not imported foodstuff' and found 'road work' for people to earn some cash. They continued to socialise across the colour bar and my christening in 1958 was attended by the governor general, Lord Twining, as well as 'Europeans, a Seychellois family, an Indian, a Goan, a half-caste and lots of Africans, some of whom were Moslems'.

This contradicts the way they treated their servants as naughty children, sacking them for reasons ranging from understandable (drunkenness and theft) to ridiculous (laziness and 'misunderstanding instructions') and, in Tom's case, occasionally lashing out. So much for treating Africans as equals, but Tom's tunnel vision would never have allowed him to question his double standards as a self-professed socialist and a colonial. Years later, however, he admitted that his socialist views were naïve and that, in his experience, hope was repeatedly extinguished by the greed of those who call themselves socialists while destroying the environment. He reckoned the only true socialism was in the Catholic Church and in Israel's kibbutzim.

It is pleasing, all these decades later, that Waugh captured the essence of my parents in their public domain. Despite their marital difficulties, Kilwa was to hold happy memories – for Tom, having his own territory for the first time was both challenging and gratifying, as Waugh noted, its very remoteness giving him the autonomy that he so loved; as for Sheila, she loved the coast and the Swahili culture. Above all, my arrival was to give them both an unexpected joy in their increasingly loveless marriage.

For by 1959 Tom was up to his old tricks with the girls. A young woman came to stay with them from Dar, and 'Tom got very sweet on her and it was most embarrassing. How silly men are! He has been quite moony ever since.' She was meant to look after me when Tom and Sheila went on a safari together, but he insisted on taking her with them, leaving me in the care of my visiting godmother, much to Sheila's irritation.

The only memories I have of Kilwa are in the photo albums, carefully compiled by Sheila: on the potty, in my playpen or on the beach with my mum, shaded under a sun hat, flanked by one of her beloved dogs. The carefree Kilwa days came to an end in 1959 when we went to England on leave.

CHAPTER 12:
DAR ES SALAAM DAYS

On their return to Tanganyika in early 1960, following their home leave, Tom joined the Ministry of Foreign Affairs in Dar es Salaam, the capital of Tanganyika Territory. He did not like it 'one bit', as he had lost the independence of being master of his own fiefdom, and now had to report to an autocratic colonial system. He was depressed, but by July he transferred to a role in the public affairs department which, as Sheila told Grace, would take him 'on safari, in contact w local newspaper editors and radio chiefs, will probably escort and travel w VIPs and keep in touch w African side of things'. Some friends thought he was 'wasted' in it, but Sheila reported that 'he enjoys it although doesn't like to admit it. His translations

from the vernacular press usually contain something rather salacious each day and people are amused by them.'

In Dar we lived at 3 Mzinga Way in a government house, with a large veranda – every now and then a snake would drop out of the bougainvillea

On home leave in 1959: Sheila with Grace and me aged two

that grew over it – a big garden, chickens, a dog named Abdulla and a cat called Poo Poo. My mother had made a comfortable and tasteful home, as she had done all her married life, starting with the tent in 1947. By the time we moved to Dar over a decade later, she had collected carpets, Arab chests and copper Omani coffee pots, to add to the books and classical recordings that had been shipped from England.

As well as a garage for our car – the Bedford truck of the Groundnut days had long since given way to the Peugeot 203, a desirable status symbol for an up-and-coming man – my mother had an African violet nursery which was her pride and joy. Joseph, the '*shamba* boy' as he was called in those days, a fearsome-looking Makonde with scarifications etched deep in his face, used to cut the grass by hand with a ferocious-looking *panga*. He and Mohammed, the cook and 'houseboy', and Maria, my *ayah* who had come from Kilwa with us, lived in whitewashed servants' quarters at the back of the compound. When I took my children there in the late 1990s, the house was inhabited by a minister and painted a sickly green, the large flamboyant flame tree by the gate which I loved to climb was long gone, and Mzinga Way was now a rutted and almost impassable track. It was hard to explain to the children that this was once heaven for a two-year-old.

All the colonial children in Mzinga Way knew each other and we formed a raggle-taggle community of naughtiness, visiting each other's houses while our unsuspecting mothers rested in the afternoons. We played all the normal games, hide and seek, doctors and nurses, cowboys and Indians – I was always the chief as I was given a wigwam one Christmas, much to the envy of all my friends – and collected shells. My best friend Denise and I would climb the flame tree and plot how we were going to steal Cherie Brown's cowries when she was out.

When I was very little my father drew and coloured my very own ABC (he was ambidextrous, wrote with right and drew with left), and he took it upon himself to have me reading before any of the other children. He also taught me German nursery rhymes. I remember being jiggled around on his foot while he sang '*Hoppe, hoppe Reiter*' lustily, followed by the great '*plumpz*' when the rider fell off the horse, and I off his foot. These were my first words in German and the only ones he ever taught me, although I was to become fluent later on.

Every Saturday morning, we climbed on the back of his *piki piki* – Swahili for scooter – and rode into town. This was our special time, to make up for the long hours he worked and didn't see me during the week. Once I was about four or five my father would drop me off at primary school on his way to work. I was so proud to be seen on the back of the Lambretta, hands round his waist, satchel on my back, pigtails flying.

Mzinga Way was in the suburb of Oyster Bay close to the beach, and we had to cross Selander Bridge to reach the old tree-lined town centre, built by the Germans before the First World War. Faded and crumbing even then, there was nevertheless a good selection of shops, mostly run by Indians. Our Saturday destination was the toyshop, where my father let me choose whatever took my fancy. This spoiling was to continue right throughout my childhood as Tom loved to play the adoring father by pandering to my every wish.

My mother disapproved of this 'spoiling' and made her feelings clear. As she wrote to her mother in a succession of letters between 1960 and 1963, 'he spoils her so and won't back me up, hence my authority is nil', and 'Tom now spoils her worse than ever – nothing she asks for is denied even awful things like bubblegum'. It infuriated her as I was 'so good' with her, 'but plays up dreadfully when Tom is around. He just can't say no to her and she knows it. Consequently, she whines and wheezles, cries and rages to get what she wants. It is most unrestful and makes me feel quite mad.' It reminds me of the young Tomy, as described by his father, Hermann: 'But I WANT cucumber salad.'

My memories are predominantly of my father, who took on the mantelle of motherhood, squeezing my mother out. Was it because he had no memory of how a father should behave and his only role model was his interfering mother, was it simply a way to spite Sheila, or maybe he simply had to be in control? Her letters home between 1961 and 1963 contain countless mentions of his obsessive behaviour, especially over meals, which became a battleground. She tried to 'put a stop to "Nanny Tom" reading [me] a page per mouthful' to make me eat and reported that I was 'much less trouble and a much better eater' with her than when my father was around; 'Tom bows to [Vicky's] crazy whim – she first has her bath, then in bed eats 4 sandwiches whilst he reads to her. Then some nuts, then a cup of milk, then cleans her teeth, then in bed with a cup of water, then we bid her goodnight.'

After a rare trip away on her own in 1961, she 'came back to a very spoilt and difficult Vicky, having every spoonful of her lunch shovelled into her by her doting papa. It is pure laziness as she can do it perfectly well. It is a great source of irritation between T and me. He WILL feed her.' I was four. In the end, because Tom was 'so pigheaded', he agreed to lunch in town for a week 'and it worked wonders. She now eats.' The last word belongs to Sheila: 'He is such a fool and behaves in such a silly way. It is a shame for the child who is a darling when properly managed.'

The constant warfare over food and the right way to bring me up concentrated their irreconcilable cultural differences. It is only now, rereading my mother's letters and remembering what I could see of how my father behaved when my half-brother was growing up, that I see a clear pattern emerging. My mother's upbringing in Norfolk,

My father as I remember him in his
fifties – good-looking in colonial
whites as he sat at his desk with
pipe in mouth and monocle in pocket

Hermann Ungar (left) with his
schoolmate Felix Loria, around
1908

The photos in my father's study of my grandparents Hermann and Grete Ungar

Group photo taken in Alfred Zweig's garden, Burg, 1 June 1924, celebrating Gustav Krojanker's 33rd birthday. L to R: Ludwig Pinner; Lilly Zweig; Hermann Ungar; Ella Krojanker; Gustav Krojanker with his dog Sherry; Frieda Zweig; Teddy Rosendal (Frieda Zweig's husband). This photo would have been taken on one of Ungar's visits to Krojanker, who also lived in Burg; Alfred Zweig, Stefan's brother, was a great mutual friend

Grete with Honza and two-year-old Tomy in about 1925

nann Ungar in 1928 , the year before
ed

Richard Kohn, Hermann's cousin and
Grete's third husband

: with Sascha, Honza and Tomy after Hermann died

Tom and Alec in Wells shortly after they arrived in England

Sub Lt Tom Unwin, RNVR, c. 1943 aged twenty; the photograph that J[kept on her dressing table all her lif[

Sheila in Germany, about the time she met Tom

Professor Walter (centre) with his family and colleagues; Tom in shadow behind him with Cdr Ja Aylen who is on the far right

etch from Tom's letters:
angri-La

Tom and Sheila's wedding photograph

Africa (clockwise from top): Tom (left) discussing planting; Tom supervising
ughing; Tom (right) surveying with Gerald Waterson, Nelson looks on; Sheila
th Nelson and the African wildcat kitten

Early colonials Tom and Sheila

Tom in bush gear on home leave

Sheila with Leslie Moore on his
island, 1952

Above: Tom inspecting the askaris
(police) as a young district officer

Below: My christening with Lord and
Lady Twining and parents

Tom escorting Julius Nyerere and President Houphouët-Boigny of Côte d'Ivoire on a state visit, 1963

ve: In the garden at 3 Mzinga
in Dar

w: Teaching me how to draw

Tom and Sheila in the garden at Zomba with me and Abdulla

and me going to school on the
bretta

In Uludağ in 1967, the first of the contentious ski trips

Tom and Di on their wedding day, September 1970

Tom smoking his pipe, in his Papua New Guinea days

Dad and me in 1993

as an unwanted and unloved child, was very strict; as a child all I remember is how *kali* (fierce in Swahili) she was compared to my father, who took 'the line of least resistance and instead of strictness just disappears'. She acknowledged that I was badly behaved when 'her Pa is around – but she's not so bad when the old dragon of her ma is around'. As an only child I was always strong-willed and grown up for my age and, shamefully, my dominant memory is of my adoring father. I have erased all recollection of the battleground between them.

I remember very few outings as a family; it was as if each parent was jealous of the other. After our weekly toyshop expedition, Dad and I would go to the Italian coffee shop – Tanganyika was full of Italians who had remained in the country after the war – and he would order a double espresso, while I would have milk. Coca-Cola was not allowed, except on Sundays when we visited some family friends, who would hide a bottle of Coke and a tube of Smarties by the gnome which fished in the pond.

On Sunday mornings, while he listened to the World Service news with its familiar 'Lilliburlero' march, I sat on his knee and he filed my nails – I used to bite them, and he despaired. I remember him painting on a disgusting-tasting varnish to try and stop me. The highlight of the day was listening to Uncle Mac and his *Children's Favourites* show. One year my best friend Denise requested a South

Denise (left) – best friends

African song called 'Ag Pleez Daddy' for my birthday; it was the most exciting thing that had ever happened, and she and I stood in front of the old Grundig radio set, singing along.

Every Sunday I went to Sunday School at St Albans Anglican Cathedral. Dad was an agnostic, he always proudly proclaimed, but my mother wanted me to go and so I did, but never with her. Afterwards, Dad and I would go to Oyster Bay for our weekly swim. At the south end of the beach was a saltwater pool, carved out of the rocks, which would fill up at high tide, so when the tide was out you could still swim. We would climb the uneven steps down to the pool and, if the tide was low, poke about on the reef, trying to avoid being spiked by sea urchins – a painful experience when it did occasionally happen as the spines all had to be removed by tweezers. Then we would go looking for cowrie shells which we would take home for my collection.

Every now and then my father and I went camping in Mikumi Game Reserve, a few hours' drive from Dar. We would set off before dawn on a Saturday and get there late morning, after stopping on the way. At night we slept under canvas – nothing like the posh safari places you get today – in very old, smelly tents, on camp beds with rusty metal legs that only lifted you a few inches off the ground, but were always made up with clean sheets and blankets, plus a canvas washbasin and a long-drop latrine (the name speaks for itself) if you were lucky – otherwise we made do with the great air-conditioned lavatory that is the bush.

Dad loved nothing better than a good fry-up, and in the morning after a drive around, we would collect wood and light a fire. I can still taste that crispy bacon, eggs and fried bread. His favourite story, which he told right up until his final years, was how after breakfast, just as both he and I had just finished 'spending tuppence', a pride of twelve lions walked right in front of us.

That is not to say I don't have happy memories of times spent with my mother when Dad was away: setting up our easels and painting in the nearby village of Msasani and, when she contracted TB in the early sixties, afternoons snuggled up together reading books – Beatrix Potter, and the *Little Grey Rabbit* series by Alison Uttley. When I read with my father, it was *Max and Moritz* and *Struwwelpeter*. Max and Moritz are two practical jokers who get their gory comeuppance when they are ground into duck food by the miller; nor do the 'pretty stories and funny pictures' from *Struwwelpeter* have happy endings for their nasty child protagonists, like Cruel Frederick who tears wings off flies and throws kittens downstairs, or Harriet who could not resist playing with fire and burns herself to death. My father's childhood favourite Johnny Head-in-the-Air nearly drowned because he never looked where he was going. I didn't realise then the symbolism of simple book choices: *Schadenfreude* versus good old British anthropomorphism.

In 1961 Tom got a new job in the prime minister's department in Dar es Salaam. It was the run-up to independence and there was much to be done. His job involved liaising with all the diplomats on behalf of the prime minister's – and later president's – office, so it was natural that he came into contact with them socially. My mother's letters reveal life to have been a long succession of cocktail parties, some of which she looked forward to, others she dreaded. Being a senior official's wife, she was expected to reciprocate, so we often had guests for drinks or dinner. She once had to accompany Indira Gandhi around Dar on a state visit as part of the official reception; and there is a wonderful photograph of my father escorting Julius Nyerere and President Houphouët-Boigny of Côte d'Ivoire on the latter's state visit

With Sheila on the beach in Dar

in 1963. Prime Minister Harold Macmillan's celebrated 'wind of change' (the phrase used in a speech in February 1960 to the apartheid South African parliament) was blowing over Africa and Dad was in his element as a high-profile European in an otherwise African environment: the public Tom at his best, in contrast to the private 'family' man at his worst. He remained working for Julius Nyerere's government well after independence.

Tom continued to take Swahili exams throughout his time in East Africa and now spoke almost perfect classical Swahili. His language skills made him popular with his African colleagues – and, later, wherever he was posted. Both my parents remembered the time he rang the office of his boss, Julius Nyerere, then president of Tanzania. Later Nyerere, who had taken the call himself, asked to whom he had been speaking. When he heard it was Tom, he was amazed and said he spoke Swahili better than any European – and most Africans – he knew.

This is the father I remember from my childhood: Tom Unwin, the clever colonial official, dark-haired and handsome, resplendent in his white shorts, white Aertex shirt, knee-length white socks, complete with garters and brown shoes, size twelve. He was the epitome of an English gentleman – except that, of course, he wasn't.

While my father appeared to relish his African days, Sheila was trapped in an increasingly unhappy marriage. She began to trade in Arab chests, spurred on partly by boredom and partly to compensate for my father's penny-pinching, as well as to have something that was her own, given that she only had minority shares in me. These large brass-studded teak boxes were much loved by the colonials, and imported from India via the Gulf to Zanzibar, which she visited frequently and where she had made friends with a blind Arab, Mohammed Matar. Soon they were in business together.

Also in Dar were Neville Chittick and his wife, Helen, who was now pregnant. In June 1961 Sheila took two jobs for the grand sum of £20 per month; the first at the British Institute of History and Archaeology in East Africa, working for Neville, and the other as editor of the *Tanganyika Notes and Records*. There were signs that Sheila and Neville's relationship was growing into more than just friendship by 1962, as Sheila was 'rather cross' that Neville had appointed a 'pretty girl who can't do shorthand and has bad typing'.

On 9 December 1961, Tanganyika gained independence from Britain and exactly a year later became a Republic. I remember the independence ceremony when the Union Jack came down for the last time and the new Tanganyika green, yellow, blue and black colours were raised – mainly because I had never been allowed to stay up so late. The following day Tom and Sheila went

State visit June 1963. Tom is just behind Presidents Houphouët Boigny of Côte d'Ivoire (dark suit) and Nyerere to his left (white suit)

to the garden party at Government House and met up with old friends: 'Tom had great fun talking to Czech and Russian visiting delegations, all very charming.' Sheila complained that he had to work throughout the holiday 'either in the office or greeting and dispatching visitors.'

Tom's long absences on official business at least meant that Mum had me to herself and could get me into a sensible routine, as she recorded: 'Tom had a week in Kilwa and we had a week of peace. I must say I resent being pushed in the background all the time and being made a dogsbody, but it really is much easier that way.' She let her guard down to her mother in January 1961 when she wrote, 'I don't really know what Tom is doing as he never writes and his phone calls have been brief and not about his activities.'

When he was about to go to Delhi in April 1962, she was relieved as it 'will mean a bit of peace for me anyway. He is extremely difficult at the minute.'

Tom breezily brushed aside any signs of unhappiness in their marriage, trying to justify his actions. In his 1961 annual birthday bread-and-butter letter to Grace, he wrote, 'these are the best years of our lives without knowing it ... V is a constant joy and in between times S and I get on quite tolerably too', but in 1962 the tone changed somewhat: 'Sheila is just about managing to put up with me. She has a hard time of it but then marriage, as you well know, is no bed of roses for anyone.'

From May to September 1962, they combined home leave with a trip to set up the Tanganyikan Embassy in Bonn. In England, Tom continued to try and curry favour with Grace, reporting that 'S is a little depressed – her usual self in fact – and not too downhearted. Life with me must be very difficult, but then she is not the easiest of people either, as you know better than anyone', and signing off, 'All our love for now, and look after yourself, dear.'

In 1963 Tom finally made it in his career. Working for Nyerere in the run-up to both independence and the Republic, he moved in 'high circles'. He was promoted to permanent secretary in the Ministry of Foreign Affairs, working closely with the president – years later he would claim in an interview that he was Nyerere's 'most important advisor' – rubbing shoulders with VIPs of all types, from the King of Burundi (Tom had to source a score for the national anthem when the government house band had lost it), to senior British diplomats, such as Sir Hugh Foot, and African leaders, including the Zimbabwean Joshua Nkomo.

All this seems to have gone to his head, as he became increasingly impossible and more elusive; at one point in 1963 he was away for six weeks in Léopoldville setting up the Tanganyikan embassy. There he met a young French secretary, with whom he had an affair. Sheila and I were alone in Dar, which she resented, and she sank into a depression, avoiding going out, not even to the hairdresser, as there was 'no point'. His guilty behaviour, including a huge bunch of flowers on her birthday and whisking her off to Kenya on his return, fuelled suspicions about his infidelity.

Sheila's mother had criticised her previously for 'doing too much' to which Sheila replied it was all for 'Tom and Vicky who are both extremely demanding and self-centred – as for the parties it is not a good thing to let Tom go on his own all the time, he likes me to go to keep the family flag flying'. He knew it would harm his career if there was any gossip about their marriage, and she wanted to keep an eye on him.

I had no idea how bad things had been in those Dar days until I made a shocking discovery after my mother's death. I found a note among her papers, carefully hidden in her largest Arab chest, describing one of their rows after a party. It was folded, signed and dated, 23.7.63. As they were walking into a reception to celebrate Polish National Day, Tom casually mentioned that he had invited

Tom with his French girlfriend, looking a bit shifty

'a certain young woman, whom I had previously said I did not wish to invite' to a big sundowner they were giving. She knew he had purposefully timed this news so that she had no chance to discuss it with him.

They quarrelled bitterly all the way home: 'I spoke to him angrily, both for his

lack of consideration for my wishes and his cowardice.' The quarrel continued on their arrival home, 'culminating in him spitting on me'. He left the house to take the dog for his last walk, but Sheila felt so angry that she locked the communicating door between the living and bedroom areas of the house. When Tom returned, he 'forced his way in, pushed me back roughly into our bedroom and continued to push me about so that I could not leave the room. He hit me twice on the head. I struggled to get out of the room, but he held me by the wrists and would not let me go.' She told him she was going to call the police, but he said that he would deny he had hit her. 'I was by this time weeping. I sat on the bed, a prisoner, as he would not let go of my wrists. He was afraid of what I would do if he let me go. I told him I was completely fed up with his ways, ever since our marriage in 1946, and that I intended to seek a divorce, asking for custody of our child.'

Reading this broke my heart. I felt so guilty at my blindness and lack of sympathy towards my mother; I simply had no idea that he had hit her. Her wish to shield me from my father's behaviour meant that she only ever hinted at the truth – and I had never asked her for any details.

CHAPTER 13:
LEAVING AFRICA

Our life in Tanganyika ended in 1964, when Tanganyika united with Zanzibar to become Tanzania. Despite setting up three foreign embassies on behalf of the new government after independence in 1961 – in Bonn (1962), New Delhi (early 1963) and Kinshasa (mid-1963) – Tom had been told that, as a Brit, he could either become a national of Tanzania or he would have to leave. While he loved the country and admired Nyerere, he felt he could not take the risk of staying.

His decision was influenced by the unrest of that year. In January 1964 several hundred radical Africans rose up and overthrew the Omani Sultan, who had ruled Zanzibar for over 300 years, in a revolution that killed thousands of Arab and Indian residents. Six days after the Zanzibar Revolution, the Tanganyika African Rifles mutinied, fired up by their brothers in Zanzibar. Tom and Sheila were great friends with Commander-in-Chief Brigadier Pat Sholto Douglas of the Tanganyika African Rifles, who escaped and came to our house with a number of officers. They parked a corporal armed with a huge *panga* outside the house, just in case. I distinctly remember the Brigadier coming and hiding under my bed, as he and his officers were in fear of their lives.

Tom insisted that my mother and I took refuge in the Canadian High Commission. There we waited all day for news that President

Nyerere was safe and for the arrival of the Royal Navy frigate HMS *Rhyl*, which had been summoned to Zanzibar the week before and whose help Nyerere had again requested. The city was in a state of anarchy with the mutineers in charge of the army, and there was trouble downtown as Arab and Indian traders were chased out and their shops looted, just as in Zanzibar.

A few days later, we were woken up at 6.30 a.m. by the sound of gunfire. We rushed down to the beach at Msasani village, and there was a massive aircraft carrier, HMS *Centaur*, accompanied by the destroyer HMS *Cambrian*, firing her guns, helicopters swarming around her like flies and swooping down on the admiring crowds for photographs. Brigadier Douglas, who had hidden on the beach until he was picked up by a boat from HMS *Centaur*, was on board and directing operations to retake the barracks by dropping men by helicopter behind the mutineers' lines. Marines were prowling the streets and, after some sporadic fighting, order was restored. The mutiny was over.

The mutiny served to reinforce Tom's decision to leave Tanzania. He had been told he would be removed from external affairs and, hot-headed as ever, he resigned. He applied for several jobs in the region, as he did not wish to leave Africa, but nothing suitable came up. In June he departed for Rome, Paris and London to find a new job, leaving us behind.

Once he had resigned we lost the house, and my mother and I moved into Neville's house as he was away at the time. She had no idea when or where she would be asked to go, and our lives were packed into twenty-six boxes, while she was delegated to sell the car, household goods and her beloved collection of African violets. To pass the time we visited Lake Manyara National Park and then in August joined Neville on an archaeological dig on Mafia Island, south of Zanzibar.

Years later, when in possession of my mother's papers, I resisted the urge to read the hundreds of letters from Neville that Sheila had kept. When I did eventually pluck up courage, I discovered a passionate record of their tormented love affair, which had started before she and I went to Mafia. What became apparent as I read through the handwritten pages was that Tom approved from the outset and that Neville was completely honest about their relationship – it was, after all, the swinging sixties and open marriages were common in Neville's bohemian circles. As he later wrote when Sheila had returned to England, 'You and Tom must come back – we're a happy quartet.'

Being alone with Neville in Mafia was Sheila's idea of heaven, even though she nearly drowned while snorkelling off the shore and had to be rescued. But for me, only six, it marked the beginnings of a great period of uncertainty. I felt that something was not right: where was my Daddy? Although I liked him enormously, why were we here with Neville? A small man with a huge hooked nose like Mr Punch and shock of unruly hair, he was nonetheless charismatic. He could never make his mind up about anything and hummed and hawed with indecisiveness – my father nicknamed him 'Hamlet' – yet he was a most generous and kind person. But I missed my doting Dad.

We returned to Dar from Mafia in September 1964 to wait for the call to join my father. Unlike other home leaves, on this trip it would be just my mother and me, sailing away from our life, leaving all our things in Dar, including the dog, to be sent wherever we fetched up. For my mother it meant leaving Neville, for, despite them being desperately in love (as all those letters made clear), he felt unable to leave Helen: he was torn – and a bit wet – and didn't want to make her unhappy; he hoped that he would be able to make the affair work while remaining married. My poor mother appeared to have little say in her future – it was still very much a man's world. I can only imagine her anguish at not being able to escape her awful marriage and be with the man she loved.

As we prepared to leave Dar, Tom had been doing the rounds in Rome, Paris and London, as well as Geneva, searching for a new job. He was not good at being on his own and, as he wrote from Rome, was depressed by the 'nagging thought that I am now unemployed'. He was at his most philosophical and introspective when lonely and, sitting in a Rome piazza, sipping his espresso, he wrote to Sheila 'how everyone should be happy in this brief span, you and I so seldom are'. When he had no audience he was able to reflect on the person he had once been but who had been subsumed by his driving ambition and search for the limelight.

While there he was conned out of £6 by a confidence trickster and felt very ashamed – it was a lot of money back then; he resorted to early nights with the *Observer*, 'that at least I can manage in bed!' In a PS he exhorted me to 'look after Mummy, and be kind to her – not like Daddy, that naughty man', and added a cartoon of himself with a halo, 'I am so good here I even have a halo' – he was feeling guilty and somewhat sorry for himself.

In Rome a former Groundnut colleague, now at the Food and Agriculture Organisation of the UN, was neither 'hospitable nor helpful'. He moved on to Paris, 'cold and grey though the girls are chic', where his connection did not show up. Full of self-pity, sex played on his mind, but he had 'no great ambitions in the amours line as not having enough confidence if it doesn't work, as is only too likely'. In Geneva he met Prince Sadruddin Aga Khan who 'was charming but said he could do nothing ... as a result I am as usual a little depressed'. He was pursuing two possibilities for his dream job at the United Nations, one with refugees and the other with the Technical Assistance Board (UNTAB) 'both of which I am considered quite suitable for'.

Between June and September 1964, he bombarded Sheila with thirty-seven letters. Here is a typically thick-skinned paragraph about his infidelities, written in July:

> In your view at least – the main fault for the failure (I
> am not speaking in physical terms) lies with me. It is
> much more difficult for me to change my spots – I have
> them, I know. But we can only deal with this problem
> in cooperation and in mutual confidence. You must,
> for example, stop making continuous innuendos and
> digs at whatever relations exist between me and other
> women. There is no point in scraping away all the time.
> There is precious little to reveal I assure you. But we are
> all entitled to a little privacy, and after all, if you ask no
> questions I need tell you no lies … because of the peculiar
> circumstances which have made me and despite my
> superficial self-assurance you know very well how unstable
> and easily disequilibriated I am. So please, please stop
> looking for bones of contention and let us live and let live.

He deluded himself that being a refugee – his 'peculiar circumstances' – was an excuse for his appalling behaviour; it was an influence, perhaps, yet it was not responsible for his inability to see anyone else's point of view or his refusal to accept any blame. This he inherited from his father – everything was seen through his lens.

He was also reflective about their marriage, and Sheila's threats to leave him owing to her unhappiness during the last year, where she hardly went out and was 'taking masses of pills'. The affair with the French girl was serious and she had wanted Tom to leave Sheila, who must have been aware of what was going on – knowing him, he probably told her as he was unable to keep secrets – and this contributed to her depression and drove her into Neville's arms. It was obviously raw and unresolved and seemed to weigh heavily on Tom's conscience.

He wrote to Sheila in response to a letter from her (not found) on 7 July, saying that he was 'extremely well-aware that almost all you say is true', but that their sexual 'problem' was only part of it as he was 'not violently in love' with her: 'I love you much more than one loves an old friend and confidante, and I love you of course as the mother of my child. I love you for all the things you are and have been to me, and for the good friend you will always be, whatever happens.' He was 'determined to try and mend things'; he was not sure he would succeed but did want to 'try very, very hard, if not for our sakes, then at least for Vicky's'.

Sheila had heard it all before when she had threatened to leave him for John Pritty. Reading this now and comparing it to his later letters, I realise he was incapable of any action that did not revolve around his own self-interest.

Poor Sheila was stuck in Dar, waiting for news. Tom was shilly-shallying, one minute asking her to delay her departure 'so I can devote my whole energy to doing what I have to do without distractions ... on the other hand I am very much looking forward to seeing you both again – especially my little Vicky who I miss very much ... I feel v unsettled and edgy and find it difficult to see myself in this state, being able to settle down to domesticity. On the other hand, it is probably just what I need. God knows.' Four days later on 17 July, he regretted 'more and more' asking her to postpone her arrival as he felt 'very lonely despite all the people

I meet ... every time I see a little boy or girl in the park I think of Vicky and I miss her very much, and when I see husbands and wives together I wish you were here'.

In London he rented a small flat in Rutland Gate and awaited his mother, me and Sheila, who was praying that the visits would not coincide. He began networking to further his search for a job; he met up with Neville, a 'nice, nice, man. I am really very fond of him – he is at heart extremely good and kind'. Neville had been, perhaps still was, in a *ménage à trois* with his friend Kingsley Amis's wife, Hilly, and Tom was catapulted into the swinging literary set that orbited around Neville's close friend, the iconoclastic, alcoholic journalist and later editor of the *Spectator*, George Gale, the role model for *Private Eye*'s column Lunchtime O'Booze.

Gale arranged for Tom to meet Peregrine Worsthorne, then editor of the *Daily Telegraph*, with a view to becoming a roving Africa correspondent. Although an avid reader of the *Guardian* and *New Statesman*, Tom was so desperate that he would consider anything. Tom also took up Evelyn Waugh's offer of an introduction to a senior executive at Shell. Nevertheless, he was holding out for a job with the UN's TAB, which he was verbally offered at the end of July, but he had to wait a full month before he had formal confirmation. Meanwhile, anxious and impatient, he explored all sorts of avenues – ranging from a tweed-maker in Peebles ('no Germans, no Jews'), to the British department of family planning, Fisons pharmaceutical company, a safari company in the Okavango and the department of trade in Bolivia. He also placed an ad in *The Times*:

> *Ex Africa – young 40, 17 years in Tanganyika, planter, District Commissioner and Foreign Service official, excellent linguist, organizer and administrator, wants responsible job anywhere.*

While waiting for interviews and replies to his advertisement, he led a busy social life. In addition to seeing old friends from Wells (but not Joyce) and former colleagues from Tanganyika days, he met up with Jeannine, now the ex-wife of Mikindani DC Alan Scott, whom he described as 'such a nice person'. She welcomed him into her upmarket circle of friends, who tried to help in the job-hunting. His letters to Sheila were peppered with mentions of Jeannine: he went to stay with her mother in Dowdeswell Manor, and he took Jeannine and Lady Listowel, a 'maddish Hungarian who thinks she is very clever, but she is a bit of a menace', to a sundowner in the Tanzanian High Commission, where he met up with President Nyerere, who greeted him 'most effusively'.

At this meeting he hatched a plan to become the UN representative in Dar with Nyerere's endorsement. He sent a series of frantic letters and cables to Sheila in Dar, urging her to contact Nyerere's secretary, like this one: 'JOAN WICKEN WHO RETURNS TO DAR WEDNESDAY WILL ALSO HELP STOP CONTACT HER LOVE TOM.' Although this didn't work out – there was already an incumbent – he did in the end join the UNTAB. He sent Sheila a jubilant cable on her birthday, 9 September 1964: 'happy birthday darling stop un job now definite but no posting so far stop love tom.'

All this took from June to September to unfold. He was now having an affair with Jeannine, going everywhere with her, helping her organise conferences and mixing with the great and the good, but felt no compunction in writing to Sheila that 'I even miss you, from time to time'. He had the nerve to say how much Jeannine was 'looking forward' to seeing Sheila and me, but simultaneously felt guilty so he encouraged Sheila to buy 'something – any price – as a bd present ... I would be quite happy to spend even £50 so long as it makes you happy darling.'

Whether because of his affair with Jeannine or because he was concerned about his marriage, he had consulted a doctor about his sexual problems to 'put me back on my feet, at least to the extent I was on them before, sexually, so that perhaps in due course we can resume our marital pleasures ... I do wish life weren't so difficult ...' He had written to Sheila in July:

> Dr Bloom says my trouble is that I am too nervy, quite apart from a fixation about the size of my J[ohn]T[homas], which he says doesn't matter. He says all I need is confidence and a partner who is not too passive. There is nothing wrong with me physically at all, and it is purely a question of not getting discouraged.

He was given pills to 'stimulate the body and sedate the mind ... It is not difficult to lack confidence, is it, in my position?' he added plaintively. His bullying and coercive behaviour was in stark contrast to this lack of self-confidence and echoes his father's neuroses.

Keeping his options open, Tom had made great efforts to see Sheila's wealthy cousin Hazel, with whom she had been so close in childhood. She was keeping a cottage for them should they move back to England. He also had taken her daughter, Daphne, 'pretty and fun', out to lunch from time to time. Poor girl, she called Tom her 'favourite wicked uncle'. He had also visited Grace in Durham and was 'dragged round Greenwall's [coffee shop], people flee from her, but she runs faster than most, physically grabs them and makes them talk to her. All most embarrassing.' He had never criticised his mother-in-law in writing before, and perhaps did so because he was irritated by his own mother who arrived in early September.

Grete's visit was not a great success; it is fascinating that for the first time he saw her as she really was, rather than the idealised mother figure of his childhood. Circumstances had changed Grete from the glamorous socialite of the Prague days into a penny-pinching refugee, who had fled Prague with nothing but her boys and her jewels in the lining of her coat. He was cross with himself for not being more sympathetic, 'but I find her a stranger and very difficult to love and cherish her. I do wish I didn't feel like this, just like you with your own Ma. Only mine is I think worse because she does not observe the conventions of this b country and this is frequently v embarrassing.'

Grete was constantly complaining:

> ... drip, drip, drip ... she is quite impossible a lot of the
> time and makes me so terribly embarrassed – as you know
> only too well. And of course, you cannot tell her anything
> at all. She is 69 and worried about her blood pressure –
> tells me she is determined to live until 120 – and I said For
> God's sake have pity on us!

He even said he felt 'physically sick and depressed' when he was with her:

> I forbid her to have anything to do with ordering of food,
> but then of course I have not ordered the right thing, there
> is too much of it, and she has to sacrifice herself by eating
> it all up. I thought she'd bust tonight! ... it is quite pathetic
> – and she will do nothing about it.

He took her and Jeannine to see performances of the German songs written by his father's friends Bertolt Brecht and Kurt Weil, but she 'did not seem to enjoy it and pocketed the sugar from the tea tray during the interval! I said, "Really Ma, how could you?" But she will never improve, and it grieves me terribly that she annoys me so and I feel so ashamed to be with her.'

By the time my mother and I arrived in Europe in September, Tom's job with the UNTAB was confirmed and we were to go to Malawi. We stayed in Durham and Scotland with Grace and my aunt, and then in London with a friend of Jeannine's, who kindly took us to a Royal Command Performance of Billy Smart's Circus. I am unsure whether Sheila knew that Jeannine and my father were having an affair but given that Tom knew about Sheila and Neville, it seems likely it was all in the open. Discretion was never my father's middle name.

In mid-November we arrived back in Dar by plane, courtesy of the UN, and picked up the dog and a new Peugeot 404 station wagon. Sheila made a flying visit to Kilwa to see Neville before we drove down to Zomba, then the capital of Malawi, just in time for Christmas.

In Zomba, we lived in a colonial-style bungalow at the end of a dusty little road, with a big terraced garden and a mulberry tree which produced the most delicious fruit. I made some new friends, settled in well at the Sir Harry Johnstone Primary School, got glowing reports and joined the Brownies. My treat of the week was the arrival of *June and School Friend* comic, sent by Grace, along with Enid Blyton's *Malory Towers* books which, together with *Tintin* and *Babar the Elephant*, were my staple reading material.

Sheila was understandably depressed after seeing Neville in

Kilwa and then moving to a strange place with a husband whose attention was clearly elsewhere. There was also some uncertainty about how long they were to be there, since Tom did not get on well with his boss, an Iranian, who was, according to Sheila, 'very middle-eastern and excitable'. She was increasingly upset with Tom, who spoiled me 'dreadfully' so that I behaved 'like an infant at times ... very shaming. He will not see how silly he is, if only to annoy me'.

He was also being 'miserly' and asking for retrospective tax contributions on the profit she made from selling the Arab chests; as she wrote to her mother, it's 'funny how he resents my good fortune – he should be pleased I have an interest which makes money'. He was probably jealous of her success as she was asked to contribute an article on chests in *Africana*, described by her as 'a pretty bum journal published in Nairobi'. Photographs of her at this time show a strained and tired face looking bravely at the camera.

There was 'one bright spot', Sheila wrote, 'a visit from Neville who came unexpectedly ... for a long weekend'. I remember picnics and expeditions with them both, climbing dusty inselbergs and kopjes in the arid bush, looking for rock paintings, eating Plumrose liver pâté out of the tin on Ryvita and getting stung by buffalo beans, hairy seed pods that grew in the wild and caused a painful rash if you brushed against them.

In April 1965, Sheila stole off to meet Neville in Dar and Mombasa with Tom's and Helen's blessings, although Helen was becoming less tolerant. After this visit Neville wrote,

Such joy you give me, and I have done little to express
my thankfulness – most of all for releasing me from my
prison. Know that always, whatever happens, there will be

something of you going with me, and so long as I live this
will do something, great or small, to light my way.

Starved of love and affection it is understandable that Sheila
was swept off her feet by such romantic prose.

In May Sheila wrote home that she was considering sending me
to boarding school. She thought I should be in a more challenging
environment and needed to escape my father's slavish devotion:
'Tom and I have such different ideas on upbringing that I wonder
if it would be best'. She may well have been trying to shield me
from the steadily deteriorating marriage. It was to be a battle royal
as Tom, convinced that I was a child prodigy, could not bear the
thought of being parted from me. He needed someone to adore
him unconditionally.

There were some other high points, according to Sheila. Ironically,
a visit by Jeannine was deemed 'a great success'. Tom took her on
safari, and Sheila was 'sorry not to go as I had to look after Vicky'.
Neville encouraged Sheila to let Tom pursue Jeannine as they both
thought this might resolve the stalemate. At the same time Neville
was indebted to Tom, evidenced in this letter of 5 October, 'Give my
love to Tom and say how grateful I am for his understanding and
forbearance over our unusual and perhaps trying behaviour.'

Sheila made several trips to Tanzania, ostensibly to pursue her
chest business, during 1965. She was still in touch with her blind
Omani, Mohammed Matar, whose family she had helped to escape
the Zanzibar Revolution. She told her mother that Tom was 'rather
fed up with my activities but reasonably tolerant'. It suited him to
have Sheila occupied with an interest of her own, to remove the
spotlight from him.

While in Dar and Zanzibar she also saw Neville and together
they went to Kilwa and to Lamu Island in Kenya. In August Sheila

discovered she was pregnant. She longed to have another baby but the circumstances couldn't have been worse: an abortion was the only solution. Neville wanted to fly down but couldn't, writing of the abortion, 'it had to be done I suppose although the more grossly irresponsible parts of me protest'. Sheila's distress is not recorded. It was an impossible situation.

Meanwhile, things came to a head at Tom's office: he discovered that someone senior to him had been fiddling his expenses and, as the public Tom was a man of principle he decided on the advice of Neville – also a man of probity – to report him. Much to his fury, he was made to feel the guilty one and ordered to retract the accusations. Unsurprisingly, he could not stay where he was. His sympathetic British boss in the UN arranged a transfer to be Deputy Resident Representative to the large UN Development Programme (as UNTAB had become) office in Ankara, Turkey.

So, less than a year after we arrived, we drove back up to Dar es Salaam, boarded the SS *Africa* and headed off to Ankara. It was a great strain on Sheila who, apologising to her mother on arrival in Dar for not writing, complained: 'Tom as usual did not help with packing at all but again/as usual was critical and bad tempered just the same. I am under the weather with packing, travelling, Tom's driving etc. but expect I'll recover.'

Leaving Dar meant leaving Neville: he was unable to see them before they left and wrote of his 'immense sorrow that you – and Tom too – are going without our being able to say farewell – yes, fare well – dear Sheila until we meet again and God preserve you and keep you happy ... what we had forged between us will not be broken. Give thanks for the days we had together ... it's not goodbye. Let our love sustain each other. Blessings on you always, sweet Sheila'. Yet again she feared she was pregnant (she wasn't) and the parting was agony.

My only memory of this trip is the Crossing the Line Ceremony (the line being the equator). This ancient marine tradition goes back at least 400 years and was to mark a sailor's first journey over the equator. In the twentieth century passenger ships would celebrate with a carnival event presided over by Neptune, god of the sea, who meted out punishments to revellers in a nod to the ceremony's violent history.

Predictably Tom, who was King Neptune, took great delight in ogling all the glamorous girls in their bikinis and dispensing the customary forfeits. Mine was to have him crack a raw egg over my head; there was a marvellous photograph of me (now mislaid) grimacing while the egg was administered by Tom, who was clad in a Gandhi-style dhoti, finished off with a white cottonwool wig and beard, made by Sheila, the fancy-dress expert. These voyages were one long party, complete with formal dining and dancing in the evenings. To look at the photos you would not have guessed my parents were on the point of splitting up, respectively so glamorous and handsome, the facade hiding the heartbreak.

The *Africa* docked in Port Said where we caught another boat to Beirut, unloaded the car and from there drove towards Turkey via Syria. The dog was under my mother's feet in the front and I, along with a pretty young German girl who Tom had picked up on the ship, in the back. It seemed my father's behaviour had not changed.

CHAPTER 14: DIVORCE

We arrived in Ankara in the winter of 1965, a grey city engulfed in smog, staying at the Boulevard Palace Hotel on Ankara's main thoroughfare for several weeks while my mother found a flat. I was now eight and went to the British Embassy school, which had only four classes and was highly unsatisfactory. The discussions, started in Zomba, about boarding school, now intensified. Tom was torn; he wanted me to have the best of everything, but he didn't want to lose me. He was still annoyed because I had not enjoyed the great educational road trip from Africa to Turkey that he had organised for my benefit. As my mother pointed out, 'what children like best is to be with other children, go to school and play!' Fed on a diet on Enid Blyton, I was dying to go to boarding school, play tricks on Madame and have midnight feasts. Life would be just like Malory Towers.

Looking back, I recognise my insistence in going to my first boarding school, Godstowe, at the age of eight, as the moment when I divorced from my parents, which in turn precipitated their parting. I must have been aware of their terrible arguments and my father's constant belittling and bullying of my mother – he was never one to try and keep it behind closed doors as his temper was uncontrollable.

I had no idea of the extent of my father's fury over my departure. He had caved in about me going to school; in his heart of hearts, despite 'much argument and unpleasantness' he knew it was for the best. But he also had an ulterior motive as I discovered all these years later: he was now determined to marry Jeannine Scott. What follows I have pieced together from the hundreds of letters which I found after my mother's death. I am convinced she had kept every single one in the knowledge that I would eventually read them, to prove all these decades later the sort of man my father was: Tomas Ungar, rather than Tom Unwin.

He made my mother's life miserable in the period leading up to our departure to discourage her from returning. He was trying to force her into the arms of Neville so that he could remarry. In the recriminations that flew back and forth between 1966 and 1972, when the divorce was finalised, there was one central disagreement over the reason for their parting. Tom sanctimoniously maintained, both in private and in public, that Sheila had left him for Neville, while Sheila insisted that it was because of his 'unkindness and infidelity dating from 20 years back' and because he 'wanted to marry Jeannine, which I was prepared to make easy for you'.

As she wrote on 6 July 1966, her leaving arose from:

> … your unkindness and verbal unpleasantness, disloyalty and indeed disinterestedness in myself as a personality, let alone your wife. You want me as a useful person to have about – not even as a mother for our child (you consider yourself better at this than I am) and certainly not as a woman with personality, a soul, or even to make love to.

Tom's constant refrain was 'you have given me much loyalty and support for 20 years … it wasn't only my fault … you have for a long time never given me any warmth or responded to any moves in that direction I might have made'. As Sheila tartly replied, all she had ever wanted was 'a quiet life for the past 20 years but with you carrying on, going off with people, and being difficult and unpleasant in the extreme', it was not possible 'couldn't you have behaved in a way which was more conducive to affection?'

Tom's final act of revenge for losing the argument about boarding school – he always had to have the last word – was to force us to travel from Istanbul to Victoria by train, second class, no sleeper. It was a terrible journey, with brutish border guards in Bulgaria, several changes of trains and no sleep. It must have been dreadful for my mother, realising as she did, that she was probably leaving her life of twenty years behind forever.

Before we left Turkey, we had a little party at our house. My parents had a rather fey English friend, Hermione, married to a Turk. Their son had been travelling overland to Australia with a girlfriend and, somehow, they were both stuck in Turkey. Hermione had not taken to the girl, a twenty-year-old from Exeter called Diana. She brought her to this party to introduce her to my parents to see if they could find her a job. I remember chatting to a young, slim redhead, beautifully made-up, which I thought was rather impressive. I had never seen anything like it before. Nor had I any idea that this girl was to become a permanent fixture in my life.

In the first letter Tom wrote to Sheila in London, in early May, he mentioned casually he had taken Diana, 'a nice girl, though over-painted … lovely smile', out to dinner, and soon every letter was 'lunch with Diana', 'took Diana to a nightclub', 'went for a walk with Diana' and so on. When challenged he replied,

Yes, I agree there is an element of self-interest in my spending so much time with Diana: but she is very sweet, very nice and I think, very innocent. I feel about her half fatherly, half male. But it is nice to spend time in congenial female company, and as she likes it too, why not? Nothing hole in the corner about it ... I make no bones about it!

He hated being alone and this was only mid-May, barely three weeks after our departure. However, his boss was disapproving and, after only a few weeks, warned Tom not to be seen out with her so often. Always pig-headed, his response was 'to go out to lunch with her most days ... cannot see what harm it can possibly do'. As ever he alternated cruelty with self-serving kindness, so on 24 May he wrote to Sheila, 'you deserve to be happy – we all do – but perhaps you more especially' and in the next breath asked her if she was considering coming back as 'strangely enough, perhaps, I do find I miss you a bit'. She had heard that before.

Tom now had three women in his life. There was also the French girl back from the Congo, who 'was not at all happy – depressed', and he was meeting up with Jeannine in Elba, who was 'looking forward to our little holiday' but was torn about 'making a life' with him. In his cavalier way he had suggested that Jeannine and Sheila should meet, although he realised Sheila would 'probably find it embarrassing'. They did in fact meet in the summer of 1966 and, Sheila said, 'we put all our cards on the table'. She agreed that she and Tom had 'reached the point of no return' but that he was waiting for her 'to fall into the arms of Neville ... which was not a present possibility'. Jeannine confessed that Tom wanted to marry her, and Sheila agreed to a divorce so long as she had 'adequate support' as she had 'no means at all'.

Nevertheless, Tom was keeping his options open, as Diana was still around in June 1966: 'She is a very sweet nice child and I do enjoy her company very much. So bright, so full of joy – a pleasure to be with'. He had the temerity to suggest in early July that Diana should look after me in the holidays if Sheila didn't want to return to Turkey; he was also planning to bring Grete over. Sheila's patience snapped in this letter of 6 July:

> You are thinking of her as your child, not ours … it is quite
> unthinkable that I should not take my place as mother of
> the family. You don't seem to consider that Vicky loves me,
> as her mother … and clung to me exclaiming 'You are my
> mummy, no-one else's mummy!' I couldn't hand her over
> to anyone else particularly a young girl I don't know. How
> can she be 'very fond' of V? They only met for about three
> quarters of an hour.

His reply a few days later expressed surprise at her 'unnecessarily bellicose letter' as all he wanted was 'peace and calm, physically and emotionally'. Diana left when Tom went to Elba and then on to meet us in England.

In the end they agreed that Sheila would come back to Turkey for the summer holidays while they sorted themselves out. Neville met Tom in Istanbul before we arrived – he was en route to Nairobi and still unhappily married. My mother always maintained the men agreed that Neville would take her off Tom's hands so that he could marry Jeannine, Diana or even the French girl: anyone would do so long as it wasn't Sheila.

Tom was extremely anxious during the summer of 1966 and was able to write considerately to Sheila, as he did when he needed a shoulder to cry on. He found the whole situation,

> … upsetting and confusing … I can't make up my mind …
> do you think Jeannine and I could make a go of it? What
> do you think honestly? I hope you are finding life more

tolerable; please never be frightened of changing your
mind: I don't mind how much you dither, because we face
a major decision in our lives and there can be no harm in
second, third etc. thoughts. Nothing in life is irrevocable
except death, and harsh words: I hope not to use any more
of them in future.

But Jeannine did not want to be involved in a divorce as she
would have been the named co-respondent. After the holidays, Tom
took me back to London to meet up with Grete, my mother went to
Beirut to a conference with Neville on the archaeology of the Middle
East, and in September both parents took me back to Godstowe.

This is the last time they were to meet for several years. Shortly
after my father's return to Turkey and the arms of Diana, Sheila
wrote to her mother:

... urged by Tom as well as by several friends I have
decided to go to E Africa for a month. The institute is
digging in Lamu and is keen for me to join. Tom has for
the past 18 months been hoping that I will go off with our
great friend Neville Chittick of whom we are both very
fond ... he is most unhappily married ... Helen is possessive
and presents difficulties. I do not for this and other reasons
think this is a possibility.

My mother spent some of the happiest weeks of her life digging
with Neville in Lamu and the nearby island of Manda. She came
back in time for Christmas 1966, which we spent with Grace, and by
March the following year, encouraged by Neville, she had obtained
a secretarial role in the Food and Agricultural Organisation of the
United Nations in Nairobi, to be with him. The move was against

Neville (centre left) on a boat near Lamu

her better judgement, but she was so in love she wanted to be near him – and hoped it would work out.

In Ankara, meanwhile, Tom was besotted with twenty-one-year-old Diana and his letters are filled with adoration and self-justification, tinged with his characteristic crudity: 'I see too much of Di ... She is a very sweet sensible girl, full of fun, and very attractive even tho her legs aren't up to the mark. But she is terribly nice and understanding for one so young. And her head is screwed on better than one might think.' He told people that Sheila had left him for another man, seeking their pity. He encouraged Di to write to me at school, 'She has somehow taken to her ... on her own initiative. She is a sweet girl ... such a comfort to have around ... knows the way to a man's heart is through his child.'

On 15 January 1967, he wrote, 'I simply must marry her. We are both very determined to do this. In some ways it seems absurd, but she has given it very deep thought and the answer is always the same.' Then he began to get impatient:

> ... it is difficult and unfair for all of us to keep things as
> they are. Especially on Diana. It also makes my position
> very difficult because most people think I am being
> thoroughly immoral when in fact our marriage is as dead

as a dodo. I have not the least feeling of behaving in a
morally reprehensible way.

A couple of days later he accused Sheila of being 'impassive and
non-uttering' as it was 'difficult for him job-wise and difficult all-
round ... Di and I love each more and more every day ... ought to
get on with the divorce ... can't see the point of buggering around.
Life with Di is such fun, and peaceful and nice that I should find it
hard to contemplate other arrangements.'

To get what he wanted he could be silver-tongued, as here on 21
January 1967:

> I am quite determined that our failure to live together
> happily shall not affect our relationships with Vicky: she
> must never feel that we love her any the less, nor that she
> is some kind of pawn between us. She must also never feel
> that there is dislike between us: just an agreement to differ.
> I swear to you I shall never say anything nasty to her about
> you: nor indeed do I feel it.

This one he signed 'much, much love your silly old Tom.'

Tom reverted to his normal character a couple of months later.
The first big row with Sheila was over sleeping arrangements
during the 1967 Easter holidays when I was to go skiing with Tom
in Turkey, on the condition that he and Di did not share a bedroom.
He was livid at being 'told how to regulate our lives':

> I accept you do this for Vicky's sake, but you are wrong ...
> I object to deceiving Vicky in what seems to me to be a
> despicable matter ... it is cheap hypocrisy and altogether
> unworthy. If it were not for the fact that I fear you would

say V can't come I would not even offer to comply with
your Diktat ... but as I must above all see Vicky again I feel
I must under protest offer to give in, with some rancour.
Having walked out on me you might now leave well alone
and try not to interfere in my life.'

He then accused her of double standards in spending 'weeks
with Neville with Vicky present.'

Sheila was exasperated:

For goodness sake get your facts right. I had warned you
many times that I was unable to stand your treatment of
me much longer. Your meanness in submitting us on the
long journey with no help in bookings was the final straw
... you were heavily involved with Jeannine and only cared
for my presence as housekeeper ... last year in London I
was living entirely alone and when I went to Mafia I shared
a *banda* with Vicky and at that time you were sleeping with
Jeannine and M [the French girl].

Worse was to come. When we eventually arrived in the ski resort
of Uludağ, Tom told her casually that I had refused to share a room
with Di, so I shared with my friend Malcolm – he saw nothing
wrong in nine-year-old me sharing with a eleven-year-old boy –
leaving him and Diana to bunk up together, 'a matter of expediency
and nothing sexual'. Sheila was 'most upset ... it brings home for
once and for all that your word means very little and that your own
wishes and desires are paramount'. She told him the courts took
'a very serious view of children being brought into contact with
mistresses, and it seems would uphold any view of mine to ensure
such a happening would not occur again'.

The threat over lack of access scared Tom and he was contrite – up to a point, as he was never one to admit he was wrong. On 25 April he finally gave her the financial information her lawyers had been chasing, although he insisted that any settlement had to take her earning capacity into account and ended sanctimoniously: 'I don't think you should start threatening me like that especially through a lawyer, without any warning. Not nice. Not over a thing like that. The important thing is that Vicky had a pleasant and happy holiday. I am sure she has suffered no ill effect at all.'

Shortly after this spat, Sheila moved to Nairobi to take up her new job. As she wrote to her mother on 5 June, 'despite initial difficulties I am very glad I came'. She felt sure 'things will work out as far as Vicky is concerned and that she will love it here, as there is plenty of riding and swimming. But,' she added, 'Tom is in another of his moods and very unpleasant again.' This was a false hope as the Nairobi years were fraught for her. The reunion with Neville was a terrible disappointment as, soon after she arrived, she found he had at least one other girlfriend plus Helen, who came and went with their two sons. To make matters worse, her work was a grind, running a typing pool of stenographers, and her new boss was, like Tom, unsympathetic to the plight of a single mother who needed time off in the school holidays to look after her daughter.

The divorce was affecting Tom's equilibrium and in May 1967 he wrote, 'it will delight you to know that I am just as nasty to Diana, although we go to bed a lot … I am slowly coming to agree with you what a horrible person I really am.' He could not resist the dig about his sex life. He wanted the finalise the divorce before the finances were settled, something that is still quite unheard of. Sheila had refused this on legal advice as she did not trust him. He thought he was being 'very generous in the voluntary payments made entirely on my own initiative'; he gave her £50 per month, not a great deal even then. He let loose one final barb: 'I am letting you sue me although you slept w John Pritty long before I was guilty of adultery w anyone else.'

He added that now she was in Nairobi, a 'source of cash would be readily available'. It infuriated her that Tom saw Neville as a means to save her from being an expense to him, although by law he was obliged to support her, married or divorced. Tom knew she would find it a 'horrid letter' but he was 'nettled at these constant prods when really I think am being anything other than mean over the whole thing'.

They both liked to play the winner in their vicious game of correspondence ping-pong. Sheila responded on 4 June:

> ... the fact that you persuaded me to return to you and that
> V was born is what constitutes forgiveness in the eyes of
> the law and this could not be a reason for suing me. It is
> difficult to see how you could have done something else
> when you were openly living with Diana. And there were
> Jeannine and M [the French girl] in between.

She finished by saying how 'terribly upset' she was with these 'unpleasant tendentious letters' and would hand them over to her lawyer in future: 'You don't realise what a struggle everything is for me, one which I am prepared to meet and overcome.'

Tom wrote as much as five times a week between my departure in 1966 and the divorce in 1972, when he was trying to score points or was desperate to see me. Sheila kept copies of her replies to him, cataloguing each insult, broken promise and evidence of financial meanness. There are simply too many unpleasant exchanges to quote them all. As the stakes rose, his letters became threatening and abusive, despite always beginning 'Darling' and ending 'all my love'.

I can hear them speak as they write – my father's furious missives rattling off his typewriter like bullets seeking a target; my mother's rather considered exhortations, despair etched in every word.

Then there was his vindictiveness, the mud-slinging he resorted to in order to have the last word: the constant dredging up of John Pritty in 1953, the only ammunition he had against her, unfair though it was; Sheila's references to his being 'unkind' and 'nasty' throughout their marriage, the two words that crop up again and again that reflect the sad truth of their relationship. All the while my father was fussing away over my welfare, my flat feet, a fungus on my arm, spectacles, the lack of regular letters from both of us, the division of the holidays and, in his thick-skinned way, giving my mother blow-by-blow accounts of his relationships with Jeannine and Di, the things they did, including lots of sex, and places they visited. He must have known that his boasting was deeply hurtful. Sheila was ground down by it all.

Tom still claimed in some of his letters that he was genuinely concerned about Sheila's welfare and correspondingly baffled about why she retaliated to his jibes. He was either extraordinarily insensitive or disingenuous – or more likely, a mixture of both. From Sheila's point of view, he was also unpredictable, his mood and tone changing from one letter to the next, depending on whether things were going his way.

Strangely, as I discovered later, Grete supported my mother during the initial stages of the divorce, saying she was 'heartbroken about goings on … Sheila dear, I want to tell you how highly I think of you, you are a very valuable person and excellent as a mother for Vicky. You will always be dear and near to me.' It was odd, as my mother barely managed to hide her hatred of Grete while I was growing up.

Grete had made it clear as soon as Tom and Sheila were married that Sheila was not good enough for her precious son and was always criticising her to her face – for her cooking or housekeeping – which riled her, as her mother-in-law's knickers were frequently festooned over the radiator in the sitting room. In addition, mother and son would speak either in Czech or German, so Sheila felt totally excluded. I remember car journeys in Austria with all four of us, Nana and my father singing lustily in the front, while my mother, beside me in the back, seethed with resentment.

Tom with Grete in London

Sheila thought she knew exactly from whom Tom inherited his amorality and duplicity, although she also recognised Tom's failings as a husband were 'like his father, he can't leave the girls alone and always has done this from the first month of marriage'. She attributed his sentimental besottedness with me to his mother, who had put both her boys on pedestals. Grete's contrary behaviour towards my mother during the divorce was fuelled by her dislike of Di, rather than a love for Sheila. She had survived her marriage to an Ungar and saw no reason why Sheila could not do the same.

My parents' very different relationships with Nana (Grete) affected my feelings for her. My mother made her attitude towards her clear throughout my childhood, but Grete's influence on Tom had been important in the early years in England, especially over the Joyce business. He still adored her, even though he found her annoying and shameful as she grew older. As a result, I spent a lot of time with her throughout my childhood, often against my will, right up until her death in 1978, as my father wanted to show off his baby to his mama. She would also come over to London (and later Turkey and the Philippines in the 1970s) from Canada and stay either with us in a rented flat or somewhere nearby.

I first met her in 1960 when I was two, when my parents had left me with Grace in Durham to go skiing in Austria, and Nana came to stay to help. Apparently the two old ladies hated each other on first sight: English Granny accusing Czech Nana of being slovenly, while Nana heartily disapproved of English cooking. It all came to a head when I fell down the stairs, rolling from the top to bottom. Granny howled with laughter while Nana was furious, convinced I had broken every bone in my body. 'But I could tell she was fine,' retorted Granny, 'and I laughed so she wouldn't cry.'

With Nana in Durham, looking very uncertain

My earliest recollection of Grete is in Vienna in 1962, when I was left with her while my parents took a trip to Bonn to set up the new Tanganyikan Embassy there. Nana had rented a one-bedroom apartment in Vienna, a city she knew well from her girlhood. She still seemed to have many friends and relatives there – cousin Hetty was visiting from

Yugoslavia at the time – but her special admirer was the head of the Spanish Riding School, Colonel Alois Podhajsky. We used to meet him there and I, horse-mad, would be entranced by the splendid white Lipizzaners as they rehearsed their intricate manoeuvres.

Nana was a traditional Czech cook: every morning she would make me *knedlíky* – bread dumplings fried in egg, followed by plain yoghurt with tinned mandarin oranges – a little girl's idea of heaven. For elevenses we would eat *Sachertorte*, a type of chocolate cake. On several evenings she took me to the Prater, Vienna's famous funfair, whose big wheel was immortalised by Orson Welles in *The Third Man*.

She had never lost her heavy accent and would proudly proclaim, 'I vas born in Prague, Owstria! Ven I vas born in Prague it VAS in Owstria' – and indeed that's what it said on her passport. Perhaps because she had known what it was like to be a refugee, or perhaps because she was naturally greedy, she was obsessed with food. She was always trying to make me eat, even when I was a teenager. 'Have some, try some,' she would cajole, waving a loaded fork in my direction. No wonder my father force-fed me as a baby and later, as a little girl, when I was quite capable of doing it on my own.

By the time I remember her, she was extremely large, with pendulous breasts, a sweet little round face, Mrs Tiggy-Winkle eyes and a cherubic smile. She wore baggy clothes, all bought from the charity shop. As she – and I – grew older, Tom was quite happy to pack me off to Canada on my own to visit her, even though I found her as annoying and embarrassing as he did. In Vancouver she lived in an apartment block which had a lovely swimming pool – which provided a welcome escape from her fusty flat. She suffered terribly from constipation and her loo always stank of the cigarettes she smoked to try and make her

Nana in the 1970s, a studio portrait done in Manila

'go'. I now regret not being kinder to her, but at the time I knew nothing of her history.

One day in Vancouver, when I was about nine or ten, she took me to the local supermarket. 'Come, I show you how it is done,' she said. I followed her in and was horrified to see her stashing candy bars and anything she fancied in the folds of her voluminous mac. 'Nana, you can't do that!' I cried as soon as we came out, thankfully without being caught. 'Vy not, zey are all silly monkeys, zese Canadians. Zey sink zey are so clever, just like you, but I am cleverer zan zey are.' This was her standard rebuke: 'You sink you are so clever – but you know nusing.' Naturally I never told my mother about my shoplifting sprees with Nana.

Looking back, I am certain her refugee status and loss of all her family had contributed to her eccentricities and behaviour; and just as they accentuated her Jewishness and Europeanness, my father would have shrunk from them as he was hell-bent on assuming his more-British-than-the-British character.

Once Tom had decided what he wanted – divorce, remarriage and joint custody – he used everything in his power to get it. He began to write in aggrieved tones how he was the injured party, as here in August 1967, 'We did not agree to part, you left me to return in 3 weeks, and never did. And then you did not wish to return. Now surely this is true. There is no benefit in rehearsing this stinking cold corpse of a marriage of ours.' He was 'cheesed off' with things but agreed he was 'an impossible person, and all this uncertainty and strain makes it worse.'

Grete was still trying to prevent Tom from marrying Di after our summer holiday in Marmaris in 1967. She wrote to Sheila that she disapproved of Di, that she was 'awful, egoistic, very silly ... , doesn't like children, nothing motherly in her at all' and that she thought she had made Tom 'see the light ... I think Diana doesn't like me. So what! I am really glad I came here and I hope I make Tom see what a terrible mistake he would make.'

It seemed that her advice prevailed briefly in the autumn of 1967: Tom felt he 'couldn't possibly marry someone who is not at least fundamentally attached to the child', and who was not 'prepared to accord V that place which she has in my heart – first place'; he reported that 'Di has got the sulks – does not like V at all which worries me greatly and seems to spell finis. I cannot compromise on this issue.' He could not juggle between 'what V wants or what D wants ... not fair during all too brief holidays [and she is] not very nice to the child, not unpleasant but completely cold'. According to Sheila, she even described me as 'plain and dull', something which riled both parents and resulted in her banishment, supposedly for good.

In September 1967 Tom forced Di to return to England and it was mooted that he should join Sheila and me in Nairobi for Christmas. But Tom was incapable of living alone – even the dog had died. As he wrote to Sheila on 10 October, 'I have not cried so much for a long time and it is not just self-pity'. He felt he had 'cut off his right arm' but deemed himself unable to take the risk of marrying Di if she did not like his beloved daughter. No sooner had Di gone than Jeannine came to visit, as she was now writing lovingly and wanted to marry him. For once Tom refused to discuss it with Sheila (who had heard this from Grete) – 'I don't have to tell you everything' – but he did acknowledge his love for Di meant that it was the first time he felt 'really married to anyone'.

Despite Di's father calling Tom 'a bad man', she returned in a few weeks and Tom now instructed Sheila to go ahead with the divorce so that he could marry his Di, 'silly, selfish, not over well-educated, a little vain … but she loves me dearly'.

Tom justified this remarkable volte-face, saying Di now understood 'Vicky comes first and of course she didn't dislike V, [was] only coldly indifferent'. As their marriage was 'physically so unsatisfactory' and Sheila still 'in love w Neville it simply has no chance of getting back on track'. He sympathised that things with Neville were not working out: 'poor N and poor you'. Indecisive as ever, he was now not sure he wanted to get married at all but was 'finally jumping in w both feet as the limbo makes me feel so uncomfortable – constant tummy upset and no appetite – lost 10lbs recently – and unhappy … constantly worrying about Di being unhappy'. This was compounded by his anxiety that Sheila was 'getting more and more disillusioned about N' and perhaps thinking about coming back: 'Don't be too disappointed in me … we all make mistakes'. How like his father he was, plagued by self-indulgent doubts.

Also in September he hired an expensive, ruthless lawyer and began to bully Sheila into submission. Sheila was having a tough time in Nairobi. Neville was still prevaricating about getting divorced, and he had other girlfriends. The same month Sheila reported that 'Helen is back, not welcome and not invited' and Neville was in a 'super-dither hoping for rapprochement' as he loved his two boys. She added sadly that she 'always knew this year would be the end of it one way or another … as N incapable of cutting himself off from the Gales [George Gale and his wife],

Helen or anyone else'. She felt 'buried beneath these fears and feelings to such an extent that I fear I shall not emerge alive'. Despite all this, Neville wrote her loving letters from England while he was on leave in 1967, casually mentioning the time spent with his new lover. He was truly impossible, yet she still loved him and he her, in his own way. She had gradually come to realise he was incapable of committing himself to one woman.

She was now resigned to leaving Nairobi although she was 'glad' she came: 'I look upon the past three years as having contained for me times of enormous happiness which have now gone by.' Tom cruelly informed her that he had seen a friend of Neville's who told him Neville was 'notorious for not dealing well w opp sex and uses his marriage to Helen as a rubber band ... which always enabled him to return to his burrow from his foragings ... I wonder if N really WAS very keen on you?'

His unpleasantness was fuelled by the very real threat of losing his job. Still in September 1967, his boss said that he 'did not take the job seriously enough' and that he was too free with his opinions. Never able to take criticism, Tom found this 'terribly upsetting' and it made him feel 'physically sick'; he claimed to be popular with his colleagues, expats and Turks alike. With rare self-awareness, however, he admitted he had a tendency of 'upsetting anyone in authority' and, were it not for school fees, he would resign. He said he had never felt more depressed and warned Sheila not to be surprised if he went 'off his rocker' and that 'if it wasn't for Vicky' he would put his head in the gas oven. It is hard to know whether these recurring suicidal thoughts were attention-seeking or real. He echoed his father's neuroses under pressure.

He agreed with Sheila's accurate assessment that in his 'state of righteous indignation you can't look at yourself objectively', replying that, 'I fear you are quite right: I am too concerned about my image – my ma says my father was equally as impossible as I am.' Luckily for him his boss retired and his new one gave him a second chance. His reprieve led to a new ebullience in his dealings with Sheila.

Tom tried to use Sheila's work in his arguments to keep me for longer – claiming that despite his being at work all day, he had the perfect babysitter in Di. This came to a head over the 1968 Easter holidays which Sheila wanted divided between the two of them. She was so miserable she felt incapable of insisting. Just recently I found the February 1968 letter in which Tom told me what to write to Sheila: 'I think Mummy is wondering a bit whether you wouldn't prefer to go to Kenya – but I think you are very happy to come skiing with me, aren't you? You said so in a recent letter or two. Tell Mummy next time you write how much you enjoy it, so she won't worry.' In the next letter he continued, 'I am longing to see you again, it will be such fun, just you and me. Don't you think so?' But this was yet another deception as Di was to join us for the holiday.

Tom had booked tickets for me to visit him for the whole of the Easter holidays, despite Sheila's protestations that she needed to see me as I was 'reaching puberty'; in desperation she even floated the idea of them getting back together again as I needed a 'steady home background among children of my own age'. She then suggested that Tom come to Nairobi over Easter to talk it all over, but he refused point-blank, saying there was no sense in discussing the divorce. 'Vicky much prefers to go skiing,' he pontificated; he wanted me to 'come home to her own room [in Ankara], dolls and cosy chats over breakfast'. He even sent a cable: 'Latest letter from Vicky quote I am so much looking forward to going skiing.'

Cunningly he wrote to Grace in March, justifying his actions in not allowing me to go to Nairobi knowing Sheila would complain to her mother: 'Vicky should have a quiet restful holiday without too much excitement and dashing about – but S is of course very fond of her … it is of course very expensive' – even though Sheila in her desperation had offered to pay. He continued, 'Sheila tried to throw a spanner in the works suggesting V needed her more than me'; ruthlessly he went on to describe their 'unhappy marriage lasting 20 years':

> I don't love her and she has for many years not loved me in the slightest … there is no warmth in our relationship and despite the fact that I have been very generous to her she still writes me acrimonious letters … but basically she has made her own bed … for God's sake don't tell her I have told you anything … but you know how fond I am of you and I want to be straight and not beat about the bush.

Sheila upped the stakes by reminding him on 26 February that he was 'unlikely to get 50/50 access' once they were divorced and if work prevented her from looking after me, then she would give it up; she would not use me as a 'bargaining point'. She requested that Tom send me to Nairobi for the second half of the holiday. She pointed out his double standards on the summer plans for visiting Grete, 'after all dashing round Canada is hardly having a quiet time at home with her dolls … You must be quite mad … you can't just have everything the way you want it … there is a price to be paid for everything'. She ended imploringly, 'I love her, and she loves me.'

As the saying goes, possession is nine-tenths of the law, and once I had arrived in Turkey, Tom replied to Sheila breezily, 'I will only send her if she is bored or seems to want to come. Do not expect her unless I telegraph to say she is coming.' He then made me write to my mother, saying, 'We haven't made up our minds yet. I should very much like to see you again, but it is rather a long way to travel for such a short time. I will see you in 3 months anyway.' Tom insisted he did not dictate this letter, which I find hard to believe as the choice of words mirror his precisely and the phrasing is rather adult for a ten-year-old. He superciliously added 'you will be happiest if she does what will make her happiest ... she has no overwhelming desire to see you – she is not at all emotionally cut up about our not being together, [she is] perfectly happy w things as they are.'

He compounded this cruelty on 20 April by justifying himself, 'the most important things are Vicky's enjoyment of her holiday, her peace of mind, her deriving maximum physical benefit of time off'. He asked that Sheila 'not jump to wrong conclusions and feel angry or hurt ... don't go off the deep end' nor make further 'unjustified imputations'. Going for the jugular, he continued it was 'unfair to accuse [him] of bad faith in the matter: V has not missed you in the slightest – not saying this in any way to hurt but to reassure ... Please don't hurt me even as I have no intention of hurting you. In only 3 months you will have V for a long time.' He finished with one final insult, 'I know how every day without her is painful [to you] just as every day without Di is painful to me.'

At the end of April, unnerved by Sheila's silence, he wrote an anguished letter: 'Please darling never do anything to hurt her' or to make 'this wonderful child suffer through our selfishness'. He acknowledged that neither of them would do so willingly but, pointing the finger, he said Sheila could be very 'unfair'. The only 'firm point in my life is V' and although he wished they could 'put the clock back', it was too late as 'you are too bitter and you lost any warm feelings you had for me too many years ago – ok mea culpa, to perhaps a major extent'. Once he had had his own way Tom could sound sincere, despite his exhortations being suffused with self-pity and sanctimony.

Sheila's reaction to being denied access to me over the holidays was a letter of considered fury; it runs to three closely typed pages, and the pain remains palpable fifty years later. She accused him of being utterly selfish in hijacking me for the whole holidays, yet he had the gall to say she was being unfair. She had always been scrupulous in giving him access to me, even when he was 'setting the supreme example of living with a woman who was not your wife' because she knew that I wanted to see him and vice versa. She was still furious about the broken promises over the room-sharing the previous year, compounded by his deviousness and amorality in asking me to 'choose between mother and father which is what you did'. Even worse was his cruelty in 'telling me that my only child doesn't show much inclination to see me but misses your mistress. You want to have your cake and eat it ... be divorced, have Diana and Vicky as well'. She reminded him that by law she would get custody and he access. She was 'a resourceful woman who, despite all this is willing to have a rethink of my life if my daughter's welfare is at stake', but she ended by saying:

> I have had 2 years of suffering in ways you couldn't even
> imagine, I have been inexpressibly lonely, no friends, living
> in uncongenial surroundings, no status save as a secretary,
> rejected by the man I had been relying on, short of money.
> I have now had to go without my only child when I so
> dearly wanted to see her. You think because of all this
> that I want to resume life with you? Frankly I dread the
> thought of your tempers, your unreasonableness, your
> unkindness ...

Sheila did not write again until June. She had to take two weeks off work with high blood pressure and nervous exhaustion. She was taking tranquillisers, and her work ramped up the pressure by starting dismissal proceedings against her for 'leaving the office without permission' and for being 'recalcitrant, undisciplined and impudent – almost laughable' as she wrote later. She was stalwartly defended by other members of staff and by a visiting bigwig from Rome, an old friend from Groundnut days. But it added additional strain, as she was put on two months' probation.

Master of mood change as he was, Tom suddenly became sympathetic about her breakdown. He was worried because he knew she could deny access in the event of a divorce, and with sole custody she could limit my visits. He was also worried about his job, as in February 1968 his UN bosses in New York were renewing pressure to stop him 'living in sin with his mistress', as Tom himself described it. He was incapable of sending Di away and, when he did, she came back.

He found it impossible to keep being nice and stupidly tried to get Sheila to agree to allow Di to accompany us to Canada in the summer holidays, a suggestion that fell on deaf ears. Grace had been drawn into the arguments and Sheila wrote furiously to her mother in June:

> ... your loyalty should be to me ... you know I speak the truth, after all you brought me up ... I certainly don't want you to hate Tom but you must realise he is crooked through and through and has been getting at V to say she would be upset if the sharing arrangements were different. He still spoils her and deals with her in the same stupid way.

This did not prevent Grace welcoming Tom to Durham with me at the end of the summer holidays, much to Sheila's anger:

[I am] surprised you are willing to have him to stay
– indeed I find it very hurtful … I have not bored or
burdened you with tales of his unkind treatment … you
would be very shocked … He believes implicitly what he
says is true and right … his sense of values are unbalanced.
He succeeds with his well-known charm to pull the wool
over your and R[osemary]'s eyes. He is not, like his mother,
straight.

It was exciting to visit Canada in the summer of 1968 and meet
my American cousins – Alec and his wife had moved to Seattle,
and now had three children. Tom wrote in September that Grete
was infuriating, an 'embarrassing pest' driving him and Alec 'round
the bend' with her lack of standards, 'yet beneath really kind'. On
this trip he persuaded Grete to support him in marrying Di, and
the tone of her letters to Sheila changed from being sympathetic
to accusing her in 1969 of being 'cruel' in not giving Tom a divorce:
'All this upsets me terribly. Very bad for high blood pressure.' Like
Tom she only saw things from her own perspective.

On his return to Ankara, Tom began to haggle over the 1969
Easter holidays. This time Sheila said there was no question of
splitting the holiday, so his tactic was to quote a letter from me:
"I shall not see you for 6 months, Daddy, I am so sad.'" Sheila
repeated her well-worn mantra that 'a happy and calm home-life
is the most important thing. And mothers are considered by all to
be more important than fathers in bringing up children.' Tom tried
everything, from enlisting the help of my headmistress to resorting
to emotional blackmail, saying how hurt he was and that it was not
enough for a child to see her father 'once a year esp when the child
loves the father as much as V loves me and vice versa'. He accused
Sheila of 'failing in her duty as a mum' and being 'unkind and cruel'

in depriving him of seeing me over the holidays especially as 'she loves me and needs me just as much as she needs you'.

When that did not work, he resorted to threats, accusing her of 'wrecking' his hopes for a permanent appointment by trying to get him sacked: 'if you keep messing around much longer it will get to the stage when I shall feel there is no point ... I hope that is what you want'. Self-righteously he continued, 'I have met no-one who says that a child – esp a girl – needs her ma more than her pa.' He went even further, linking access to money and threatened to sue *her* for divorce if he didn't get his way.

Sheila bravely stuck to her guns. She was fed up with being bullied and being told, as in February 1969, 'it was not the act of a good mother or a good woman denying a father access. I don't want to create any trouble, but Vicky's preference is to go skiing ... wish I could write in anger – but more in sorrow ...' They flung half-remembered quotations at each other: Sheila to Tom, 'So long as one is true to oneself, one cannot then be false to any man'; to which he shot back Oscar Wilde, 'Truth is never pure and seldom simple' [*sic*].

Unable to win this battle, he simply cut off her allowance, which he claimed was 'voluntary' and he was under 'no obligation' to pay until they were divorced. He didn't want 'V to be made unhappy by her parents' follies ... never doubt my love for the child. She means more to me than life itself. Give a thought for poor Daddy who will be sad bec[ause] he won't see his daughter.'

CHAPTER 15:
A NEW START?

In February 1970 Sheila flew to London for the long-awaited divorce hearing, writing rather poignantly:

> ... this is probably the last letter I will write to you as your wife, remember that I began with loyalty, love and affection, all of which you turned sour, and even then, only after a long, long time when I was helping you get to the top. Now you are at the top (for it doesn't look as if you will get any further) you forget all of this. It certainly seems unworthy of the idealistic young man I married 23 years ago – but, then, you are not the same person.

Tom was annoyed she had flown to London at his expense and likened their divorce to 'the clinical death of a patient who has been in a coma for years'. He assured her he would not be a bad influence on me as he still believed in 'peace, justice and decency ... still doing what I wanted to do in 1946 working for an organisation devoted to peace and the betterment of man'. He added that his biggest drawback was his 'excessive honesty', which applied to his feelings about Di – 'sometimes I wonder whether I am any good at being married ... perhaps I am one of those people who should live alone ... pity I can't marry Vicky as she and I understand each other so well'.

The continuing and protracted negotiations in the run-up to the divorce are painful to read. Despite Tom's assurances in August 1969 that he would 'never if it is in my power deny you reasonable funds if you are in need', he was, according to Sheila in October, 'easily swayed to abysmal depths when you listen to your lawyer'. He insisted on a settlement on the 'basis of current income' and refused to 'undertake to make up any shortfall' if she got a less well paid or part-time job – even if it were in order to look after me – because he also had 'a future to consider'. He would make 'ex gratia payments if and when appears necessary … you may think I am an absolute bastard, but you are not right … you might also consider that your difficult attitude to my seeing V does not help at all even tho you know it is V's wish to see me 50/50'.

But absolute bastard he was. Using confidential information about her citation in Neville's divorce (for Neville had finally bitten the bullet, though not in order to marry Sheila), which made Sheila the 'guilty party' and therefore entitled to nothing in English law, Tom blackmailed her to split the holidays equally. As she had no room for manoeuvre, she was also forced to agree to a paltry £1,000 p.a., from which he deducted life-insurance payments, leaving her with a net of £600. Meanwhile he continued to live a spendthrift lifestyle.

However, when the documents arrived, the commitment to split the holidays had been added minus the agreed wording: 'if our geographical positions allow it, without long and arduous travel for Vicky'. Sheila protested, and Tom's reply was 'don't muck about now or I know [my lawyer] will advise me to stop the monthly payments'. Poor Sheila gave in.

Ironically Tom had sent Di home, in fear for his job once again. Even Sheila was 'shocked that you don't seem to be missing her … Seems pointless that the divorce is on its way if you are not keener on the girl involved.' Tom retorted, 'as you know only too well, I am a difficult swine'.

Sheila's final letter on 2 February 1970 reads like an epitaph and reflected the depths to which they had both sunk emotionally and psychologically. She felt 'really very sad indeed' despite the inevitability of their divorce; the most wearing thing over the past three years had been her struggle 'alone and unaided' against 'the powers of darkness'. She was saddened that he didn't think he had changed since 1946:

[You have not] grown up enough to consider and judge every action not only in relation to yourself but also in its effect on others ... It is very sad for me for I judged you wrong. I was enormously influenced by your altruism; you gave me a new approach to life which seemed much more sound and basic than my own rather shallow one – But through the years it seemed your attitude was more a way of gaining approbation for the man rather than for the effect of the thoughts or belief; your constant use of schadenfreude and lack of consideration for the feelings of others has always appeared at cross purposes with the kindness and consideration which is also given out. Who then do you do it for – yourself or for others? Though I think you are a long-shot from your mother, nonetheless, I think her upbringing has had an effect – refugees yes, but you were much better off than most. Her feeling for money influences everything she did – and though in many ways she is a remarkable woman, I don't think a balance of her character would come out to her credit ... what really I am trying to say is that home influence does have an effect even if we don't know it (my own upbringing, poverty-stricken in purse and attitudes, held me back for years and probably still basically touches me) and so in relation to Vicky – what are the values you wish her to assume? Having her is not enough. Your mother loves you yet what has she given you beyond family solidarity and security based on the rewards of her wits? In old age you find her tedious, self-absorbed. Is our child going to think of us like that? I am often ashamed of myself in sometimes not being able to rise above my troubles … What is she going to think of you – this very aware and somewhat bright child of ours? Even now you pull down the curtain between reality and what you think/want things to be like – Pull it up before it is too late … So, you see why I am upset and saddened by what seems to me your wasted opportunities – the ardently altruistic young man with so much promise. Materialistically if you leave the UN in September it would be near disaster for us all; yet if it made you find your soul, perhaps it would be worth it … Perhaps I didn't then know you well enough and perhaps what I thought was my great love wasn't sufficient to accept what I found. Blessings always.

This despairing letter shows that my mother deeply understood my father, in particular his inability to be true to the good person within him who had been suppressed by his desire to succeed at any cost. He had lost all empathy for his loved ones as part of his emotional make-up; his compassion, maybe once deeply felt, now extended only to those outside his family, to satisfy his need for public approbation.

The letters continued until their divorce in July 1970, yo-yoing back and forth. Sheila was almost always depressed and unhappy,

Tom alternately sympathetic, hectoring and untruthful. Yet again he lied to her over a skiing holiday in Switzerland in 1970 when, despite assurances to the contrary, Di came along because she 'works hard looking after me and deserves a break'. He had sneakily written to me at school to ask if I minded and told Sheila that I 'did so want her [Di] to come because despite being a bit daft she was great fun'.

Sheila was livid at his using me again, but there was little she could do as he had already delayed my flights, limiting my time in Nairobi. She told him she knew 'perfectly well that I can apply to the court to prevent Vicky visiting you whilst you are living with Diana. Nonetheless I find this so distasteful I would rather allow her to come knowing full well I could never rely on you to send Diana away, even if you promised to do so'. In the future, she told him, she would instruct her lawyers to forbid me from 'coming into contact with whomever you may be living with ... your behaviour is insupportable ... please don't write me a self-vindicating letter ... I know you believe you are right, or you wouldn't behave like this'.

Meanwhile he continued to spoil me at boarding school in High Wycombe where huge parcels would arrive from Harrods – on my tenth birthday he sent me a Cindy car, a Cindy horse and a Cindy bed, an embarrassing largesse for any girl; then there were the unsuitable gifts, an engraved leather weekend case and leather washbag. Just as Grete embarrassed him, so I also found this ostentation hard to take. He thought money could buy love.

Just before the divorce was finalised in July 1970, there was one final spat: first, Tom accused Sheila (wrongly) of holding up on the decree absolute (the legal document ending the marriage) and, in retaliation, on 24 June she threatened to get her lawyer to obtain payment of her air fare for attending the divorce hearing – 'which was what you wanted' – and the allowance he had cut off in a fit of pique, which 'you have never paid but abjectly apologised for the deception'. She could not afford to lose either.

Tom's response was classic: 'So you are being nasty again … you are not thinking of V's welfare you are only trying to get your own back … I will hold you financially responsible for any loss I may unnecessarily bear by your shenanigans. I am referring your letter to [my lawyer] for advice'. Sheila replied despairingly that she was 'deeply shocked and distressed that things between us should come to this. It seems you have not only lost your soul, but your heart.'

The decree absolute was not the final act in this chapter of unhappiness. Tom was rattled, as he had been hiding from Sheila that he was to get married that autumn. Despite assurances that 'I continue to hold you in very high esteem not only as V's mummy but someone to whom I owe much and who has shared many difficulties with me', the wedding was planned on Sheila's birthday. He thought he could get away without her finding out – he even swore me to secrecy – but as he had invited several of their mutual friends, including Neville, it was inevitable that one of them would tell her.

Sheila was livid:

Ok you are going to marry Diana but I much object to Vicky being in on this and the whole thing being knowingly kept from me. It seems very conspiratorial and I do not like – or wish – Vicky to become involved in such dealings. You are teaching her to take sides which is always something I have tried to avoid. If you thought it would hurt me, then you shouldn't have told V either.

Sheila was deeply concerned about the deception, as she wrote on 13 September, accusing him of dishonesty. His involving me in the 'subterfuge' of his wedding was setting me a bad example and was evidence of his typical 'lack of judgement'. She was 'terribly worried about Vicky's grownup-ness which can only be laid at your door' and they 'had to agree' about the 'make-up' and 'low décolleté dresses', as it was only 'asking for trouble, travelling alone as she does, for her to look 17 when she is only 12'. In despair she finished, 'Poor Vicky I wonder how she will survive such a background. Don't forget that she was born for me – you didn't want her. And at the moment, and perhaps for always, she is my one joy in life.'

He replied, after the wedding, with his usual breeziness when he had the upper hand:

I agree about the wedding, but I really physically couldn't keep it from V. She quite understands the position in her usual adult way and is v balanced, settled and pleased about it all ... you were not forgotten as Vicky and I toasted you in sparkling wine during the reception and frequently talked about you lovingly, believe it or not!

He even took Di up to Durham to see Sheila's mother, Grace, with the justification that Grace invited her and that they were 'well received'. He wrote to Sheila, 'Your mum is a real brick, and a realist, too. So, don't be cross with her, will you ... Don't try and find fault with everything I do ... I usually act from the best possible motives and of course I have no intention of hurting you in any way'. During this visit Tom convinced Sheila's mother that the divorce was all a result of Sheila's unreasonable behaviour in leaving him. It was the ultimate betrayal and Sheila never forgave her.

I had a rocky start at Wycombe Abbey, my new boarding school. We left the wedding directly after the reception in Exeter, Di's home town, and drove all the way to Buckinghamshire for the first day of term. Instead of the school uniform I was still wearing my wedding clothes and was plastered in make-up. I got a rocket from the housemistress, but a lot of kudos from the other girls. Tom naturally would not have thought about how difficult he made life for anyone else, not even his beloved daughter. He just had to have his way.

I had hoped that the letters would stop after the divorce, but they kept on writing for a further two years, and were as acrimonious as ever. In December 1970 Tom moved to the Philippines as deputy resident representative of the UNDP office. His divorce and remarriage satisfied the New York head office and he was finally offered a permanent contract, a full five years after he joined the UN.

The holidays continued to cause problems. In March 1971 Tom wrote it was 'quite ridiculous that I stand not to see Vicky in April … frankly I am disappointed in this performance of yours – not in the best Sheila tradition'. For once Sheila got her own back by asking me if I wanted to go to both Manila *and* Kenya for the holidays, and I refused, saying it was too far. Tom had the nerve to say it was 'quite unfair to put such a strain on the child, to choose between us'.

The familiar discussions about money continued. Sheila wrote in July 1971:

> … it is all very well saying you bear me no resentment – why should you? It is all fine words; you may say you still love me in a funny way, but you are quite willing to force me into working as hard as I do, tricking me out of my maintenance money to try and force me into a divorce, and to cheerfully owe me £400 which I very much need. If you really, as you

say, wish me well – why don't you do something to confirm it? Do you expect me to work until I drop?

Tom defended his position:

... about the £300 [he had rounded it down] [I] will send it as soon as I can send it from my current account BUT please stop talking about me owing you this money. I paid you for many years on an entirely voluntary, and generous, allowance: I stopped paying it at one time and was ashamed of the subterfuge to which I resorted because I didn't have the guts to tell you ... but I have never been ashamed of the actual stoppage in payments which I believe was justified and effective. I was under no obligation at any time to pay you anything.

He falsely claimed she earned as much as him 'after I deduct all the payments I make for you and V ... Now don't go writing again that my letter upset you: it's nothing new and nothing that hasn't been said before. You know I mean well and am fond of you.'

As ever he was the master of sanctimonious self-delusion.

Meanwhile I was precocious for my age and started to run wild. During my holidays in Nairobi Sheila could not afford to leave her job or take a part-time one. The combination of my fares and the cost of living in Nairobi meant there was little left over each month, for she was only on a secretary's salary. Sheila was concerned at her inability to look after me and was trying to leave Kenya and return to England; Neville was now living with the another woman, even though he continued to visit Sheila when it suited him. But it was hopeless. She was worried that I 'may inherit the Unwin promiscuous streak and need being kept an eye on,' as she wrote in

May 1971. She was seldom at home and I enjoyed 'wandering around [Nairobi], dressed in funny clothes'. She was concerned about my circle of older friends who 'tend to egg [you] on'. She was trying to get the balance between 'clamping down' and making her 'opinions known ... I adore having her and she simply loves it here, but it is a worry wondering where she is when I am at work ...'

For once they shared anxieties over my welfare and Tom's reply did not point the finger of blame. He agreed 'one cannot control too much', although he was concerned about 'all this "joint" smoking all the young people here do nowadays'. He thought I was aware of the dangers and he had pointed out a heroin addict injecting himself on a bus as evidence of his responsibility as a parent. But he passed the buck back to Sheila, 'you might have a guarded word when you see her next'.

I was desperately unhappy at Wycombe Abbey and lobbied to leave more or less as soon as I arrived. Sheila was supportive and blamed Tom for spoiling me, as he had ceased to treat me as a child years ago, 'mainly for your pleasure'. He had indulged my 'whims' and 'didn't think of the effect it would have – and so she left being a child too early'. She concluded:

> It is no wonder she is unhappy in a restrictive boarding
> school. I have written to Vicky and suggested she
> tries to think less of herself and more of others, that
> happiness comes from within and that one just has to
> try a little harder ... I know it sounds hard and I am truly
> sympathetic, but she has to make an effort herself. I shall
> put her down for Bedales, it does no harm.

Tom was adamant that I should not leave, not even after O levels. He threw his weight around, said he had consulted a

UNESCO friend who had advised him that I was in the best school in Britain. He only wanted the best for his daughter, putting my unhappiness second.

> If she thinks she is on the way out she will, as is quite
> human, take far less interest in WA and try less hard to fit
> in … I do feel strongly she should stay. If you keep referring
> to the possibility/probability of her transferring to Bedales
> you will just make her feel less steadfast in her outlook.
> Not good I think.

Used as I was to getting my own way, this put me in a terrible sulk and I began to resent my father's refusal to listen.

In late 1971 Di became pregnant. Ever the coward, Tom prepared the ground in a letter to Sheila in December by disingenuously saying he would like to have another child but 'am frightened … age and my instability in matters emotional. I am like a badly working car meter – the needle flickers from + to - constantly. Yes, I was born a fool, I am sure.' However, in the next letter he announced 'our great news':

> I think it's a good idea but I have a queasy feeling about
> it all … but Di is so happy that it makes me accept it … I
> was as you know, equally reluctant at first [with Vicky]. I
> am just frightened about my emotional instability – and
> if Di and I were ever to part it would make it so much
> more traumatic … but she puts up with the bad-tempered
> bastard that I am so magnificently that she deserves a VC.

I found the letter announcing the birth in August 1972, filed separately in its own plastic envelope, indicating its significance for Sheila: 'You may have heard I have become a papa again – a fine bouncing boy of 7½lbs called Alexander. We shall call him Sasha – or Alexander the Greatest ...' As ever when things were going his way, he was ebullient – considerate and caring, discussing Sheila's plan to return to England so I could leave Wycombe Abbey, attend a day school and live with her. He was keen for me to go to university, become a doctor 'and do shorthand-typing, secretarial work and domestic science' in my year off, although I had already been talking about becoming an archaeologist, thanks to Neville's influence.

I was left to my own devices in my holidays spent the Philippines during the summers, split by agreement, of 1971 and 1972 while I was in my early teens and I got into a bad set. They had both feared this would happen, Tom writing defensively that it was not he who gave me 'a bad example',

> ... [it] was yours in leaving me: I lived with my mistress
> – ok (in separate rooms so far as V was concerned) but
> I did marry her and it was in fact a much more moral
> relationship than yours with Neville, if one is going to
> cast stones. There was no innate immorality in what I
> did, especially as the final outcome and the intention
> throughout, was what one calls moral – the impediments
> merely being you and the law!!

Nothing was ever his fault.

Sheila asked him what I got up to in Manila:

> Didn't you tell me yourself that she goes off to clubs and

sits for hours and hours with other young people smoking pot? If she's going to come to harm, which heaven forbid, she will come to harm; there are no flies on the young ... but I think Vicky respects her parents, and wouldn't want to do anything that would hurt us ... If you think you didn't give her a bad example you must be off your nut. The bad example stemmed from your impossible behaviour, your cruelty and unkindness, which made my life a misery.

Respecting my parents was not part of the equation: I recall being the mistress of disguise in order to be a successful subversive – a real goody-two-shoes outwardly (head of house at prep school, head of year at Wycombe Abbey, the youngest dormitory monitor), but revelled in escaping to my secret world, free from my squabbling parents, where smoking weed, dabbling in other drugs, including heroin, and having sex with my various boyfriends, provided sanctuary. I replaced my formerly doting father, who now had another baby to fuss over, with adoring boys. I revelled in being the centre of attention.

But I have no doubt that Tom was at fault for

The sultry teenager in Manila, in the décolleté dress I made myself

what happened next: I was furious with him for not listening to me about school; my nose was out of joint with the arrival of the new baby. I knew I would no longer occupy first place in my father's life. Moreover, I felt very sorry for my mother who was miserable and depressed; the shortage of money in our Nairobi home was palpable, while Tom lived profligately; I begged my father to give my mother more money, to no avail.

The crisis which had been building since their separation came to a head, when I was arrested in November 1972 at Wycombe Abbey for arranging a shipment of marijuana between two friends, one in Kenya and one in Devon. I had met the latter while waiting for my brother to be born. The police came for me the night we returned from half-term and I was whisked away from the dormitory after lights out, never to return.

The episode had Kafkaesque qualities. I was exiled to the school sickbay until it was decided what to do with me. While I waited, I took an English O level, for which I gained an A grade. After a few days my mother's cousin Hazel came to pick me up in the Rolls-Royce, driven by her chauffeur. I found the letter my distraught mother wrote to me after the event and now feel the shame I couldn't at the time. Although I appeared much older than my fifteen years, I was nonetheless rather naïve and did not understand what I had done was wrong: I was simply helping friends, blinded by a crush on the Kenyan boy.

Despite being a juvenile, the case went to the Exeter magistrates' court and I was fined £100. It was a horrific experience. On arrival I was led into the cells below the court, furnished with a concrete bench and a steel loo. I sat there for what seemed like hours until the case came up. Then I was taken by a policeman, like a criminal, up into the dock where I sat next to my co-accused, the Kenyan boy, who had been arrested on arrival back in England. I was lucky as Hazel's husband, Tony, had paid for a top London QC, whereas the others had to get by on legal aid. The CPS enthusiastically read out excerpts from my letters and diary to show what a depraved girl I was, much to my – and my mother's – embarrassment. One of the two other defendants went to jail, and the third got a hefty fine.

My mother was forced to leave Nairobi earlier than planned to come and look after me – the Court was prepared to slap a care order on me had she failed to do so. The letters between my parents stop shortly before my arrest. Dad had written to me weekly at school, mostly about Di and the baby – he was at this stage still calling me his 'favourite child as Sasha is not a child yet, just a conglomeration of cells ... has the makings of turning out just like his dad!' – and his letters continued throughout my teens, as did mine to him.

I remember his fury at what had happened – not with me, but with my mother, my Aunt Rosemary, Hazel, the school, in fact anybody whom he could blame except himself. I recently found the cables and letters Tom sent to his lawyer, raging that 'Sheila purposefully kept me in the dark', and that he was 'actively discouraged from coming as I was assured she would only be warned'. He was convinced that 'with my presence and with better legal advice things might have taken a less serious turn'; everyone else felt he would only damage my case with his record of volatility and intemperate behaviour.

He was particularly annoyed that the courts confiscated my passport and placed me in Sheila's care. She cabled him: 'regret owing bench ruling Vicky unable to visit Manila this Christmas'. At the bottom he scribbled 'hypocritical bitch' and 'it is quite obviously spite'.

Looking back, I do not think it was a coincidence that the

incident occurred at the same time as the birth of my half-brother, Sasha. I knew I was about to be displaced in my father's affections and was making a subconscious attempt at a last hurrah, a 'look at me!' gesture. My parents' separation and divorce had exacted a heavy price, and this was how it revealed itself.

The one positive outcome was my immediate expulsion from Wycombe Abbey. A cynic might wonder at the lengths I went to achieve my goal.

CHAPTER 16:
UNITED NATIONS MAN

Our lives changed once my mother came back to England. I had spent the two terms preceding my O levels in a comprehensive school in Lyme Regis – the only place that would have me. Hazel lent us her cottage in Branscombe, a pretty village by the sea in East Devon, where I had spent many half-terms. I managed to pass my nine O levels despite everything. Surprisingly, Miss Fisher, my dragon of a headmistress at Wycombe (she always rather admired my spirit) had put in a good word on my behalf and I went to Oxford High for my A levels, which had been my latest plan. Hazel gave us a small cottage in Stadhampton, just outside Oxford, in lieu of leaving us money in her will.

At last Sheila was able to give up work, not voluntarily, but because in her early fifties she was deemed too old. She did occasional temping, as my father refused to increase her alimony despite being relieved that I had a full-time carer, and he was now able to see me two or three times a year. So, he got the best of both worlds.

In the end Sheila took him to court at vast expense and managed to get an inflationary increase as her payments were not index-linked. I always resented that he could be so mean, as we lived in a state of near poverty, forced into vegetarianism and lacking in treats and nice things. It was make-do and mend. My poor mother was understandably depressed at having to leave Kenya and Neville in such haste. Only in my twenties and in the throes of more adult relationships did I have any idea how much added misery my actions had heaped on her already fragile disposition.

I saw little of my father during my holidays in the Philippines: he was always escaping domesticity for the office as his job was demanding – supervising UNDP's development projects – which left me at home with Di and the baby, so I contacted my friends. Despite my trial, I had not changed and was still running around with older boys and taking drugs. My father suspected nothing. Occasionally he would organise holidays and expeditions around his field trips, especially when Nana visited. My boyfriend Alfredo trailed along on these outings, resplendent in tight jeans and

Tom reviewing one of his research projects in the Philippines – on coconut disease

winkle-pickers (he was a DJ on a local radio station), quite unsuited to scrambling around volcanoes or in and out of boats. Tom put up with it all with a mix of good nature and exasperation. It was the price he had to pay for my un-grumbling company.

My letters from my exotic holidays to my mother barely mention my father and are more like a travelogue with references to friends and parties. I am touched by my caring tone and solicitousness, fed by my own guilt at having taken her away from the proximity of the man she loved, even if the affair was over. In her loneliness she would have enjoyed my scrawly missives sent, as per my training, once a week.

In my teens I was fed up with Tom's endless fussing and his terrible temper, when he used to lash out and hit me. One clout around the ear in Manila, when I was about fifteen, sent me reeling and I almost fell. I remember it well: we were sitting at the table having lunch when a row erupted, and I started walking out of the room. No one did that to Tom, so he belted me round the side of my head. Afterwards he changed back into adoring Dad, begging forgiveness, unable to explain why he blew a fuse. This sort of behaviour resonates with the stories of husbands who abuse their wives, and I wonder now how many times he hit my mother.

I found a cache of letters from my father to me after my expulsion right through to my starting at Cambridge. They remind me that he still held enormous sway over my emotions, but they also reveal his controlling nature and his obsession with my future, which had to conform to his wishes. They are all loving and invariably signed 'all/tons/lashings of my love and millions of kissies from your adoring/devoted/proud/loving/rather cross (on one occasion) Daddy', surrounded by alternate black and red kisses. He fussed about me being 'sloppy and unbusinesslike', for not writing to him regularly enough, 'you tripehound ... you blighter' and exhorted me to listen to his advice about my future:

> ... shan't push you in an unreasonable way ... hope you will
> always leave a little room in your thoughts for the wishes
> of your pop and mum & realise that what we say is only to
> make your life better and easier & not to satisfy some silly
> bees in our own bonnets ... Although in some ways you

think I am an old fogey – and no doubt I am – all those decades of accumulated experience do stand for something and should not be entirely ignored as irrelevant.

All these letters included a weekly note from Di, chatty, newsy and friendly, naturally mostly about Sasha. I find it hard to remember now what they meant to me – on the face of it, we seem to have had a good relationship, but I wonder what I really felt, getting weekly news bulletins on the progress of my half-brother from a woman I sensed had never really liked me. Perhaps as we both matured we realised that there was a middle ground of tolerance and mutual understanding for who we were and the respective positions we occupied in my father's affections.

Both parents remained concerned for my moral welfare. When I was almost seventeen, Tom sent me a copy of a letter he had originally sent to Sheila, to prove he wasn't an 'old fogey', where he said that, 'so long as she doesn't end up with a baby there is, I should think, no harm in having occasional intercourse – of course I have no idea whether she does or not but it wouldn't in this day and age surprise me. And presumably she takes the pill so there is no risk of conception.'

Tom began to exert the same controlling tendencies to keep me under his influence that he had used with Sheila. He was quick to side with me in any spat I had with her, for instance over my use of the telephone, her restriction of which was more, I suspect, induced by poverty on my mother's part than a desire to stop me speaking to my friends. Nevertheless, I felt very peeved by this and complained bitterly. He was all sympathy, and couldn't resist a dig at Sheila – he put it down to her 'over-developed sense of British ethic'.

He was determined that I should go to university and for a

long time was distraught that I wanted to go on the stage; then I acquiesced and, as a sop, agreed to do Swahili and anthropology at the School of Oriental and African Studies (SOAS). He did not understand that university is about acquiring skills rather than a career, 'don't know how wise you are to put SOAS down as 1st choice … in effect you know no Swahili at all and your knowledge of Africa is touristic'.

He was placated when I decided to try for Cambridge to read anthropology and archaeology, due to the influence of my Oxford student boyfriend, and of Neville:

> What happens in the next 3 months is probably of gt
> importance for the rest of your life … I only managed
> without a degree because I work hard, am not too stupid,
> and because (and this is the only real reason) after the
> war, service as an officer tended to be accepted in lieu of
> academic qualifications.

The kudos was now more important than the career.

My A level results were poor as I spent all my time with my boyfriend. My father was surprisingly sympathetic as I was still allowed to sit the Cambridge entrance exam, 'Never mind! you must be even more disappointed than I am … but as long as it doesn't prejudice your chances for Cambridge all may yet be well'. His letters were full of exhortations to 'buckle down for the final spurt … put school and work absolutely first' and 'love and lots of kissies darling and WORK!' He tried to pull strings to abet my smooth transition by arranging for me to go and see an admissions tutor for 'advice', exhorting me not to 'scoff at your Dad's good ideas'. I did not go, much to his annoyance.

On my eighteenth birthday in 1975, shortly before the Cambridge entrance exam, he wrote,

> ... you are my favourite daughter and I love you very much and I am proud of you and I wish you all happiness in the next year which is quite an important one for you. You are a good sensible girl (usually!) and I trust that the decisions which you will be making will always be wise and kind. Above all I hope that you will continue to be in excellent health and the joy (I am not mentioning the headaches) you have been to your parents which you have been so far.

Of course I had no idea he had another daughter.

He had the knack of keeping those heartstrings tight.

*

But as I began to slip away from his control, I took less heed of his wishes. His one overarching desire was that I do a shorthand and typing course. He had booked me in to Mrs Thomsett's Secretarial College in Oxford for three months, without consultation, during my gap year in 1976. Instead I got a job in the pub in Branscombe, where I had my cousins and lots of friends, and went overland to India via the Hindu Kush with the boyfriend.

He started reasonably enough when told of my decision; he was 'disappointed and cross', mostly because it meant he didn't qualify for the UN allowances for having a child in education, but he regretted that 'you will not get the sec training'. As with Sheila, he did not like being thwarted: 'Are you trying to have it all your own way?' he asked plaintively. Even Di was brought in on the discussion: she implored me to sort something out for her sake as I imagine his bad temper was on full display at home.

He then decided that I should do a College of Further Education course after my trip; again I refused. He was 'disappointed that no arrangements made for CFE course … I'm not going to be stupid or get cross, but I do hope you will bear what I say in mind and act accordingly'. In other words, he was going to get cross, which he did in his next letter where he gave me both barrels, showing how he fully expected to be obeyed not only by me, but by Sheila as well:

> I am not resentful although it has cost me a great deal of money … a bit of a con trick … it was always understood that you would come back and do a full-time sec course for about 3 months … AND THAT ARRANGEMENTS WOULD BE MADE BEFORE YOUR DEPARTURE. I think both you and mum have let me down over this … BIT off …

Subconsciously I knew he was flawed. I resented being a pawn in the game of my parents' broken marriage, being shoved from here to there, on and off planes, doing things that no child should do like hanging round airports in the middle of the night. At the age of eighteen I went to university and tried to escape this past. If only it had been that simple. The scars of my upbringing are cut deep into my psyche like traditional African cicatrices and left visible damage. Several years of psychotherapy and psychoanalysis eventually led me to a better understanding of my own unhappiness, and an insight into theirs; but forgiving my father was more complicated.

Tom's next post was as UNDP Resident Representative (head of mission) to Papua New Guinea in 1974, where he stayed for seven years. It was his most senior position to date and Papua New Guinea was quite like Africa in many ways – the Australians had only just granted independence and it had many colonial vestiges, including wearing white shorts and long socks to work; there was much to do in development terms, and he oversaw projects as diverse as crocodile farms, silkworm production and vocational training. The nascent guerrilla war between the Free Papua Movement and Indonesia in the western half of the island, Irian Jaya, resulted in a refugee crisis which he leapt in to resolve. This had been caused by the UN's botched handover of the former Dutch territory to the land-grabbing Indonesians, who committed horrific human rights violations against the indigenous population – including aerial bombardment, use of napalm, arbitrary detention and rape – with the result that many Papuans fled over the border to Papua New Guinea.

His letters bear witness to how well he rose to the challenge of a government keen on appeasing the Indonesians and which wanted to send the refugees back. Perhaps it reminded him of the politics of appeasement in the Second World War and the consequences it had on his family. In May 1977 he wrote that he was 'extraordinarily busy with 100s if not 1000s of refugees'. He had been 'raising hell' and got the Prime Minister Michael Somare, to overrule Foreign Affairs and agree to him seeing the situation: 'I don't know where I am going but it should be interesting and above all useful in that I may save the lives of many people who might otherwise be pushed back into a very uncertain fate.' He caused a row between Somare and the Foreign Minister and said, 'I'm just doing my job and not for myself either: for their own brothers.'

He gave a long account of his adventures in Bensbach and Suki, hundreds of miles west of Port Moresby, the capital, and right on the border with Irian Jaya, where his landing was denied despite the assurances of cooperation. He had to turn back and resorted to getting Di to ask Somare via the NZ High Commissioner, who had to interrupt a state dinner, to revoke the order. After his visit, he gave a press conference and numerous radio interviews, with his voice being 'beamed over the world'. He felt 'glad to have stuck my neck out. It may have saved some people some unpleasantness and it has greatly enhanced the reputation of the UN in PNG'.

A signed photograph of Tom being given a farewell gift from Papua New Guinean Prime Minister Julius Chan

His Papuan PA, Mary, exemplifies the loyalty and respect he commanded in his public persona. She posted this on my Facebook page in response to his obituary in the *Daily Telegraph* in 2012:

He was number one. Workaholic, wicked sense of humour! Everything was way ahead, the speed of his action. He treated all his staff with great respect. We excelled so well with the West Irian refugees, one of his favourite responsibilities since we didn't have UNHCR [the United Nations High Commissioner for Refugees] at the time. I know now why because he was a refugee himself.

She remembered the time when he was giving a speech at a government function and found a teaspoon in his pocket. Mary suspected he had picked it up instead of his pipe. 'Your Dad was the best'.

His deputy in Papua New Guinea, Kevin McGrath, also remembered Tom fondly. He recalled the occasion when he was first introduced to him at cocktail party in New York the late 1970s. 'I've just met my new boss,' he enthused to his Slovak wife, 'he is so British, you wouldn't believe it.' 'And I've just met this charming Czech,' burbled Olga, 'I simply must introduce you!'

Kevin treasured Tom's reputation as the author of witty and irreverent cables that amused and irritated his UN bosses in equal measure. Tom used this mechanism to thumb his nose at authority and the idiocy of UN protocols. One of his most notorious cables was sent at the culmination of a three-year battle against a bureaucrat at headquarters, a certain Mr Gonzalez. After receiving no reply to an urgent matter, a frustrated Tom re-sent the correspondence and was thrilled to receive a reply. 'At last I have met Speedy Gonzalez,' he remarked to his colleagues.

But his favourite – I found a copy of it tucked into his files – exemplifies his needling of the UN's political correctness, an anathema to him. The Papua New Guinean government had put up a project proposal with the word 'indigenous' in the title, which UNESCO objected to. Knowing that the recipient of his cable was Indian, he wrote:

> Government insists on maintaining word indigenous in
> project title which they say correctly describes nature of
> project. With due respect UNESCO must leave judgment
> of what Papua New Guineans find pejorative to Papua New
> Guineans. They are after all blacker than you and eye [sic]
> and if they think its [sic] inoffensive who are we whiteys
> to quibble.

As ever, he relished pushing his luck with his superiors – in this case playing the race card in a questionable manner.

Kevin recalled the occasion when the Senegalese Secretary General of UNESCO was coming on a visit and expected kid-glove treatment. He was surprised when Tom met him at the aircraft steps, clad in his uniform of white shorts and long socks, without the customary chauffeur. It made him uncomfortable to have the resident representative driving him to his official appointments; Tom of course thought this was a great joke. In fact, after this incident, the two of them got on well.

I enjoyed visiting my father in Papua New Guinea as by this time I was studying anthropology at Cambridge. His access to government at the highest levels enabled me to interview PM Somare and the Foreign Minister, Ebia Olewale, for my dissertation. I was able to piggyback on his trips to the interior and visit some wild and inaccessible places.

The public, humanitarian Tom was on show throughout his UN career. He refused to wait for authorisation from head-quarters to issue tents, food and blankets to refugees, as this often took months, by which time the victims were either dead or had fled further afield, and he was frequently censured by either New York or Geneva for his insubordination. He bequeathed me his 'personnel' files containing his corres-pondence with his UN and UNHCR bosses, latterly Kofi Annan who, despite Tom's intransigence, be-came a friend.

Yet he retained the habit of rubbing people

With my father on a motorbike

up the wrong way. While he was running UNHCR in Uganda in the early 1980s, someone in the organisation apparently plotted to have him dismissed; he accused Tom of intriguing with President Apollo Milton Obote's staff and of currency violations, called him a 'crook' (one thing he certainly was not) and of being a 'danger to the government'. As Tom wrote to his boss, the man was 'crazy, a cretin, illiterate and highly dangerous'. On another occasion he took up the case of a perfectly capable 'discreet and mature' Ugandan secretary, while Geneva wanted to renew the contract of an 'unintelligent, not especially hard-working – not specially anything in fact' expatriate worker. He must have been a real pain, his trademark of having the final word in evidence at work as well as domestically. He was not one to obey rules, something I admired in him and which rubbed off on me, also to my detriment on occasion. Whether this is genetic or the way I was brought up, I can't say.

I got a job in publishing with Heinemann in London in 1979 after I left Cambridge. I had met Ross there and we married in Branscombe in 1983. Hazel gave us the reception as a wedding present. We could not trust Tom to behave so we asked Neville to give the father-of-the-bride speech. Sheila and he were reconciled and were planning to move to Cambridge together. He had been a surrogate father to me in many ways – he always asked after me in his letters and sent me love, and I adored seeing him when he turned up periodically. At the last minute he was unwell – he was to die suddenly in 1984 – so Hazel's son, Michael, my favourite cousin, did the honours. Tom was allowed to walk me down the aisle.

After this, contact with my father became sporadic, and the flow of loving letters with it. Now that the UN had stopped my airfares, the invitations also ceased. The only time I visited him in the field was shortly before the wedding when I was sent by Heinemann to Uganda to negotiate a World Bank educational books contract. I decided to combine the trip with some holiday to spend time with Dad..

While I was there one of the first mini-genocides of Tutsis living in Uganda kicked off. Tutsis had fled into Uganda during the Rwandan genocide between 1959 and 1962 when the Hutus overthrew the Tutsis. They had settled in Uganda but were forced to register as refugees in camps, a decision reversed during Idi Amin's regime. When Obote came back to power, he accused the Tutsis (or Banyarwanda as they are known) of supporting the Amin regime and he used this as pretext to either force them into camps or expel them altogether. Over 50,000 fled, thousands of cattle were stolen or killed, and many people murdered.

This was happening as I arrived in Kampala for my official visit. As Tom was the UNHCR representative, the Banyarwanda were his responsibility, so he set off for the trouble spots on the border with me in tow as my meetings were not for several days hence, together with the Rwandan refugee representative, Phocas Ntayombya. At that time Uganda was all but closed to foreigners, in particular to journalists.

It was a frightening journey, with multiple roadblocks manned by drunk, stoned youths who insisted on searching us, and roughing up Phocas as much as they dared. Everywhere we went we passed deserted, smouldering huts and landscapes devoid of people. This had been rich and fertile country, teeming with herds of the Banyarwanda's beloved Ankole cattle – now all gone.

Appalled by what I had seen, using my National Union of Journalists affiliation (publishers were part of the union), I managed to get a story out on the World Service when I visited Nairobi for work a few days later. While I was away I was declared *persona non grata* by the Ugandan government but managed to slip back over the border into Uganda just in time for my meetings at the Ministry of Education. It was farcical.

Meanwhile, a member of the High Commission's military police popped round and said there was a price on my head, and I should leave as soon as possible as I was not safe. Nevertheless, Tom and I decided to bluff it out and went to the Independence celebrations the next day. As we stood in the line-up, Vice President Paulo Muwanga gripped my hand fiercely and hissed, 'You should not interfere in matters that do not concern you.'

The following day, at the airport waiting to board, a young man approached me. 'Are you Vicky Unwin?' 'Who wants to know?' I asked coolly, my heart hammering. I felt like I was caught up in a spy thriller. 'I just wanted to thank her on behalf of the Ugandan people for the great service she has done by telling the world how terrible things are in Uganda under Obote.'

After this my father was declared *persona non grata* as well and asked to leave Uganda. He got in real trouble with the UNHCR – UN officials are not allowed to upset the host government. This is why it often appears so toothless.

At his official farewell party, Vice President Muwanga said to my father: 'Tom, goodbye and good luck. You have been without doubt the worst UN man we have ever had here.' To which he replied with his characteristic quick wit, 'Coming from you, sir, that is a great honour.'

Consequently, he left the UN under a cloud. I always felt guilty about it as, on my return, I had given World Service interviews and written an article for the *Guardian*, 'from a special correspondent'. Obviously, people knew who it was. Dad never held it against me; indeed, he was proud of what we had done together in revealing Obote as a monster: in the subsequent civil war, the National

Resistance Army uncovered the mass graves of his opponents in the Luwero Triangle. Idi Amin had been deposed by another dictator, cut from the same cloth.

I tell this story as it shows how much my father and I had in common and how we were on the same wavelength, politically and emotionally – prepared to take risks for what is right. This was the father I remembered from my childhood, when it was just me and him, but it was one of our last moments of intimacy.

Years later when I was working for the Aga Khan Fund for Economic Development as Media Director, President Museveni summoned me to discuss the reasons why he had closed our new Ugandan television station. During the to and fro I said, 'By the way, Your Excellency, my father Tom Unwin sends you his best wishes.' A great beam lit up his face - 'Ah Tom Unwin, he was a good man. He helped our people.' Museveni's mother was Munyarwanda. The negotiations ran smoother after that.

We remained in touch and I saw him when he was on leave from his various consultancies in Cambodia, Darfur and Sabah between 1984 and 1997, and from two refugee programmes in Sudan and Sierra Leone in the late 1980s and early 1990s. When not abroad, he was living in the home he and Di shared in Somerset, the gloomy Fort of the Foreword. He felt frustrated and bored in England and only truly fulfilled when working. His final role, from 1992 to 1997, was running the EU in Kyrgyzstan, which he and Di both loved. I always regretted not visiting but I could not afford it, with two small children and a mortgage to pay, courtesy of a small legacy from Grete who had died in 1978.

Part 4

Things fall apart

CHAPTER 17:
THE SECOND GREAT SECRET

As Tom grew older it was hard to recognise the once sharp and articulate man of my youth. With age his character traits become more exaggerated – in particular his thick skin and inability to see anyone else's point of view.

This was the cause of the tremendous rift between us after he retired in 1997, when we did not speak for months. It started when Tom disinherited me in my late thirties in favour of Sasha, his son by his marriage to Di. Tom said that I didn't need anything as I had done so well for myself, whereas my brother needed help. I remember remarking tartly, biting my tongue with fury, 'So I get punished for being a success.'

Occasionally he would flash with good humour, eyes

A rare family photo with Tom, Di, Sasha and the Dalmatians, Emma and another Nelson, mid-80s

lighting up, when something or someone sparked his interest, but otherwise he sat quietly in his study obsessing about Sasha. Despite having been a devoted father to me, he seemed little interested in his grandchildren, Tommy and Louise, born in 1988 and 1989 respectively, funnelling all his energies and love towards his son. Looking back on my mother's letters, I realise it was an extension of the tendencies he had displayed when I was growing up. Nothing else seemed to matter so the rest of us – me, my children and even his wife to an extent – were all playing bit parts in his life and were largely ignored. It was deeply hurtful. It made me wonder what had made him like this. Was it the trauma of being a refugee, or was it just the way he was? I needed to understand.

Tom had been diagnosed with Parkinson's in December 2000; his lifespan was now uncertain, so it became critical to find out about his Czech heritage before he died. Cousin Helen's surprise visit in 1997 had ignited my interest but the secrets of the suitcase were not revealed until 2009, so I was still very much in the dark about his past. Hoping it would trigger his memory, in October 2002 I took Tom along with the family – Ross, Di, Sasha, Louise (Tommy was on a school trip and unable to join us) – to Prague for his eightieth birthday. The joke was I had miscounted, and it was his seventy-ninth – something I only discovered as we raised our glasses for the birthday toast.

He had only been back once since he left in 1939, and that was during the communist era. He had many Czech friends whom he had met in his UN career, and several of them had returned to Prague. While he was in Ankara he befriended Alexander Dubček, the Czech leader of the Prague Spring of 1968, who had been exiled to Turkey as ambassador. Tom always said that he had been arranging for Dubčeks defection, but the Russians had arrested his family, so he was forced to return to Czechoslovakia and a life in the political wilderness as a forester.

In 2002 we were met at the airport by Mirek and Hana Juna, Czech friends from Turkey who had now returned, with the traditional welcome tray of schnapps and cake. Mirek was a brilliant physicist and violinist but he had been demoted to a lavatory cleaner in his university after the Russian invasion in 1968. His wife, Hana, had been luckier and retained her post as a psychologist and, with it, a fine flat overlooking the Vltava River where we ate Dad's favourite Czech dumplings and boiled beef with dill sauce, washed down with shots of schnapps.

The couple were thrilled to look after us on this memorable visit. Together we walked the streets, my father full of schoolboy memories. As we strolled past the statues on Charles Bridge he exclaimed, 'Look, this is the statue – we called it somebody's farted', and indeed, the burghers of Prague were looking aloofly into the distance as if escaping from a bad smell. Louise bought him a roughly carved plaque which read 'I love my Grandpa'. It sits in my study today, alongside the Hermann Ungar library, his Remington typewriter and copies of my father's all-time literary favourite, *The Good Soldier Schweik*, Jaroslav Hašek's comic masterpiece about the experiences of a Czech conscript during the First World War.

We sought out *U Kalicha*, named after Schweik's favourite bar, where we sat at long tables and helped ourselves from the trays of glasses going around, while elderly men sang rousing Czech folk songs. Tom was in his element, singing lustily and downing the beers and Becherovkas in quick succession. He thought they were all free and was horrified when the bill arrived. Just like his mother, he loved getting something for nothing – a stark reminder of their wartime poverty.

Despite his earlier protestations of memory loss, it was quite apparent that Tom remembered much about his early life, so it was thrilling to track down the apartment in Masaryk Quay, formerly

Rieger Quay, where he had grown up and where Grete had given her soirées and had run her lingerie business.

We talked our way into the grand art-deco building and climb the staircase with its fine wooden bannisters. 'This is the one, I'm sure,' said Dad, as we rang the bell. The door was opened by a middle-aged Goth, balding, with long, greasy hair, tattooed and clad entirely in black leathers, who was working away at what looked like a gay porn site in the main room. Mirek asked how long he had lived there; we were shocked to learn that his mother had taken the flat during the war, which probably meant they were collaborators. The large, elegant flat had been divided up between the two of them. He was not particularly friendly, especially when we told him that this had been my father's home before the war. The awkward silence that followed hung heavy in the room and we left soon after. My father didn't contribute much – probably the memories played on his mind.

Tom managed to recall the street of his grandfather (Grete's father) Heinrich Stransky's small factory. Mirek drove us there, and we walked along until Dad stopped and said, 'I think this is the place.' There was not much to see: a house, which used to be the office, and an archway leading to a courtyard, where the manufacturing took place. It was all rather run-down and depressing. Hard to imagine it as having been the humming business centre of one of Prague's richest men.

We visited the Jewish quarter and, at my insistence, the synagogue, Dad with some reluctance, feigning ignorance of Jewish traditions and culture. I was not allowed to reveal his secret and he did not tell us that his father was buried in Prague's Jewish Smíchov-Malvazinky cemetery – it would have been an admission of his heritage. Ten years later I returned, after Tom's death in 2012, and found the desecrated grave.

*

Meanwhile Tom and Di lived on at The Fort, his life punctuated by visits to hospital and the doctor. He was by now very crippled and couldn't get out much. Di continued to be a good wife to him, cooking him his favourite meals and taking him out to lunch at the pub where he always had pork belly, or to the local curry house for his favourite Madras, washed down with a Beck's beer. It can't have been much fun for her as he was as bad-tempered as ever, but she just ignored him with good humour. The highlight of his life was his daily call with and the very occasional visits to and from Sasha, who was now living in Portugal, running a surf school, but was always broke, as was Tom, who had got through his pension lump sum and was living off capital. Di had at some point bought some timeshares and, while he was still mobile, they would go off on various holidays; I also lent them our Swiss mountain apartment on several occasions, which he loved. He enjoyed the morning walk to get a paper, and an espresso sitting in the sunny terrace of the local café.

On that May evening in 2009, after my father had handed over the suitcase of secrets, he was deeply depressed and clearly feeling both mortal and vulnerable; all of us were expecting him to die any day from his Parkinson's. He was now sleeping on a bed in his study, could only move with a walker and was having terrible drug-induced hallucinations. The worst of these was a recurring vision of being in a room which was suddenly invaded by a gang of Nazis toting guns, all part of a Norwegian delegation. It was so real he could see them and have conversations with them, but he was bewildered by the appearance of these ghosts, a merging of the war and the UN. His past was beginning to haunt him with a vengeance and he was confused and gloomy. He had lost the will to live and was preparing for his death by unburdening himself of his anxieties.

'I have something I want to discuss with you,' he said after supper, as he shuffled into his study that summer evening. He was eighty-five and had rather gone to seed, the way old men often do, missing bits when he shaved, and wearing the same shirt for days on end. After all, he rarely went out and no one came to visit him (except family), so what was the point?

He opened a drawer in his desk, pulled out a thick envelope and, leaning heavily on his walker, slowly moved towards his reclining chair. He began to talk.

'When I came to England at the age of sixteen, we lived in Wells. I was working in the factory, mother was cooking for the workers and Sascha [his brother] was at school. On my way to and from work I met a beautiful young woman called Joyce, several years my senior, married with a husband away at the war. I used to carry her shopping and run errands for her; soon it developed into an affair. Then in 1943 I joined up and left Wells. She became pregnant, but Mother always said it couldn't be mine as the dates did not fit so for years I thought nothing further of it.'

He told me how decades later a friend from Wells had tracked him down, saying that Joyce wanted to be in touch, but he was living abroad by then and it was too complicated. What he meant was that he had left Wells far behind when he joined the Navy; he was now successful, twice married and had two children. He certainly didn't want his life 'complicated' by the reappearance of Joyce and another child.

When he retired to Somerset, he realised that Joyce lived nearby in Glastonbury. They made contact and he used to visit her. It was in the course of these visits that he became convinced that her daughter, Bonnie, was indeed his daughter. I remembered him telling me about an 'old bird' he used to visit from time to time, a friend from his wartime days. I had assumed it was because he was bored, and it gave him something to do, an act of charity – which in a way it was.

This Bonnie was by now a sixty-something woman (older than Di) with her own children, divorced and living in America. The complication, he said, was that she now wanted to be recognised as his daughter and, in particular, to meet me, her sister. This implied that he was in touch with her too.

Tom, feeling he was liable to die at any time, was now concerned with what he should do, especially as he had never told Di the truth about Joyce, let alone that he might have another daughter. Crippled, he now relied on her for everything to make his life bearable. It would be a terrible shock and he was nervous about causing ripples in the household. Di thought Joyce was an old wartime friend whom he visited monthly, laden down with wine, cheese and chocolates, just as he did when he saw my mother – he loved to be the distributor of largesse as it made him feel better about the wrongs he had caused, and Joyce looked forward to his visits.

He showed me some recent photos of Bonnie and asked if I wanted to contact her. I saw a slim, middle-aged woman with shortish blonde hair and a jolly smile. She looked perfectly nice, but beyond that I couldn't 'see' anything, nor did I want to.

After the shock had sunk in my immediate reaction was denial: denial that she looked anything like me, or that she was my sister. Meeting her was out of the question. My knee-jerk reaction was that she should get a DNA test so that we could see whether this was all worth worrying about or not; I was too taken aback and angry to think straight. I also felt a huge sense of betrayal – not unlike my mother must have felt when she learned that she had been married to a man with a secret past; now here I was with a father who had a secret child, and I had a secret sister.

Dad wasn't even apologetic, just worried about the repercussions and what his wife and son would think of him if they found out. Yet again I was being asked to join him in a web of deception, just as we had ganged up against my mother all those years ago. He was not interested in how I felt about this, only in the damage it might do to him and his reputation – as with everything else he only saw things from his own perspective. His public persona yet again more important than the private one.

He wanted me to help him solve his dilemma by talking to his trusted lawyer and friend, in whom he had already confided the whole sad story and with whom he had lodged a letter to be handed to me after his death. He had been, he said, in two minds whether to discuss this secret with me. But he needed to share the burden with someone, someone whom he could trust, a family member, and who better than me? I think he meant me to be flattered, but it was hard to feel the honour of being 'chosen', given the distance between us.

I returned to London, with the suitcase, but my excitement over its contents was rather overshadowed by this bombshell. My father had insisted I take the photos of Bonnie with me while I mulled it all over. I immediately confided in Ross and showed him the photos. He spotted the strong family resemblance, especially

Bonnie and me; two peas in a pod

in one photo of Bonnie where she looked like an older version of me. She even had the same gap in her teeth that both I and Louise were born with, although mine disappeared when my second teeth grew, and Louise's had been pushed together with a brace. We are so alike that Facebook always prompts 'tag Bonnie' when it comes across a picture of me.

I began to feel some empathy for Bonnie – she had never known what it was to have a father and she was unsurprisingly desperate for that acknowledgement of kinship. And Tom would have been a hugely attractive father to suddenly call your own, with his rather swashbuckling lifestyle, good looks and charm. He gave me a letter from her that was signed, 'Love, Always and Forever'.

I called the lawyer. If we asked her to get a test, it would formalise the situation and then the truth might come out in the open; Tom might feel forced to confess to Di and she would undoubtedly be furious at his deception, just like all us other victims of his lies. There was also the question of Sasha – although we agreed he was unlikely to be shocked, it was obvious that my father did not want him to know, perhaps he felt ashamed. This turned out to be another obfuscation as Bonnie told me later that Sasha already knew, as Dad had naïvely thought he could introduce Bonnie's son, David, to Sasha when he visited Portugal, and the truth had come out one drunken evening, when Sasha said something like, 'I feel like I know you somehow', and David had replied, 'It's not surprising as you are my uncle!'

The lawyer advised that as my father was about to die we should hold back the test until after the funeral. He did not want any potential graveside scene. He had thought it all out in order to protect my father; he was particularly concerned for his reputation after his death. I told him I would think it over and decide what was for the best. He thought Tom sneakingly rather liked the idea of having another daughter, hence his wish to make sure that I knew about her.

In the end a mixture of common sense and curiosity prevailed: I decided to telephone my half-sister Bonnie.

Early one Sunday morning a week or so later, heart pumping, I picked up the phone. 'Is that Bonnie Fogel?' 'Yes,' answered an American voice. 'This is Vicky Unwin calling from London.' I did not need to tell her who I was or why I was ringing.

'I am so glad you called,' she said. 'I have all the paperwork ready for the DNA test.' She and Dad had obviously been in contact. I was surprised – it had been agreed that I would consider the most logical course of action, but as ever he had jumped the gun and acted in a rather underhand way.

'There is no need for that,' I said, 'I believe you *are* my sister. I've looked at the photos, and my husband and the lawyer both agree there is a resemblance; we also think that Dad is in no doubt, although he is in such a dither that he can't accept the responsibility just like that, as it has so many implications.' Bonnie was hugely relieved that we had recognised the family similarities: she knew from the moment she first met Tom that he was indeed her father – one, they look alike, and two, 'his character was me … suddenly I found out why and who I was.'

It was surreal listening to this voice that never seemed to draw a breath, down a wire, from over 5,000 miles away, and trying to take on board that this was my sixty-five-year-old sister whom I did not know about until a week ago – she had known about me for twenty-five years, had seen photos of me and my family, while I had been kept in the dark for decades.

During the course of the next hour and a half, Bonnie told me her and her mother's story as she knew it. When Joyce became pregnant in 1943, she said Grete persuaded Tom it couldn't possibly be his, reminding him of Eddy's one-night reappearance. Joyce was completely abandoned, on her own with three small children, for Tom was by now in Caversham with the BBC.

Then in 1944 Eddy came back – for good. Joyce had heard he had been in jail for deserting, however in fact, he and another army chum had run away with a couple of girls; Eddy's was the wife of an SS officer. He subsequently left her and had a son with another German woman. His rage on returning home and finding Joyce with a small baby was terrifying. He grabbed a pan of boiling water and threw it at the pair of them, narrowly missing them both. Joyce felt she had no choice but to leave.

First, she changed her name to Unwin by deed poll, so she must have planned all this quite carefully. Then she sent the older girls, aged six and four respectively, to Eddy's sister in a taxi, saying she would send for them. Finally, she stole away with only as much as she could carry, plus Bonnie, and headed for London.

Joyce kept it well hidden from Bonnie but was heartbroken at losing Tom. We know she saw him on at least two occasions in the 1940s, both of which would have filled her with despair. The first time Joyce surprised him was in London, at the digs where he was staying, shortly before going to Africa in mid-1947. She was let in to wait as he was not at home; imagine her dismay when he came in accompanied by a woman, Sheila, 'who obviously had proprietary rights'. She stayed only a few minutes.

Soon afterwards Tom visited her in Oxshott where she had found a job as a housekeeper – probably just before he left for Tanganyika. As Joyce recalled to Bonnie decades later, 'We talked like it was old times and almost happy, and he came to our room to see you. I'd said, "Here's my baby" but he lifted you sleeping from your cot and said, "Our baby".' That was the last time Joyce saw Tom for over forty years.

Joyce above all wanted a good home and a father for her beloved daughter. She saved her money and hired a marriage broker who found her a match, a farmer needing a wife to help him run the farm. Joyce should have been forewarned when her new husband threw his mother downstairs on their wedding night, but stubborn, stupid even, she moved in with him. He proved to be cut from the same cloth as Eddy Farrell. Aged only ten, Bonnie remembered being in the bath when she heard her mother scream and she ran downstairs, covered in soapsuds and stark naked, to see her stepfather holding Joyce up against the wall, so she seized a kitchen knife and threatened to kill him unless he stopped beating her mother. They left the next day.

From this point on Joyce led an unsettled life, changing housekeeping jobs with frequency. Because she was poor, she managed to get Bonnie a free place at a boarding grammar school in Lyme Regis – the very same one I went to after being expelled, although it was a comprehensive day school when I was there. Bonnie would blossom under the care of teachers who gave her self-confidence and encouraged her love of literature, which, years later, was to set her up for future success as founder and director of the Washington DC–based children's theatre company, Imagination Stage.

After leaving school, Bonnie joined Marks & Spencer as a trainee in the personnel department and, in another twist of fate, ended up renting in Belsize Park, where I have lived since the mid-1990s. While at M&S, she fell in love with Dick Fogel, a Jewish student from Cornell, who was doing an MA at Sussex. They were married in Hampstead but not before she discovered she was not legally Bonnie Unwin, but Bonnie Farrell. Joyce had not been able to register her birth except under the name of her legitimate husband. Like her mother, she changed it to Unwin by deed poll, so she could have it on her marriage certificate. Bonnie moved with Dick to America but looked after Joyce from afar. Bonnie and Dick had bought Joyce a council house in Glastonbury, near Wells, as she wanted to move back to where she had lost her heart to Tom. Eddy Farrell was long dead.

Bonnie was happy at first in America but suffered panic attacks. These became so bad she could not go to a restaurant for three years. At the heart of these anxieties was the fear of becoming a mother herself. Joyce had never cuddled or hugged her and had been completely self-absorbed throughout her childhood, unable to provide the emotional security a child needs. After extensive therapy, Bonnie and Dick had two children, Sarah born in 1972 and David in 1976. But Joyce's circumstances had inflicted too much damage on Bonnie, and Dick left her for a childhood sweetheart after twenty-four years of marriage. Nevertheless, she had inherited the best attribute from both her parents: that ability to survive despite all adversity. So, Bonnie threw herself into her work and being a wonderful mother, and later grandmother.

Joyce had always told Bonnie that her father was Tom Unwin, but that he was dead, a war hero, yet strangely her mother received no war widow's pension Throughout her time in America Bonnie had begun to doubt her mother's story; Joyce had told so many lies over the years. Was it possible her father was not really dead? She needed to find out but knew that Joyce would never tell her the truth.

CHAPTER 18: BONNIE FINDS HER FATHER

I was horrified by Bonnie's story, and equally appalled that my father had known all this for at least twenty-five years, if not all his adult life. I felt furious that he had abandoned Joyce and his daughter to poverty and a life of service. Later Bonnie told me she remembered me saying, with reference to the deception pulled off by Grete and consequently by Tom, 'The Unwins are all liars, they are dreadful people.' I was impressed that Bonnie had managed to throw off her shackles and become a successful entrepreneur.

I was biting my tongue while I listened to all of this. What I wanted to know above all was how she found her/my father. She told me she discovered the first real clue about her father at her aunt's funeral in 1980. She had rushed back to England to accompany Joyce who felt it her moral duty to attend despite the bad blood between the two half-sisters; but Bonnie had always adored her beautiful opera-singing aunt and was eager to go and pay her respects to the only other family member she had ever known and had now lost.

At the funeral her mother introduced her to Bert Banting, one of her aunt's closest friends, and said casually that he had been a great friend of Tom's – they had been in the Home Guard together in Wells as young lads, patrolling the silent city streets in the blackout. As soon as her mother was out of earshot, Bonnie sought him out. She told him that she really wanted to know more about her father, who Joyce had always told her had died 'a hero's death' during the war; she had been laying flowers on the cenotaph in his honour for decades. His reply was to change her life.

'Tom dead! That's a rum one. Of course he's not dead. I haven't seen him for years but the last time I heard of him he was living in Africa.' Bonnie's reaction was a mixture of delight and despair: joy that she did have a father who was alive, but hurt, bewilderment and downright hostility towards her mother who had lied to her for so long and to her father who had never sought to see or expressed any interest in his daughter.

So, she asked Bert to try and find him, but not to tell her mother. Little did she know that Joyce had asked Bert the exact same favour, with the strict instruction to keep any discoveries from Bonnie.

It took Bert two years to track Tom down to Kampala, where he was living with Di and the young Sasha. Bert paved the way for their reunion by meeting Tom on one of his leaves in a London pub and filling him in. As soon as Bonnie received her father's address, she started writing to him and he responded. In his second letter he gave his account of the events which led to Bonnie's existence. He claimed that he was,

> ... just under 20, had never been with a woman before and
> we used to play knees under the table ... kids' stuff ... we
> flirted and fooled a bit ... I was infatuated and flattered
> that [Joyce] should take notice of me, and I remember her
> taking me by the hand to her marital couch which from
> that time on we occupied from time to time. I couldn't tell
> you how often, perhaps ten, perhaps twenty times. I was of

course terribly naïve about all this, but she told me she was very unhappy with her man, I think she told me he used to beat her, and I of course adored going to bed with her.

Typical Tom, making himself out to be the victim.

He said that there were 'two schools of indoctrination' about the baby – Joyce's that it was his, and his mother's that it wasn't. By this time, he claimed, he was in the Navy and had fallen in love with my mother – another lie as he did not fall in love with Sheila until 1946 and Bonnie was born in 1944. This is what he wrote in a letter to Bonnie on 5 June 1982:

It maybe that I wilfully suppressed all knowledge about Joyce and yourself because I wanted to marry Sheila. I was never really 'in love' with Joyce. I suppose it was a purely physical thing. Of course, I liked her very much. What did I think of her? Attractive, a bit bizarre, I always thought she was a bit crazy, used to go for long wild lonely walks in the woods: I think I went with her once or twice on moonlit nights. However, as I said my memory is sketchy. My 'going away' I think had nothing to do or perhaps not much to do with Joyce, I simply went to Africa to turn swords into ploughshares esp. as Czechoslovakia had gone Commie. So, I didn't really 'leave her' as I was never 'with her' … Perhaps I was being a bit intellectually dishonest. I honestly can't remember … Perhaps I am trying to tell it to you as I remember it. I had no idea that I was 'much the most important person in her life' as you put it. I don't think anyone has mentioned her name to me since, I suppose, 1947. Though when my mum died three years ago I found, among her things, an old photo of Joyce and it made me wonder. Probably when we meet you will be very disappointed with the funny, tubby old man you will find. Unlikely you will find him 'vibrant, amusing and adventurous' as do my supporters.

This latter self-deprecating yet boastful observation was disingenuous in the extreme, as in 1982 Tom was still handsome and certainly not 'tubby'. He always sought reassurance to boost his self-confidence. And he must have felt extremely nervous at this turn of events.

They were to exchange letters for a further two years before they finally met.

Bonnie was becoming increasingly frustrated by the delay, as they did not meet until Tom moved back to his house in Somerset after leaving Uganda, very close to Glastonbury where Joyce was living. Finally, in October 1984, Bonnie received the summons she had so eagerly awaited from her father to meet him at the Royal Over-seas League in London on 19 November.

Their first meeting remains imprinted on Bonnie's memory. As she walked towards him he, always early, was waiting for her outside in the mews, 'Henry VIII-style, with arms akimbo, hands on hips and his pipe jutting out from his mouth'.

She said it was the longest walk of her life, and I can believe it: the closer she came to him she could see that this was indeed the man from the photograph her mother had kept on her dressing table her entire life. As soon as he saw her he said, 'Even if I didn't believe you were my daughter before, now I believe it. You walk just like my Vicky!' He took her in his arms, enveloped her in a massive bear hug, and she cried – cried from the relief at not being rebuffed and finally meeting her father. Her search was at an end.

They spent the best part of the next two days together, cementing their relationship. She was bowled over by his charm; he seemed genuinely interested in her, answered all her questions and complimented her on her looks, something her mother had never done. That was Tom to a T: he had the knack of making you feel like the most important person in the room, something my daughter Louise also inherited from him. He was intimate and put no restrictions on his new relationship with his daughter – aside from the huge one of keeping their secret from me, his wife, Di, and son, Sasha.

She adored him from the moment she set eyes on him:

As soon as I met Tom, he was immediately elevated to a hero in my eyes, my heart and my mind. He made me whole and gave me the confidence and support I needed to feel good about my myself. My world changed as a result of meeting him. I was so happy to have him in my life! This was clearly where I belonged – in the family of this dashing, worldly, charming man. And this glorification of him lasted, though it was tempered in later years.

Over the next twenty-five years she never challenged anything he told her about his relationship with her mother. She was simply so overjoyed to have a father at last that she was prepared to avoid any discussions which might alter her hero worship of this marvellous man, her father. From the moment we first started talking in 2009, I felt compelled to give her a more truthful picture of her father – something I have always felt conflicted about, even though there are no malicious or jealous intentions.

The delight in finding her father at last had been dampened

because she felt she was betraying Joyce. Bert had also told Joyce how to contact Tom, and she had finally written to him, two years after Bonnie first made contact with him, sending photographs, and then telephoned him. As he wrote to Bonnie later, he would have much rather 'kept life uncomplicated and without dramatic overtones and memories of the past, some of which in retrospect I wish had been different':

> ... I have returned the photos [to Joyce] with a little note,
> but I don't, for the time being (especially as I am in much
> confusion at the moment) want to start being badgered by
> meetings. Your mum always had a very romantic streak
> in her and used to be much given to quixotic gestures.
> I thought I had better drop you a line to tell you what
> happened, lest you be accused of keeping things from her.

Typically, impatient before he met Bonnie, Tom had arrived unannounced on Joyce's doorstep and got her out of bed. She had sent him away until she had 'made herself beautiful' and they had a 'very pleasant two hours together – she is still the sweet person she always was and looks splendid too, even without saying "considering".'

Later he wrote to Bonnie, 'She is a bit bothered by the fact that you have not mentioned to her that we have been in touch for some time now'. As Tom had forbidden Bonnie from telling her mother this was cruel in the extreme. Tom's duplicitous treatment of both women is shocking, caught up as they were in their respective webs of deception.

Poor Bonnie felt both jealous and betrayed, yet held out a secret hope that this rapprochement might lead to a family life at last. Before that could happen she and her mother had to have a heart-to-heart, something Joyce found impossible due to her lack of empathy or ability to feel affection for anyone other than Tom. The meeting was angry and accusatory on both sides, each feeling the other had betrayed them, both competing to be the centre of Tom's attention. Bonnie was concerned for her mother, who was now relishing the rediscovery of her lost love, while Tom was more cavalier and treated it more like a renewal of an old friendship. Joyce's servile promise not to 'make trouble' infuriated Bonnie – Joyce was still afraid of damaging *his* reputation, which was particularly galling as she and Bonnie had suffered so much in order to protect Joyce's. And what about the name Unwin, now that Tom was back? Wouldn't people recognise it and think it odd? Tom, always able to lie easily, casually suggested they could pretend to have been married once, during the war, an untruth that pleased Joyce greatly.

Time passed, and gradually Bonnie and her mother adjusted to the status quo, each able to delight in the entry of Tom into their lives, and to enjoy their own relationship with him and, best of all, the times when all three of them were together. Tom, now retired, lived so close to Joyce that he visited her frequently and, when Bonnie was over, he would see them both together in her tiny Glastonbury cottage, where they would sip a sherry, before going out to a pub lunch, just like a 'real family', although the excited daughter in the back seat was well over forty. And it was useful having Tom nearby, as he could monitor Joyce's failing health.

He admitted that as Joyce got older and increasingly barmy (she had the beginnings of dementia), he found these visits a chore. He told me later that he found Joyce 'a pest'; as he wrote to Bonnie:

I find it very boring, and at times embarrassing to take her out … but I feel I owe her. It is certainly no thrill for me. I see her for about three hours each month which is about all I can take, but she gets so much pleasure out of our little outing that I think it must be worthwhile and will count among my few good deeds when the fast-approaching final reckoning comes.

As his health deteriorated he was unable to drive to visit Joyce during her final years, although he did telephone her.

Bonnie then went on her own to visit Tom in Somerset, something she continued to do until he died. She called him frequently and wrote often. Whether Di cottoned on I have no idea, but we know she tolerated Tom's frequent visits to see Joyce, just as she did the ones to my mother. She even drove Tom to see Joyce shortly before she died in a nursing home in 2008.

Tom was one of the first people Bonnie called when Joyce died. She was disappointed by his lack of reaction of any sort apart from relief. He did not say any kind words about how much he had cared for her, nor did he send flowers to the funeral – he who had always sent Joyce bouquets on birthdays and Valentine's Day. Bonnie says it was as if he felt he had repaid his debt over the past twenty years – and more.

Bonnie feared she would be abandoned again now the slate was clean. In the aftermath of Joyce's death, Bonnie wrote to Tom and asked that he acknowledge her as his daughter and make the introduction to me:

> ... it seems that [Vicky] and I share talents and looks and perhaps it would be interesting to her also. She seems to have an enquiring mind ... although I recognise that Vicky may have no interest in meeting me. But I am hopeful that will not be the case. Again, I respect your wishes for

privacy, but it occurred to me that you may want to control this and speak to Vicky about it earlier rather than later ... or never.

And that was the catalyst for my father's confession.

All this I have pieced together over the past few years: the bare bones of the story are as Bonnie told me on the phone that day; the rest in subsequent meetings and emails, and from the memoir she wrote on her mother, *A Sun for My Soul.*

It is extraordinary that she never bore our father any ill will for the way he treated both her and Joyce, nor attached blame to him for their poverty while she was growing up. Once she had met him she was in his thrall: he was 'worldly and urbane', had 'interesting ancestors', and he had led an 'exciting' life in contrast to her mother's diabolical relatives, and 'country mouse' lifestyle.

She believes that Tom felt guilty about Joyce and for all the suffering he had caused, and in her he had a soulmate of sorts: she was the one person who knew him when he first arrived in England, a simple Czech refugee, before he became anglicised and sophisticated from his time in the Navy and then the Colonial Service. To him, she represented a very important part of his life, those first happy, innocent days in England, having escaped from Czechoslovakia, living with his beloved mother and brother, with not a care in the world apart from the daily grind of the factory and playing soldiers with his Home Guard chums in his free time. Poor Joyce could not have known that the happy-go-lucky youth she loved had ambitions beyond settling down in Wells.

CHAPTER 19:
MEETING BONNIE AND
FAMILY RUCTIONS

All this was in June 2009; from June to November my mother's life took centre stage. For years she had been saying that she wanted to move out of her delightful cottage in Branscombe (she had sold the Oxford house and bought a cottage in Devon), as she felt the garden was too much for her; she had bad arthritis, with each hip replaced twice, and now had spondylosis. I had tried to talk her into moving closer to London, back to Oxford perhaps where she had friends, as it was difficult for me to see her as often as I would have liked.

She was adamant that she wanted to remain in Devon and she found a little flat in a Victorian mansion that had been converted into sheltered housing in nearby Sidmouth. We sold her cottage and Ross and I went down to move her. Within a couple of days, we had everything unpacked, all her pictures hung, ornaments in place, her TV and radio working, and she seemed delighted.

Just nine days later I received a phone call from the manager of the property saying my mother had suffered a massive stroke and had been rushed into hospital in Exeter.

It was heart-breaking to see this elegant, vivacious woman, my mother, paralysed down one side, incontinent and unable to utter more than a few words out of the side of her mouth. Yet I knew her brain was still active as she was worrying about what had happened to her earrings. After a couple of weeks in intensive care, she was moved to a rehabilitation centre in Budleigh Salterton but shortly after had another series of strokes which put her into a coma and she never regained consciousness. She died seven days later on 22 October 2009; we had, on medical advice, withdrawn feeding tubes.

I was with her every day, sitting by her almost lifeless body, watching it go blue at the extremities as life seeped away. It was horrible. Luckily all the family had a chance to say goodbye during those weeks before she lost consciousness, including Tom, who was brought over by Sasha to pay his final respects. Despite her paralysis her bright eyes acknowledged the irony of her ex bringing his son to her deathbed. And as for Tom, despite all that had passed between them, he was visibly upset.

It was soul-destroying having to pack up and dismantle the new home we had lovingly created so recently. There had been some items we had not yet unpacked or even looked at, including several large black bin-bags. Peeking inside I found bundles of letters, held together by elastic bands; recycled A4 envelopes, dated in my mother's handwriting, containing more letters; and plastic bags full of yet more letters. A cursory look showed that these were from my mother to Grace, written during the war, which she intended to use as a base for a memoir, plus the ones she had sent home from Africa; then there were all the letters I had ever written to my mother from the age of eight until quite recently, when telephone and email took over; finally there were envelopes full of letters from my father and her friends, including hundreds from Neville.

There was nothing to be done with them at that point, so I

simply put the sacks safely in my car to take back to London with me.

In the interim, I heard from Bonnie that she was to visit England, as she did once or twice a year to catch up with her old M&S girlfriends. Although the visit was scheduled for only a week after my mother's cremation, we agreed to meet, partly because I knew Tom wanted this but mostly because I was curious to meet this stranger who was apparently my sister.

Several friends had urged extreme caution; even if money was not an obvious motive (and one that I had dismissed immediately), they were concerned that a woman searching for a father, someone whose upbringing had been so disturbed, was liable to be extremely needy, and I could be letting myself in for something I had not bargained for, at a time when my emotions were raw from my recent loss. But I was not to be swayed.

On 12 November, my doorbell rang. I opened the door to see a slight figure dressed in grey, face hidden under a huge brimmed hat – my rain hat, she exclaimed nervously. I was immediately struck by how slim and elegant this woman was, yet she retained broad Slavic features and that characteristic gap between the teeth that I had recognised immediately. The first few minutes were a babble of inconsequential niceties driven by our mutual anxiety.

Bonnie's memory of our meeting chimes with mine. Her heart was pounding as she climbed the steps of our house. She had dreamed of meeting me for so long. What if I didn't like her? What if she didn't like me? She rang the bell and, she wrote later, 'the door opened and with it my world. There was Vicky smiling at me and looking every bit the younger sister!'

Where do you start with someone whose DNA you share but whom you do not know at all? I figured that, true to form, my father had hidden his Jewish background from Bonnie. We had covered much ground already but not the Jewish heritage. She was intrigued by my revelation, but strangely unsurprised as her mother had always said Tom was Jewish. However, when Bonnie had asked point-blank at their first meeting, he denied it, saying Joyce was being 'fanciful'.

Bonnie's husband Dick was Jewish, and they had brought up their children in the faith, even though she had not herself converted. She was fascinated by this coincidental new aspect of her bloodline. So, I brought out all the old photos I had found and sorted from the suitcase – including the beautiful photo of Joyce that Tom had found among his mother's effects which she had not seen before – and the various books about Hermann Ungar, which have a historic collection of photographs, and gradually this led to a more relaxed form of chatting about the past, and the present.

Joyce

Naturally she had a grandiose view about our father, a perspective born out of only seeing someone once a year. While not trying to disavow her from her hero worship, I felt it was necessary to round out his character a bit more: to tell of his terrible temper; how he had hit both my mother and me occasionally; of his obsession with our half-brother Sasha; of his workaholic tendencies which led him to neglect his family.

But mostly we pondered on his inability to face up to being Jewish and the suppression of his father's literary legacy; the latter a result of the former. Bonnie could not get her head round the denial of his roots and his symbolically locking his past up in a suitcase.

But what to do with this knowledge? We felt at ease with one another, each of us, from time to time, glancing at the other and starting with surprise at a mannerism or a look that seemed to reflect oneself. So it seemed natural to try and understand his secrecy but simultaneously to celebrate our shared history and to resurrect the reputation of our grandfather.

We recognised that this would have to wait until our father was dead, but we both knew that this was not far off: he had been shattered by Sheila's death. Even though he had been married to Di for forty years, years that she had stood by him and loyally supported him, even at his most trying, those early years at the end of the war and the pioneering in East Africa had formed a special bond between him and Sheila. In addition to his visits, he would also call her weekly and they would reminisce about the old days; he called her 'number one wife', she called him 'the old devil'.

I think she forgave him, but never forgot his terrible behaviour. Otherwise why would she have continued to see him, to cook for him, to receive his weekly phone calls, but also have kept the letters that bear witness to his true character? Somehow, she found a compassion that resonated with the memories deep within her of the young, handsome officer, whose insecurities gave him spots, of the idealistic socialist whose vision led them to Africa – the man she fell madly in love with. The same went for Joyce who, despite all, also forgave him.

Before we could make any headway with our plans came the first of many disruptions. There was a painful triangular row between

Tom, Sasha and me over a misunderstanding to do with a job that I had hoped my son, Tommy, was going to get in our Swiss village, but which Sasha took, thanks to my introduction.

I was mortified that Tom sided with his son. Naturally he did not see it that way: 'It's a free world,' he said. I had slammed the phone down in fury and he decided to break off relations with me. 'You put the phone down on me. Nobody does that,' he said childishly, when I asked why he had stopped calling me on Saturdays, the ritual that had taken the place of the weekly letter.

He then refused to come to Sheila's memorial service as I would not invite Sasha – something I knew she would not have wanted. I had told him this at the outset. The original plan was for Tom's nephew-in-law, Darren, to drive him down and come back later to collect him. For a while I thought he would come; he called two days before to ask about the dress code but come lunchtime on the day itself, I had still heard nothing. Stuck in Branscombe with no mobile reception and no email, at 12.30 I turned to Ross and said that we had better go up the hill where we could get some signal; this we duly did to find a Facebook message from Sasha containing a pompous tribute from Tom, essentially all about himself and not about Sheila.

Message sent on 26th Nov 09 on the occasion of the Commemoration of Sheila Unwin's recent death: I am deeply moved by being unable, at the moment, to be there with you and your friends. We started life in the Navy on completion of the war by getting married in 46. We then went to the Groundnut Scheme in a far distant country of which we knew little, where, living in tents, artificial settlements, we tried to produce, in a Maoist way a kind of ultra-modern socialist mechanised agriculture in the midst of untested rainfall, soil mechanised equipment and endless herds of Masai cattle finding a meagre living in the absence of adequate water: but above all there was no pilot scheme which would have produced a negative answer to the possibility of success. After four years in the wilderness I obtained a govt post as a district officer and went on from there. What I really want to say is that for 25 yrs we supported each other and enjoyed life. We also produced a wonderful child and contributed as best we could to the welfare of a charming people. But above all we grew more and more to appreciate Nurse Edith Cavell's words from the stone pedestal whence she preaches in Charing Cross Road: it is simply that 'above all things is humanity'. Sheila followed this.

I did not read it out.

Bonnie was extremely supportive throughout this traumatic time. Given that her first loyalty might have been to her long-lost father, she was objective enough to see that Dad's behaviour was shocking. After he stopped calling me on Saturdays, I began to try and build bridges and even tried to have a face-to face meeting with him. What had upset him was a misunderstood remark about Sasha's background in that first furious phone call.' Dad thought I was referring to his Jewish antecedents and that I was being anti-Semitic; I explained to him at great length that I was referring to him, our father, being a poor role model, as he had hidden two great secrets for most of his life: the denial of being Jewish and the existence of a half-sister.

I had written an email to Sasha who showed it to Dad, but this served no purpose other than to further infuriate him. He wrote me an aide-memoire, taking my email point by point and refuting it, as if it was an issue between him and me, not between two siblings. I told him how hurtful I found this, and that parents are not meant to take sides between their children. But it made no difference. After we had gone through the email over the phone, and I thought I had answered all his points calmly and logically, he sent it back to me with a snitty cover note:

> I have been through my file note with Sasha and we can find nothing wrong with it; but much lamentable and unpleasant abuse in yours. The order of banishment [of Sasha from our home in Switzerland] is well noted but with much regret – I just cannot see the need for all this. Have you changed I wonder? Why? Sasha and I hope that a fairer wind (in both senses) will fill our sails in 2010.
> With love and in sorrow Dad

His manner of dealing with it, as if I was one his members of staff, compounded the hurt of taking his son's side. I found this note recently and it made me weep all over again. He referred to this incident for the rest of his life, always blaming me and refusing to see any other point of view. This was the side of Tom my mother had always referred to when she said, as she did from time to time, 'if only you knew what kind of a man your father was', and I would roll my eyes heavenwards.

I decided after much soul-searching that we should go to Somerset for an early Christmas celebration with my father as a way of making up; the one thing I learned from my mother's sudden death was the regret of unspoken words.

Shortly before we left for this visit at the end of 2009, I got an anguished call from Tom, saying he had run out of money again.

He was quick to make amends when it suited him. Ross and I had already administered first aid earlier in the year by looking at his cash flow and working out how much he and Di had to spend every month while keeping a little bit back for a rainy day.

He was living beyond his means, with an expensive house to run and using credit cards freely. Nothing we said seemed to influence him and I was worried that we would have to bail him out financially. It now transpired that, with a £9,000 tax bill, he was clean out of savings and only had his pension to live on. Our Christmas visit would at least share some goodwill even if the hatchet was barely buried. My father needed me, and I desperately wanted proof that he still loved me.

We patched things up on that visit. Tom was only too happy to hand over responsibility for his finances to Ross and Darren, and made various undertakings to control his outgoings by trying to follow a monthly budget. But no sooner had we left than he rang the banks and reversed all these decisions. Financial worries were to dog him for the rest of his days and were a major contributor to the depression that descended on him for the final two and a half years of his life.

In the meantime, Ross had got a new role with Deloitte in Geneva and I was to go with him. We arrived in time for Christmas. Sasha was already working in the ski shop in our mountain village; I was still smarting from the recent row and all four of us agreed that we should not invite him to Christmas dinner. However, I realised that someone had to act the grown-up here, and if it wasn't going to be Tom, then it should be me, so a few days later I invited Sasha to a family supper and he came. I gave him a cashmere sweater to break the ice. Dad rang him (not me) in the middle of the meal and was relieved at the rapprochement.

CHAPTER 20:
NO WORST THERE
IS NONE

Up until this point I had managed to piece together most of the family history from written records, my mother's letters and the odd interview and chat with my father, but I felt the need to accelerate the process. It was now spring 2010, and I would visit Dad on my frequent trips back from Geneva, especially after I broke my hip in March of that year and spent most of the summer in London. He was riddled with Parkinson's and cellulitis, sporting two huge swollen legs, bandaged right up to his poor blackened toes. I was increasingly worried about his condition. He was still sleeping downstairs in his study on a rather grotty single bed, several yards away from a loo, which he could only reach using a walker. It could take him twenty to thirty minutes to get to it in the night, so he had a bottle in his room, making the whole set-up rather unsavoury.

I was so concerned that, under the auspices of getting a proper assessment of what help he might be entitled to, I summoned the social services. They said that as he had capacity, whatever the situation, there was little that could be done apart from the provision of a carer twice a day unless he asked for any intervention.

The final straw came one morning when Di came downstairs to find him lying semi-conscious in the hall, with a bloody gash on his head and a broken window. No one could tell what had happened, but I was now on high alert. Shortly after that he had to go into hospital to receive some intravenous antibiotics for his cellulitis, and I managed to get everyone to agree that it might be best for him to go into respite care for a couple of weeks in the charming Nynehead Court, which was nearby. He never left.

It was a struggle to get him to stay there, and he behaved like an angry child for the first week, throwing tantrums and peeing in the wastepaper bin in protest. We only succeeded with Ross and me footing the bills until he could repay us from the proceeds from the house, which was now on the market. All agreed that downsizing and selling The Fort was the answer to his shortage of money.

Once he had settled down he loved it at Nynehead. First, he was adored by the staff, with whom he flirted tirelessly – many were from Eastern Europe and he talked to them in variations of Russian, Czech and Polish to their great delight. Secondly, he had an endless stream of visitors, something he felt was not particularly welcome at The Fort. Bonnie, for instance, could come and spend hours with him without feeling anxious, and I visited when I could, sometimes with Tommy and Louise.

He found it hard to read, so I gave him one of those continental newspaper holders straight out of a Prague café when he had difficulty folding his *Daily Telegraph*. I enjoyed listening to his reminiscences; in my quest to find out more about his early life, I began to make tape and video recordings, well aware that he represented the last of a generation that went to war and was a fund of memories that needed to be recorded for our family's benefit and for posterity. Louise loved to help with the filming, and was equally fascinated by the stories. This is when I recorded his wartime recollections and his memories of Africa, which augmented the material contained in my mother's letters.

However, Dad's ill health, financial worries and the move to Nynehead Court continued to be a major distraction to me from researching and writing about our heritage; comfortingly, in all of this my relationship with Bonnie became increasingly important. She and I seemed to be on the same wavelength; even her rose-tinted specs about our father were becoming somewhat opaque as she became more realistic. She enjoyed discovering a reason for her black moods – she ascribed them to Hermann's darkness – and she also saw that we were both strong women, inherited from our mothers. She understood that Joyce and Tom could never have been together in his twenties and thirties – she was too quiescent and did not have strong intellectual opinions like my mother; but the relationship might have worked once our father had established himself, as it seemed to have with Di. Joyce was rather similar, an attractive woman, a good homemaker and housekeeper, which is what it seemed my father wanted from a wife, just as his father had shunned intellectual women.

Bonnie came over for her annual visit in the late summer of 2010 and we sat in the garden, eating grilled peaches and prosciutto and drinking chilled Sauvignon. Louise dropped by to say hello; she was thrilled with the discovery that she had a secret family, a Jewish heritage and an illustrious grandfather. Like Bonnie, I think she felt it explained something she couldn't understand within herself – her propensity for mood swings and depression, being highly strung internally and yet, like all of us Ungar/Unwins, retaining the ability to radiate a huge personality and *joie de vivre*.

So, life carried on: Tommy now had a job with a media company; Louise was enjoying her work in retail and living in Clapton, DJing and mixing with the arty East London set; Dad was settled in Nynehead and, although finances continued to be a worry, they were at least under the watchful eye of Darren, who lived next door to his care home. Relations among us were restored despite the no-go areas concerning criticism of his family's profligacy which continued. And then on 2 March 2011 our lives changed forever.

*

It was a Wednesday morning and I was preparing for my routine Geneva day, in my workout kit, doing emails, when I heard the key turn in the lock. 'What have you forgotten?' I yelled as I heard Ross racing up the staircase.

'Terrible, terrible news.' I knew that meant a death and thought it must be one of his elderly parents, or even Dad, who had been ailing for some time. 'It's Louise – a terrible accident – she's dead.'

And so began a pain that is so unendurable that you feel you cannot go on, that life cannot be lived with such a huge hole in it. The shaking and screaming gave way to numbed silence as, somehow, we managed to get on a plane from Geneva to London, hiding behind sunglasses, and bolstered by one gin and tonic after another. Three of my dearest girlfriends greeted us as we opened the door, as well as our beloved Tommy, whom I simply enveloped in my arms. It was he, together with our house-sitter, Mandy, who had opened the door to the policeman at 7.30 in the morning; it was Mandy who had to ring Ross with the awful news.

It is hard to remember the first few days, as we simply went through the motions, seeing the police, receiving endless visitors, sleepless nights and, the worst experience I will ever have, seeing our Louise's body in the morgue, laid out under a sheet, her face all bruised from the attempts at resuscitation. We couldn't even touch her as she was separated from us by a glass partition.

There is no pain close to the death of a child – as I was to write later in the *Sunday Times*, for a mother, in particular, it is like losing a limb, for the baby you carried and nursed is ripped away from you. There were times when I felt I could not go on and just wanted to curl up and die; suicidal thoughts lurked in the recesses of my mind, but of course there was Ross and Tommy, who were also in torment, and I knew such thoughts were self-indulgent.

I recall one of my lovely friends racing through the door, bearing two roast chickens and vegetables, another making a huge grocery delivery but refusing to come in; others arriving, bearing emotional support as well as practical assistance. In the Jewish fashion of sitting shiva the house was full of people for well over a week, and we were never left alone apart from when we tried to sleep. There was the funeral to arrange and all the legal requirements to attend to, just as for my mother.

Slowly the story unravelled, about how Louise was entertaining a few friends to supper, to celebrate submitting her application for Chelsea College of Arts. One of them had brought over the party drug of choice, ketamine, which they took after dinner. Louise carefully weighed out the powder to ensure a safe dose. But she was not informed enough to realise that her long stint off any form of drugs during her recent trip in Australia – not that she was a regular user by any means – made her more susceptible to its effects than her friends who were more frequent users.

Three of them had to work the next day, and left about 10.30, while her girlfriend stayed over. They watched episodes of *Never Mind the Buzzcocks* to wind down and the friend retired to bed, but Louise decided to have a relaxing bath and continue watching *Buzzcocks*. About an hour or so later the friend became aware that Louise was not in bed and rushed into the bathroom to find her peacefully submerged under the water. She called 999 and tried to resuscitate her, but it was too late.

Because this was an unexpected death the full weight of the law kicked in: the friends were arrested; the body had to have a post-mortem and could not be released immediately; there had to be an inquest.

To write this I have returned to the diary I wrote during the dark days that followed Louise's death. The pain is visceral even today – my feelings pulse out from the pages, bewildered, distraught, grief-stricken and suicidal. My response was to go public, to cut off the media interest before it started and to try and educate other young people about the dangers of club drugs and legal highs. I joined forces with another bereaved mother, Maryon Stewart, who founded the Angelus Foundation and began the process of dissemination – via the press, the radio and the television. Shortly afterwards, in July 2011, Amy Winehouse, who was part of Louise's Camden set, died from alcohol poisoning and, as she had a history of addiction, we collaborated for a time with her father, Mitch, and her stepmother, Jane, who set up the Amy Winehouse Foundation.

We built a website in Louise's memory where we posted an account of her funeral, photographs of her taken by us and friends, film and video clips, articles and recordings. Tributes and comments from all over the world flooded in; it was comforting and healing. Here is the obituary I wrote, published in the *Guardian's* 'Other Lives':

> *Our daughter, Louise Cattell, who has died suddenly, achieved more in her 21 years than many of us do in a lifetime. Born in Oxford, she grew up in London where, as a teenager, she immersed herself in the Camden music scene. She became a photographer who, from the age of 14, covered bands such as the Cribs and the Mystery Jets before they became well known, while simultaneously DJ-ing with her partner Kylie – they*

were known as Pure Filth – and appearing with the likes of Theo Adams and Roots Manuva. She did all of this while attending Francis Holland school; amazingly she got good GCSEs, three A-levels and made a marvellous Malvolio.

Her other passion was art: she completed a foundation course at the London College of Fashion and was in the process of applying to art school, having taken two years out to work in the industry. Slogging away at New Look as a visual merchandiser, she nevertheless was an indispensable production assistant during several London Fashion Weeks, where she worked on prestigious shows such as Giles Deacon, Julien Macdonald, Jaeger, Fashion for Relief, Irwin & Jordan, Matthew Williamson and Fashion Fringe. Her teachers recall her coming to school aged 12 with green hair, and being sent home, only to return with a subtle shade of aubergine, which they let her keep. Every day was an occasion to dress up, and the hair was central to this. She was thrilled to get through to the second round of The X Factor – with a very short lilac 'do'.

Little Lou, as she was known, had a huge heart and compassion for others: she supported friends through anorexia, agoraphobia, cancer and depression. She was an expert dancer and hula-hooper. At her humanist cremation, as we belted out the words to Cabaret, her photo watched over us: dressed up to the nines, beer in one hand, camera in the other. It was a fitting send-off to someone who never sat alone in her room. Louise is survived by us and by her brother, Tommy.

One of the great joys, paradoxically, that embraced us in the aftermath of Louise's death was the love and support shown by her friends. It was as if they transferred all their emotions to us, and we were hugely comforted by them.

Louise

A few days after we returned to London, more than a hundred of them turned up for an impromptu wake at our home, and we hugged and howled, laughed and cried, sang songs and played music. They were instrumental in organising her funeral, from designing and printing the memorial programme (packed full of photos of Louise from babyhood to the present), to organising the playlist (just like a DJ set) and reading poems and eulogies. They sorted out Louise's flat – I was incapable of going there for weeks – and helped us arrange a keepsake day so that they could all own something of hers.

They were constantly with us, holding our hands, just as we held theirs, throughout this traumatic time. It was wonderful to see how loved our daughter was. In many ways they were more of a comfort than some of our contemporaries, who found it hard to empathise in an appropriate way, no doubt because they could see into the abyss – the trauma of losing a child – and were unable to cope with their own emotions, let alone ours. But the young see things differently and for that we were, and still are, forever in their debt.

My father was unable to provide any comfort whatsoever.

Looking back through my diary I am reminded of several phone calls I had with him where he tried to intellectualise Louise's death:

> Dad tried to analyse things on the phone, started telling me that he couldn't understand the 20% of Louise that he did not recognise with a hint of criticism about her wildness … I had to shut him up, not interested in his analysis, just want to remember her as I want to remember her. He then said he couldn't understand how we didn't know about her great kindnesses to others – if it had been Sasha he would have boasted about them!

He was incapable of empathy, of understanding that his granddaughter's generosity was not for external gratification and that, in giving, the only reward that matters is to oneself.

Just when I needed a father to take me in his arms and hug me, he was unable to do so. Maybe it was his way of coping, but it was like a slap in the face; he was only able to see Louise's death through the lens of him and Sasha, never asking me how I was feeling or coping, although Di, who adored Louise, was devastated and offered a degree of comfort on behalf of them both. I was glad my mother was no longer alive as she would have been heartbroken. She and Louise, both quirky and artistic, had a special bond.

On Midsummer's Day – Louise's favourite day of the year – we held a memorial with eulogies by myself, Ross and Tommy, performances by her friends and memories and tributes from the guests, in the Quaker style. Louise's friends turned up in throngs, as did ours. Bonnie managed to coincide one of her visits with the ceremony, and Tom came up, chauffeured by Darren and accompanied by Di but no Sasha. I caught an awkward moment when Bonnie greeted her father, just like a casual acquaintance, as Di looked on.

Things soon began to go sour again between Dad, Sasha and me. Sasha had brought Tom to the funeral but since then he had gone silent after his return to his surfing job in Portugal. I told Dad in one of our now-resumed phone calls that I felt hurt by this, but Dad brushed it aside, saying 'he's very busy, you know'. I replied, 'No one is ever too busy to do those things which are really important. I know he and I have had our differences, but I have held out the hand of family to him, inviting him round for Christmas ... blood is thicker than water, so I am very hurt.' Dad was unmoved.

This state of impasse continued for the rest of the year. Then we found out from someone in the village that Sasha was to work in the ski shop over Christmas. I still felt raw about the row over the job and Tommy, and I fell into a deep despair. Ross wrote a calm and polite letter to Sasha, pointing out how hurt we all were by his lack of support since Louise's death and his failure to attend her memorial service in the summer, given the help we were providing to the family by paying the nursing home fees and helping draft Tom's will, as Ross was now a Trustee of his estate, along with Darren.

When I challenged my father over Sasha's silence, he said it was all my fault as I had been so horrible to him and he was still deeply hurt. Yet again he took his son's side; I simply could not get through to him that the loss of our beloved daughter superseded any other grief. I told him that until he began to show love and support for our family I felt unable to speak to him, and Ross would be the intermediary. My despair was too deep-etched.

In the end, I summarised my view of the situation to Dad in a letter where I told him that if he was serious about being a better father, then he should start seeing more than one perspective on everything and that he should have ensured Sasha came to the memorial. I told him we refused to respond to his emotional blackmail, about how 'unhappy' this state of affairs made the two of them:

> How unhappy do you think Ross, Tommy and I are? Our
> wounds can never be healed over Louise (try to imagine
> how you would feel if Sasha had died age 21) and you
> should have supporting us as your primary objective
> instead of laying into us and asking us to offer olive
> branches; these are not in my power. As I have said before
> an apology is simply a form of words; actions are real.
> … you have made no effort ever to see our point of view.
> And it's never been more critical than now; I don't want
> you to end your life with us being estranged, but you have
> not really been a proper father during the past few years, or
> indeed a proper grandfather to Tommy in the first instance,
> and to Louise's memory in the second.
> I will always love you as you are my father; but I am
> rather fed up with being daughter, second class. I hope
> that you will ring me to have a conversation borne out of
> mutual love and respect rather than accusations of blame.

The letter made no difference; my father refused to support us over our first Christmas without Louise.

*

Then an unexpected development: I received a call from Nynehead Court, the care home, saying that Tom had been caught trying to organise his departure to Switzerland for an assisted suicide. When confronted by the furious owner, as this was and still is strictly illegal in Britain, Tom had told him that I was aware of his plans.

I had known that Dad was depressed about his inability to provide for his family after he was gone, and felt that the care home was an unnecessary drain on his last remaining finances. I had told him that he was entitled to live out the rest of his days in comfort and reminded him that he was asset rich though cash poor, since he had four properties with plenty of capital tied up in them. I was not willing to be a proxy to this discussion – at that stage that was all it was – and would certainly not accompany him to Switzerland; moreover, the whole thing was expensive, and finally – selfishly, maybe – I was not able to face a third bereavement within a year. It was obscene that he felt he had to kill himself in order to provide for them.

We were summoned to a meeting with the owner, who wanted to make sure Tom understood the seriousness of the situation, that he was putting the owner's business at risk by his actions. As I recorded in my diary: 'Dad said afterwards that he couldn't understand what all the fuss was about. Thought people did this all the time and didn't believe me about charges of murder and manslaughter. For a clever man he is very single-minded, perhaps selfish is more accurate, although he feels he is being selfless.'

The next time I visited there was a new bombshell: Dad was going to move to a nursing home in Portugal where it would be much cheaper and where he could see Sasha every day, Di could visit and so could we. We pointed out all the difficulties: no NHS, lack of good medical support, cost of medication, insurance issues, lack of visitors, friendly nurses, language barriers ... but we were told it was none of our business.

The next day I had a quiet word with Dad and tried to remind him that he was entitled to spend the rest of his days in comfort and where he chose. He was not convinced; he seemed so concerned about Sasha's inheritance that all else was inconsequential.

At this stage Sasha suggested in response to a letter from Ross that we should meet in Champéry, where he was working during the half-term holiday. He looked pale and thin as we sat down with our drinks. We immediately started discussing the Dignitas issue; he was shocked as he said he had no idea, and was appalled that Dad would consider taking his own life. We then moved on to Portugal – he had done some of his own research and agreed that it was a false economy and that Tom loved Nynehead. We suggested Tom needed to concentrate on realising some assets by selling at least one of the four properties to fund his care.

It was only then that we got on to Louise. I was already in tears trying to get through to Sasha that all these shenanigans were simply adding new layers of pain on to a grief that was so deep it was unbearable. He finally understood and we both cried and hugged, and peace was made.

Portugal was ditched as a silly plan; the new one was to take Tom back home if the house remained unsold for much longer, although we were still prepared to foot his nursing home bills. This was not an attractive proposition for either Di or Dad when they thought about it carefully. The next scheme was to move him to Manchester where Di had a friend with nursing homes. I went to the UK to discuss it with them, a few days after Ross's shocking and unexpected diagnosis with prostate cancer. Battered first by Louise's death, the row at Christmas, and now this, I simply felt unable to cope with any more family matters. Reluctantly, I shrugged my shoulders and said, so be it.

A few weeks later, after Ross's successful operation, we returned to England for a wedding. I had been receiving disturbing calls from Nynehead, telling me Dad was crying and didn't want to go to Manchester; the move was set up for that same weekend. The owner of Nynehead had been trying to talk Tom round, even offering to match the fees of Manchester, but to no avail. He then called in the social services who, while advising against the move on health and psychological grounds, said there was little they could do as Dad had capacity. We were all powerless. I had tried talking to Sasha, but he took his parents' side, saying that if that's what his father wanted, then that was that. I tried to tell him about Dad saying one thing to him, and another to his carers, and of his distress.

In the middle of the wedding I received a call from Darren, who was so upset about the situation he had consulted a neighbour, who was a barrister. They had managed to track down an emergency High Court judge in order to get an injunction over the weekend, preventing his move to Manchester, pending an official hearing. However, in order to lodge the papers, I had to write a statement, which I duly did.

Meanwhile, the barrister wrote and delivered a letter to Di to try and convene a meeting. It seemed that Nynehead believed that there was no care plan in place, the new home had not even made a needs assessment, and did not seem aware that Tom was wheelchair-bound. In preparation for the move his local nursing care had been cancelled, including the dressing of his legs, which were now swollen like tree trunks; he also had an infection and was confused and rambling.

Dad then called me and was furious, claiming that no one had consulted him and how dare I go behind his back. I told him we were responding to Nynehead's reports of his great distress at the move. We had been trying to get through to him about the offer on the fees issue, but he was incapable of retaining any information at this stage. Meanwhile all his things were packed and ready to go.

By now the doctor had issued an incapacity order and there had been a terrible meeting where Di accused Darren and me of colluding against her – which was true I suppose, but we were concerned that what was being arranged was not in Dad's best interest. The medical professionals and Nynehead thought it posed a health risk to take an eighty-nine-year-old man so far away from his friends, his devoted carers and the place where he was happy, to an unknown city, where he would receive few visitors and would have the additional trauma of both moving and settling in.

We decided to go down and see my father on the Sunday, the same day the Manchester staff were coming down to do the last-minute assessment and care plan. We needed to gauge his frame of mind.

At lunch Dad was delighted to see us. He enjoyed a Beck's beer, roast beef and crème brûlée – 'the best I've ever had'– but Angela, the duty manager, told us Tom was still very upset. She had reassured him saying, whatever Vicky has said or done it's because she loves you very much and she is doing it in your best interest. She believed he took it on board, and he was not angry at lunch. Ross attempted to explain everything to him again in a calm and rational way and he appeared to take it all in.

Just as we finished we got word that Di was on her way, so we scarpered to Darren's house as we had no wish for a confrontation. It was chaotic with papers everywhere, on the table and floor, statements from several people, including Tom's friends, all bearing witness to his great unhappiness at the impending move. I decided to join Darren as the applicant as it did not seem fair to let him take the brunt of everyone's anger. He understood that leading up to the current emergency, I had not been able to process it all, being entirely taken up with Ross's operation and recovery. I was also still in a state of deep mourning due to Louise's death, only a year ago.

Finally at 4.45 p.m. on Sunday 27 May, we were granted an order forbidding his removal from Nynehead until a hearing on 2 July in Exeter. A court solicitor was appointed for Tom. We thought that was that for the time being. We also learned that, following its assessment, the Manchester home could not take him on account of his disabilities; they were a care home rather than a nursing home, they said.

So it had all been for nothing. What a fiasco.

*

Phone calls at 3.30 a.m. are never good news; in this case it was Angela from Nynehead with the news that Dad had died shortly before. It was two days after I had seen him, the Tuesday following the Sunday. He had been in the loo and had rung for help, so she and two other carers rushed in and took him back to his wheelchair, where he simply closed his eyes and stopped breathing. Angela was holding his hand.

I felt completely drained – shocked but not surprised. I was unable to take it in. Poor Darren felt eviscerated but we all agreed that we had done the right thing; it would have been terrible for him to die alone, en route or on arrival in Manchester.

Di called me and told me that Dad had not wanted a funeral (this I knew) and wanted to donate his body to science – this I also knew as he had written a note: 'What to do with the old b***** when he's gone'. However, in a final twist of fate, Nynehead was so surprised by his sudden death that Angela called in the police and coroner to do an autopsy. So his final wish was denied.

Di arranged for the cremation to take place without consulting me; we were flying to Africa for a holiday that Thursday and would not be able to attend. However, I realised that death is more about the living, the survivors, than the dead, as I had discovered. I would honour and remember Dad in my own way, even though the past few years of our relationship had been a roller coaster, mostly on the descent.

I spoke to Bonnie as soon as I heard the news. By a strange and lucky coincidence she had spoken to Dad a few hours before he died and reported that he had seemed fine. I had also spoken to him in the afternoon, trying to reassure and explain to him what the court order meant, and why we had done it. The last thing he said to me was, 'I don't know what to believe, you tell me one thing, Di tells me another. I simply don't know who is telling me the truth.'

The autopsy results showed he had suffered an embolism, a blood clot to the brain, exacerbated by the fact that his legs had not been bandaged for a couple of weeks.

I am still devastated to think he doubted my motives in trying to prevent him the stress of moving to Manchester. It was dreadful that, in his last weeks, his self-esteem was so low that he was prepared to end his life through Dignitas or to accept a much lower quality of life in a strange place. He had become illogical, confused by his Parkinson's drugs and one infection after the other. His doctors had been advising him that he was eligible for full-time nursing via a continuing care order, as he was now facing the last few months of his life. We had been telling him the same thing, but his ears were shut.

Whatever the rights or wrongs, it was a terrible way to die, unsure about his closest family. I was glad that the lovely ladies of Nynehead were there to hold his hand and help him on his way, that he was not alone at the time of his death.

AFTERWORD

Tomas Ungar, born in Prague in 1923, died Tom Unwin in Somerset in 2012, aged eighty-nine. I regretted that I had not been able to demystify my father properly before his death; now I was all the more committed to finishing my research and putting to rest the demons that had so characterised the final years of our relationship. It was to be a way of coming to terms with all my own bereavements.

*

Di organised a memorial for Tom at the Chelsea Arts Club in October 2012. It was a warm occasion, despite relations between Di, Sasha and me remaining strained, and there were some fitting tributes from friends, former colleagues, including one from Groundnut days and Kevin, his deputy from PNG. A pianist played his favourite Viennese waltzes. We ended with a German song 'Servus' (meaning 'good day' in Austrian German), at his express request. This is his translation:

When you're leaving
Just say 'Servus'
It's the nicest thing to say
When you have to go away
Just the little
Word of 'Servus'
No adieu and not goodbye
Farewells always make me cry...

Just the little
word of 'Servus'
It's the nicest thing to say
When you have to go away

It was only at that point, with the sun streaming through the skylight and the autumn leaves framing it, looking at Dad's photo, that I began to cry for the first time. The photos of him, in his late fifties/early sixties, smoking his pipe, smiling gently, were just how I remember him before his face was ravaged by the Parkinson's mask, which was only broken by his merry smile, never far away. The stresses of the past eighteen months had left me unable to mourn properly for him until this point. The grief for Louise was still so overwhelming.

*

Di and I had agreed that we should scatter Tom's ashes in Prague in November. In deference to his great love of Africa, I had suggested I could also lay some to rest with Sheila and Louise on Manda Toto, a small island off the Kenyan coast, which I did a year later. In the end Di and Sasha did not come to Prague.

Ross, Tommy and I had arranged to meet Hana, Tom's Czech friend, now widowed, and her son, Michal, in Prague. We were going to scatter the ashes on an island, overlooking the Vltava River in Prague, just by the National Theatre, below the Charles Bridge and opposite the art deco apartment where my father grew up

It was miserably cold, not helped by my silliness in bringing a nice dress but forgetting to bring tights, so my legs were bare. Hana's chosen spot overlooked the apartment, with an unimpeded access to the water, where the current was less sluggish.

Ross unwrapped the coffee tin containing the ashes and with a couple of quick swooshes the ashes swirled on to the water; Hana threw in a blood-red rose. I thought of Dad, and how pleased he would be to be returned to his home. Hana and I gave each other a big hug, and Tommy put his hand on my shoulder and said, 'That was nice, Mum.'

I took a last look at the ashes as they bobbed gently downstream and silently said goodbye to all that remained of my father, my chest choking with emotion, and tears pricking behind my eyes.

We had some time to kill before lunch, so we strolled over to the Charles Bridge. As we walked I told Hana

Deceptively British, towards the end of his life ...

how I always felt Dad did not grieve enough for Louise. 'Oh no,' she said, 'he rang me every week, he was so upset, and apologised continually for calling to talk about it, but he had no one else to talk to. He was so worried about how you would cope, but proud at how you did and the positive actions you took, but still devastated for you.'

It was so frustrating to discover all this after his death. Why couldn't he have talked to me and comforted me like a normal parent? The cynic in me says that he was really looking for Hana's sympathy for himself rather than showing any empathy for me.

He had not, however, told her about Bonnie. Hana strongly

believed that the loss of his family and his homeland, never spoken about, had affected him greatly. He had told her, in a rare admission of honesty, that Sheila's leaving was more because he had never been a good husband and he could not stop himself from being horrible to her. He did not say why: I think it was another manifestation of his insecurity, his need to assert himself.

We agreed that because of hiding his past – Hana knew all along he was Jewish, as she was, and had tried to get him to tell people – he found it impossible to show emotions apart from being the jester, the charmer. I told her this was just like his father, so it was perhaps genetic rather than a result of survivor guilt. When I interviewed him shortly before his death, he confessed that he hid his Jewish origins from his children because he didn't want us 'to be burdened unnecessarily'.

I was heartened by Hana's information on how deeply Dad had felt Louise's death, but saddened by his inability to communicate and share his sense of loss with me. It would have brought us together towards the end of his days and rebuilt some of those broken bridges, those childhood arcs of shining love that had shattered as we each cut our own paths through life, survivors of our own respective histories.

*

In March 2013, two years after Louise's death, one year after my father's, Ross and I moved to Singapore. Looking back, neither of us was coping particularly well and we were getting on each other's nerves. We were both aware of the statistics on marriages not surviving the death of a child and were determined it should not apply to us. Arranging parties on Louise's birthday and her anniversary gave us some comfort, as we wanted to keep her memory alive, but nothing could replace the void in our lives. As I noted in my diary, 'Perhaps it is just another form of escapism, but so what? It fills the time, which stretches out uninvitingly into the future, never-ending and always lacking the one thing I would give anything still to have ...' We were still stuck in the groove of bereavement.

I needed a project to give my life a structure but felt incapable of continuing with the book on my father, which I had now been researching for almost ten years. The wounds were still too recent. I had started to go through all those envelopes of letters between my parents, but they only reinforced my increasingly negative view of him. They were all written at the time of their divorce, close-typed or handwritten, page upon page. Just reading a few lines here and there as I sorted them made me put them on one side: I was simply not strong enough. The anger and accusations that came tumbling out of them were as potent today as when they were written. They would have to wait.

So, I decided instead to edit my mother's wartime letters as a kind of dress rehearsal. It was strange working with my mum's familiar handwriting and I could hear her voice loud and clear in my head as I read. Comforting but also unnerving, yet it felt like a completeness: I had neglected my mother after her death, just as I had during her life, and I needed to make amends.

*

Then, out of nowhere, my bubble was catapulted into outer space. As I wrote in my diary in November 2013:

> Yesterday I was diagnosed with a soft tissue sarcoma of the calf, and here I am today in hospital having had a biopsy and a PET scan, waiting to hear the prognosis ...
> Last night I could not sleep, hardly surprising really. 'Why me?' As Louise would have said, 'It's not my fault.' What have we done to deserve all this bad luck: the deaths

in close succession of my mother, Louise, and then father, with Ross's prostate cancer in-between? He at least is now clear. I have never believed in God and I certainly would not be tempted to do so now!

It's 3 am and I am sitting on my lounger overlooking our softly-lit pool, all calming turquoise and gently fading pinky/mauve lights, the palms gently rustling in the breeze, and breathing in the scented tropical air. Out of nowhere a big storm rolls in, forked lightening and soft rain. I begin to think how much I love my life, my husband, son and friends, and I am not ready to go just yet. So much travelling to do, so much laughter and joy to be had …

I decided to come back to London and be operated on by one of the world's best surgeons. All my calf muscles were removed but, thanks to him, I still have good use of my leg and am alive, despite the cancer being found in my bloodstream and the poor statistical prognosis. I am sure the cancer was caused by the effect of the successive bereavements on my immunity. As I write this I am still clear.

After six and a half weeks of radiotherapy, I was ready to return to Singapore. I was exhausted and needed to devote myself to recovery, and finishing my mother's book was therapeutic. It was only after the publication of *Love and War in the WRNS* in 2015 that I felt strong enough to get back to my father. I began to open the envelopes containing my parents' letters.

As I read them for the first time, fifty years after they were written, I felt, as I said earlier, a deep sense of shame that I had not supported my mother more. I felt helpless and hopeless; in my head I was shouting, 'Don't let him get away with it! Stand up to him!' But she was so wretched and beaten down by life – her awful job, the loss of her both her loves, being poor and lonely and missing me dreadfully – that she was quite incapable of doing anything other than expressing her fury and misery in writing; and every time she attempted to strike back – as when she kept me for that Easter holiday – he retaliated like a spitting cobra going in for the kill, topping and tailing his poison-pen letters with a venomous 'Darling' and 'All my love'.

I could hear Sheila's howls of anguish slicing through the decades like a sword. For the first time, I got an insight into the bitterness and pain that drove my mother's last forty or so years, why she would say darkly, 'I could tell you some dreadful things about your father that would surprise you. He is not a nice man, you know', and I would say, 'I don't want to hear them', and block my ears. I had this image of my handsome, golden father, the father of my youth, my hero and number one supporter, clouding my brain.

The sheer misery of those letters haunts me and rouses deep-seated and hidden emotions. As I noted in my diary, when I was making lunch one day:

> ... I felt a searing pain of the loss of Louise and how unfair
> it is that she is not here. It is at times like these I can hardly
> believe I ever had a daughter, that her name was Louise,
> and that she grew from a darling little bundle with ringlets
> into a moody teenager (just like me) and then into a
> charming and beautiful adult ... and now she is gone. And
> then I cry – but what is the use, there is no comfort to be
> had anywhere ...

It was only through this mammoth task of chronicling my parents' lives as laid out in their letters that I have managed to find some healing and respite from my own feelings of guilt towards my mother but also towards Louise. It is impossible to escape that haunting feeling of having failed her in some way – a fatal way that indirectly led to her death. Was it because I was not a good enough parent? Did I imbue her with an independence that she was not ready for, because I projected my own childhood experiences on to her without taking account of our different characters and the different times?

I will never know.

*

At first I thought my father had been a classic victim of survivor guilt – the guilt *he* felt at surviving, while his family perished. But the more I read his letters, and about his father, Hermann, I realised he was a product of his genes. The shared characteristics are uncanny, given that my father was only six when Hermann died: the neuroses; the hypochondria; the agnosticism; the bravery; the idealism; the feeling like an outsider; the desire to belong; the insecurity; the flirtatiousness and sexual philandering; the strange ideas on parenting; the need to be the centre of attention at all times and to show off; the craven adulation of famous people – for example, Nyerere (by Tom) and Thomas Mann (by Hermann); the casual misogyny and unhappiness that they each caused their respective wives; the warped and cruel schoolboy humour.

Reading accounts of Hermann's pranks, if I close my eyes I can hear my father – is it simply a case of vulgar Czech and/or Jewish humour or something else? The tortured and unself-confident man seeking to find pleasure in another's discomfort to distract from his own? As a refugee and outsider in post-war Britain and, later, in Tanganyika, my father shared many of Hermann's feelings of not belonging to the accepted social order. It brings to mind the Czech ambassador incident with which this book opened. Deep down, he never felt really British, despite outward appearances.

If genes play such a large role in forming character, what does that say about what my children inherit from me? And Bonnie's from her? The only comforting thought is that we are both much more self-aware and can compensate for our shortcomings. For Louise, perhaps, this came too late. Having grown up with Nana, I realise that Dad's obsessive attitude to parenting came directly from her and is therefore something Bonnie and I have both managed to avoid in bringing up our children.

Bonnie adds an insightful perspective as I struggle with my own feelings of failure. She says I am too hard on myself, that I should credit myself for breaking the cycle; that, despite my depression, I behaved like an adult in a way that Dad never did; I picked a good husband and made marriage work, which was and is a great gift to both Tommy and Louise. Whatever blame I feel, she thinks it's a miracle that I have made it thus far, given my chequered childhood, and I should 'pat myself on my back' and pay tribute to poor long-suffering Ross, who has supported me throughout my life. With no parents to give encouragement and offer solace over my bereavements, it is a comfort to have an older and wiser sister, as well as a loving husband.

Bonnie believes Tom was a narcissist, just like his father, and to some extent his grandfather, Emil. Growing up without a father, all he ever wanted was the unconditional love of his family, his co-workers, his direct reports who, as his PA attested, adored him (gardeners and messengers notwithstanding). It might explain why he was so poor at managing upward relations, falling out with his bosses, people and institutions in authority, and his lack of empathy and inability to see another point of view – all classic narcissist characteristics. And when that love ceased to be unconditional, for instance when I began to have serious boyfriends, a husband and then children; he couldn't bear being marginalised.

This would explain why our relationship deteriorated once I was married and the children were born, why he transferred all his attention to Sasha, and why he paid scant heed to Tommy and Louise. He was jealous of them for taking me away from him. Perhaps there was also an envy caused by Tommy's cruising through life seamlessly – clever and athletic at school, funny, charming and extrovert.

It is more difficult to explain his relationship with Louise. You would think that as a girl, and my daughter, she would remind him of the joy I brought him as a child. He would kiss her, and greet her warmly, always calling her LouLou but, as with Tommy, the relationship was never grandparenty; it was fond but at arm's length. The kids would never, ever have volunteered to go to The Fort without us – they were not made to feel particularly welcome and had to be on their best behaviour in the dark and sombre house – whereas they were happy to spend time with their paternal grandparents and, to some extent, with my mother although, being much older, she was unable to cope with them on her own when they were younger. Both my parents' damaged childhoods rendered a free and easy relationship with their grandchildren difficult.

Dad's intellectual analysis of Louise's death – 'Tell me, I really don't understand why Louise felt the need to take drugs' – made me catatonic with anger. I stormed out of the room saying, 'God, you really don't understand ANYTHING. Like Mum said, you are so dense.' Here was this man, my father, her grandfather, sitting there like an innocent, as ever unable to see the whole picture, life from others' perspectives, not just his.

It is poignant to remember how thrilled Louise was to discover she had Jewish blood; how excited to learn she had a secret auntie; and how ecstatic she was to read Hermann Ungar. But how ironic to think that, perhaps, in these discoveries were the seeds of her destruction, epigenetic depression playing its role.

I have often wondered if our heritage finally caught up with Louise, that she was the victim that I should have been, that it skipped a generation. At the time when I suffered from depression, my kids were the same age as I was when my parents split up; my depression led to years of erratic behaviour, now thankfully tempered. Just as I imitated my parents, one's only role models in life according to my therapist, was it any surprise that at

The loving grandfather?

the age of fifteen, the age at which I was expelled from school, Louise first started hanging out with what my mother would have called 'a bad lot' and my father 'a fast crowd' and experimenting with drugs? Like me she was also arrested – for possessing a cigarette-case full of spliffs, a borderline amount for personal use.

I vividly remember that evening, when her distraught friend Anastasia rang us late at night and said she was at the Kentish Town police station where Louise was being held, and how we rushed down there, to be met by a kindly police officer. He said that he had 'frightened the life' out of Louise to make her realise the severity of what she had done, but because she was so young, he would let her off with a caution, if we agreed to getting her some counselling. It felt frighteningly familiar. I recognised her naïvety and her wish to push the boundaries from my own childhood and all I wanted to do was protect her.

Now, thinking about the hundreds of Dad's letters, it is quite clear that his single-minded world view, with himself and his opinions at its epicentre – he always in the right, the wronged party in any dispute – was to shield himself from revealing the man he really was. Tomy Ungar's reinvention of himself into the public figure of Tom Unwin buried his secret self to protect his reputation. 'Good old Tom' was a magnet that drew an admiring crowd of friends and supporters – and many of those reading this will find it hard to recognise the man they thought they knew.

Outwardly he appeared to fulfil the character he had invented, yet beneath the protective thick skin lay an inability to see anyone's point of view; a lack of empathy, taking no account of anyone else's feelings; a superficial commitment to refugees and victims of persecution while ignoring the victims in his own family. The effect of his denial was octopus-like, with its tentacles strangling his closest relatives – none of us immune to his personality nor from the damage caused by his deceptions. This was the private man, Tomas Ungar, who was prepared to suppress everything in order to succeed. Just as his father's darkness was revealed in his writing, Dad's was only visible to those closest to him: yet in public the two men were beguiling, good company and much admired.

Writing and researching this memoir has given me the solace and catharsis that I have been searching for all my life. I have tried to seek my mother's forgiveness for my seemingly callous treatment of her; I have honoured my dead forebears by tracing their sad history and brutal end; I have contextualised and put behind me the terrible rift between my half-brother and me; I have paid tribute to my tortured grandfather, Hermann Ungar. In doing all of this I have discovered my sister Bonnie and formed a bond with her that only sisters can know, that will outlive all the deaths that this testimony bears witness to.

But most of all I have forged a deep understanding of the events and inheritance that moulded my father into the man he was: the Czech-born perfect Englishman, oozing charisma, compassion and charm, whose carapace hid deep-seated insecurities, a violent temper and a depressive streak, who could simultaneously be a demon and a devoted dad. Rediscovering, after half a century, the letters he wrote to me, regular as a Swiss watch, while I was at school, feeling the love and devotion radiating from the blue airmails or the crinkly UN-headed notepaper, with their red and black 'kissies', fills me with the warm glow of that unique father–daughter bond that was exclusive to us for so many years. It remained, to a lesser degree, to the very end when I was the one he could rely on to advise and safeguard him from his deep-seated anxieties.

My only regret is that his first daughter, Bonnie, was not able to share that all-enveloping love that a father has for a daughter until she was well into her thirties. Sadly for her, and for him too, it would be a different sort of love, idealistic yet tinged with guilt and shame, and scarred by years of denial. I am glad he made amends and tried to atone for the wrongs he did to both Bonnie and Joyce, albeit years too late. It is hard not to judge him harshly for his actions, yet Bonnie has forgiven him, so who am I not to?

*

I visited Prague with Bonnie in 2017. I had always wanted to introduce her to our heritage, to the Prague of her father and grandfather. I also wanted Bonnie to meet Hana, who knew Dad so well. Hana was thrilled to see us and to reminisce about the times with Tom in Turkey. It brought him to life for Bonnie, another side of the father she barely knew.

I had lined up the genealogist Julius Müller to devise a tour of Prague for us. He emerged from the tram, dapper in a light jacket and fedora, face wreathed in smiles. With doorbell-ringing chutzpah, we delighted in masquerading as a trio of dangerous criminals as we broke and entered our way around the Prague residences of our grandfather and father. As we wandered round, I thought, these are the streets my father took to school, where he was sent out for ham and pickles for the soirées, where he took the tram or the bus to see his friends and grandparents, the river where he larked about in boats.

We passed the island where we scattered Dad's ashes in 2012; I took a photo and conjured up the last time we had visited Prague together, and then his committal to the waters of the Vltava.

*

When I had first spoken to Julius about this trip, the previous October, I had casually mentioned that we would be going to Boskovice: 'I don't suppose you want to come?' Oh, yes, he said, he would be very interested as he had never been there and offered to drive us down.

Boskovice in summer is even more attractive than in winter – the pastel-coloured houses in the Jewish quarter twinkle in the sunshine, the cafés and shops are open, both locals and tourists basking in its warmth. I was disappointed to find that the pub in the family home, the Kaiser Haus, has been replaced by a crèche. On the other side of the front door there is a fancy jeweller's. The house itself had also been renovated since my visit in 2012, converted into offices and flats.

Bonnie had a surprise for the curator of the synagogue. She revealed that the original Boskovice Torah is now in her synagogue in Bethesda, Maryland. After the war over 1,600 Torah scrolls were rescued and brought to Westminster, where they were restored and then distributed throughout the world. It's uncanny that the Boskovice Torah ended up in a far-off city where Ungar diaspora live.

We also walked up to the Mensdorff-Pouilly Chateau where our great-great-great-grandmother Jetty taught the Countess French in the early 1800s. Mozart wafted through the open windows and into the courtyard. We were taken back 200 years: superficially nothing seems to have changed – Boskovice is still a small market town and, from this distance, there is little modernising to be seen. The countryside looks like it did in our grandfather's time, with wooded hills and small fields, purple with pyrethrum, grain ripening in the sun. There was a pair of palomino ponies pulling a plough, a foal trotting beside them. I closed my eyes and allowed the images from my history to flit through like a kaleidoscope: Hermann, Grete, Tom, Uncle Alec, and all those ghosts that we are bearing witness to.

As we parted company at Prague airport, I contemplated the significance of this visit to each of us: to Bonnie it was the missing piece in the jigsaw of her life, rediscovering her father's past, visiting the village of his forebears and his childhood haunts. For me, I had fulfilled my father's dying wish to reintegrate Bonnie into the family, or at least my family, to be the sister to her that she always wanted, and that he wanted me to be. Despite his flaws and his deceit, our father has brought us together and left a legacy that cannot be undone.

THE FATE OF THE UNGAR/STRANSKY/KOHN FAMILIES

While writing this book I managed to trace the fate of Tom's immediate Ungar, Stransky and Kohn relatives. Here I summarise my findings on the family members mentioned in this book; they are also charted in the family trees. With thanks to cousins (Ilana) Kitty Strauss and Helen Stransky, to the Jewish National Archive in Jerusalem, JewishGen, Yad Vashem, the Theresienstadt Martyrs Remembrance Association and the United States Holocaust Memorial Museum in Washington DC. I was pleased to be able to discover what happened to Helen and Peter Stransky's parents, my great uncle and aunt, and tell them before they both died in 2020.

UNGAR FAMILY

Emil (Tom's grandfather) died in 1941 of natural causes, prior to the transportations. He was buried in an unmarked grave in Boskovice.

Jeanette (b. Kohn) (Tom's grandmother) was transported from Boskovice to Terezín on 19 March 1942, then to Auschwitz on 25 April 1942, where she was probably gassed on arrival since all records cease. She was seventy-nine.

Felix (Tom's uncle) was transported from Boskovice to Terezín on 19 March 1942 with Jeanette and his wife, Marianne. He and his sons were part of transport of 1,000 prisoners from Terezín to Warsaw on 25 April 1942. They stayed there for three weeks, in the Great Synagogue, and then the SS began rounding the men up and taking them to Treblinka, where they were forced to build the concentration camp. Soon all 1,000 prisoners had been sent to Treblinka, but only 300 men fit for work were spared – the rest were gassed on arrival and their ashes used to fill the potholes. Of the surviving 300, only nine young men survived, the rest having been clubbed to death or stabbed with bayonets.* It is not clear at what stage Felix and the young brothers Hans-Georg and Otto were murdered.

Marianne (b. Knopfelmacher) (Felix's wife and Tom's aunt) was transported from Boskovice to Terezín on 19 March 1942, and to Auschwitz with the rest of the family. She survived the war but it is likely she died shortly afterwards as there are no records of what happened to her.

Hans-Georg and Otto (Tom's cousins and Felix and Marianne's children) see above.

Gerta (Tom's aunt) committed suicide in Palestine in 1946 on learning of the fate of her family. Her husband, Amnon Rudy Kleiner-Zair, died in 1977 in Israel.

Blanka Totis (Tom's first cousin once removed and Hermann's first love) survived Terezín, married Dr Vilem Haas and died in Budapest 1978. She had adopted Gerta's son, Petr, as Gerta was too poor to bring him up in Palestine, and he took the name Haas when Gerta emigrated in 1926.

---

* As documented in *Ghetto Theresienstadt* by Zdenek Lederer (Edward Goldston & Son, 1953).

Petr Haas (Gerta's son and Tom's cousin) joined his birth parents in Palestine in 1939 but shortly after he volunteered to serve in the Sixth Company of the British Army's BPO. On 13 June, 1942, Gerta received a telegram: *Corporal Peter Haas, 15500, a soldier in the British command of the German division, is missing in battle in the Western Desert.*

STRANSKY FAMILY

Heinrich (Grete's father) died in Prague, 1933, of natural causes.

Pauline (b. Gehorsam) (Grete's mother) was removed from #6 Joseforska, Prague (not their house, maybe they had been hiding there) on 6 July, 1942, was taken to Terezín and from there to the death camp Treblinka on 19 October 1942. No record of her arrival, so we can only assume she was gassed immediately. She was sixty-nine years old.

Otto (Grete's brother) fled from Prague to Náchod in September 1939, having divorced his wife, perhaps for expediency. In July 1942 he 'escaped to the woods' but was recaptured six months later, as he appeared in December in Terezín before being recorded as dead – from 'meningitis' – on 16 January 1943.

Luisa (b. Weinmann) (Grete's sister-in-law) was transported to Terezín in early 1942; according to their documents she was 'deported June 10, 1942 to Ujazdov; all women were moved to extermination camp Belzec* and murdered by the gas. Last day of her life shall be considered June 30, 1942.'

---

* Belzec was in Poland, and only operated between March and December 1942, yet between 430,000 and 500,000 Jews are believed to have been murdered there.

Helen Stransky (Grete's niece and Tom's cousin) escaped aged four to England on the Kindertransport in 1939; moved to the US from Canada and then to Israel where she died in May 2020.

Peter Stransky (Grete's nephew and Tom's cousin) escaped aged two to England on the Kindertransport in 1939; lived and married in Canada; died shortly after his sister Helen in May 2020.

Richard Weinmann (Luisa's brother and Helen and Peter's uncle) fled Prague and emigrated to Canada with his mother and Helen and Peter. Later he went to the USA, where he died in 1957.

KOHN FAMILY

Ludwig (Tom's favourite great-uncle) was transported from Třebíč to Terezín on 22 May 1942 and then to Auschwitz on 26 October 1942. The family tree assumes he died soon after.

Tilly/Ottoline (Tom's great-aunt) her fate is not recorded, but probably murdered on arrival at a concentration camp.

Richard (Tom's uncle and stepfather) was arrested in Prague in September 1939 and transported first to Dachau for two weeks and then to Buchenwald where he did hard labour and died on 18 August 1942 at 4.10 a.m. of 'tuberculosis'. The Washington Holocaust Museum holds extensive records of his imprisonment.

In addition to the ten close relatives listed above, a minimum of fifteen Ungar/Stransky/Kohns were murdered in concentration camps. But this is a conservative estimate as the records do not yield death dates for many family members of the appropriate generation, and I have not gone back to more distant relatives of my great-grandparents' generation, the Biachs, Knopfelmachers, the Landaus, the Loewys and so on: the number would be too great.

Kitty Strauss gave me this letter addressed to Erich Konrad (i.e. Erich Konrad Kohn), Tom's first cousin once removed (see Kohn family tree), who had escaped to England before the war. It illustrates perfectly the horror of the Holocaust, especially as it is about my own family. It is written on airmail-type paper, now very hard to read; several of the pages are damaged and the last page is missing so it is tantalisingly incomplete. It is not clear who the writer was, but probably a member of the Kohn family, as the writer refers to 'my dearest son Dr. Kohn', although the term 'Uncle' might well have been used out of respect for this stalwart member of the Jewish community in Jemnice/Jamnitz. As Erich wrote to Kitty, 'I cannot say how sad I am that Uncle Ludwig whom I adored [Tom's favourite great-uncle Ludwig] had this tragedy to experience before being murdered himself.'

> *Jamnitz, 7. 7. 46*
>
> *Dear Mr. Konrad!*
>
> *Mrs. Dussik gave me your address and told me that you would like to find out about your family, which is understandable, but regrettably I can only relate sad news. Poor Richard [Kohn, Erich's cousin and my father's uncle and stepfather] was taken away as early as 1940, and he kept going, in spite of all the suffering, until he died in 44 in Osweicim [Auschwitz – this is not true as we know he died in Buchenwald in 1942] from pneumonia [again, TB, according to the Nazi records], without any medical treatment; and it's all right to say it – he was released from his suffering. But uncle Ludwig never found out about it, he kept up his hope for Richard. The aged father had to bury your cousin poor Enno [probably a nickname for Ernst, Richard's brother, who died in Auschwitz in 1941]. On 18.V.42*

we were all, 51 of us, transported to Třebič, the collection point.

On 20. we were locked into sealed train carriages and took off, we did not know where to. In the evening we were allowed out and in the pouring rain, with our rucksacks on our backs, we hiked from Bohnschowitz for about 1½ hours to Theresienstadt, there we were crammed into barracks. The rooms were meant for 6 people, but we were 25, in 3 boxes, stacked above each other, accessible via a ladder, these were the beds. Everyone was allowed 50kg to carry, including bedding. The food: early, black, so called coffee; noon: an indefinable soup, 4 to 5 potatoes, half of them inedible, accompanied by something they called dip/sauce. Evenings just like the mornings, half a loaf of bread for 3 days, 50 g of sugar, 30 g of Farina [milled wheat made into a kind of porridge] per week.

I'd rather not describe the physical and psychological suffering. Your father [Dr Emil Kohn who had died in 1933] and Ludwig had been my school mates, we were happy in J [Jamnitz] whenever we could get together; the dear uncle was constantly flustered/shaken, every time he hugged me and cried that we had to meet here. In the autumn of 42 he was already standing in line to be taken away, but Dr. Zucker intervened (Enno's friend) and he was taken out of the line; soon after even Zucker had to go and during the next transport poor Ludwig too; I don't know who else of your family were there, but the uncle once came to me and complained/mourned that all of the relatives had already been deported and that only he was left. Wanda who had been married to Ludwig's son Ernst [the one who had been murdered in Auschwitz in 1941] with her child [Sasha] and [new] husband [Pavel Freund, Wanda had remarried and she and her son Sasha appear also in the records as Freund] arrived later; but grandfather could not be happy for long because he had to go into the unknown; Wanda and family had to walk in 44, only her husband could save himself; the fate of all from Jamnitz is the same, some to Poland into the Pogroms, some mostly gassed. I would have written to you earlier, but my pain was much too great, I have lost 4 sons, 1 daughter, 2 grandchildren, the daughter-in-law, my dearest son Dr. Kohn, who also treated your father, suffered the same fate. It is a miracle that I am alive, I spent 7 months in hospital and there I did not forget it. With regard to the property of your loved ones, sadly it was all confiscated ...

May they rest in peace.

SOURCES

PRIMARY SOURCES

Taped and filmed interviews with Tom Unwin, Ilana (Kitty) Strauss and Helen Stransky

Family photographs and albums

Letters and papers: To and from Tom & Sheila Unwin; to and from Joyce Rochefort Unwin; between Bonnie and me; my letters to and from my parents; to and from John Pritty; to and from Neville Chittick

Numerous academic papers, unpublished papers, letters etc. from my father's collection

BOOKS

Feigel, Lara, *The Bitter Taste of Victory*, Bloomsbury, London, 2016

Fogel Unwin, Bonnie, *A Sun for My Soul* (self-published), 2016

Helm, Sarah, *If This is a Woman*, Little, Brown, London, 2015

Klemenz, Nanette, *Hermann Ungar*, Bouvier Verlag, Bonn, 1981

Klemenz, Nanette, *Hermann Ungar. Ein Monographie* [Hermann Ungar: A Monograph], Bonn, 1970

Sebba, Anne, *Les Parisiennes*, Weidenfeld & Nicholson, London, 2016

Serke, Jürgen, *Böhmische Dörfer: Wanderungen durch eine verlassene literarische Landschaft* [Bohemian Towns: Excursions *through a forgotten literary landscape]*, Zsolnay, Vienna/ Hamburg, 1987

Sudhoff, Dieter, *Hermann Ungar: Life and Works* (available in translation at www.hermannungar.com)

— (ed.), *Hermann Ungar, Sämtliche Werke* [Complete Works], *Vol. 1: Romane* [Novels] (2012), *Vol. 2: Erzählungen* [Stories] (2015), *Vol. 3: Gedichte, Dramen, Feuilletons, Briefe* [Poems, Plays, Short Prose, Letters] (2011), IEGL Verlag, Hamburg

Ungar, Hermann, *Bankbeamte und andere vergessene Prosa, Der [The Bank Clerk and other forgotten prose]*, ed. Dieter Sudhoff, IGEL Verlag, Hamburg, 1989

—, *Boys and Murderers*, trans. Isabel Fargo Cole, Twisted Spoon Press, Prague, 2006

—, *The Class*, trans. Michael Mitchell, Dedalus European Classics, Cambridge, 2004

—, *The Maimed*, trans. Michael Mitchell, Dedalus European Classics, Cambridge, 2002

—, *Gartenlaube, Die [The Arbour]*, Rowohlt, Berlin, 1929

—, *Der Rote General [The Red General]*, unpublished but performed play, 1928

—, *Romány, menší prózy [Novels and short prose]*, trans. Jaroslav Bránský, Kulturní zařízení města, Boskovice, 2001

Ungar, Max, *Tradition und Entfremdung: Die Lebenserinnerungen des jüdischen Privatdozenten Max Ungar* (Tradition and Alienation: The Memoirs of the Jewish Private Lecturer Max Ungar, English translation by Miroslav Imbrisevic (available online on www.hermannungar.com) ed. Mark Hengerer, Studienverlag, Vienna, 2011

Waugh, Evelyn, *A Tourist in Africa*, Chapman & Hall, London, 1930

Wood, Alan, *The Groundnut Affair*, Bodley Head, London, 1950

ARTICLES

Berguaer, Elisabeth, 'Sexualität in ausgewählten Werken von Hermann Ungar und Ludwig Winder' [Sexuality in the works of Hermann Ungar and Ludwig Winder], PhD Thesis, University of Vienna, 2011

Bránský, Jaroslav, 'Boskowitzer Motive im Werk des Dichters Hermann Ungar' [Boskovice motives in the works of Hermann Ungar], *Litteraria Pragensia*, 2, 1991, pp. 89–97

Chew, Mieke, 'On Hermann Ungar's forgotten books', *Music and Literature*, July 2014

Hoffmann, Dirk, 'Wer war Hermann Ungar?' [Who was Hermann Ungar?]. *Zeitschrift für Deutsche Philologie*, 2, May 1991

Patkova, Eva, 'Hermann Ungar 1893–1929: Skizze einer Biographie [A Biographical Sketch], Prague, Charles University German Department, 1966

ADDITIONAL RESOURCES

JewishGen, Yad Vashem, Beit Terezin/ The Theresienstadt Martyrs Remembrance Association and United States Holocaust Memorial Museum websites:

https://www.jewishgen.org/new/

https://www.yadvashem.org/

http://www.bterezin.org.il/

https://www.ushmm.org/

ACKNOWLEDGEMENTS

My research for this book has spanned many decades. Along the way I have been helped by many people whom I wish to thank publicly.

In Prague Julius Müller not only helped me find my long-lost relatives in the National and Boskovice Archives, but also showed me round the city of my father and grandfather; Thomas Schneider came across me while doing his research into the novels of Hermann Ungar and we had great fun trying to break in to the Smíchov Malvazinky cemetary to find Ungar's and Heinrich Stransky's graves. Howard Sidenberg of Twisted Spoon Press, one of Ungar's publishers in English, also helped point me in the right direction, as did Michael Mitchell, translator of Ungar's novels for Dedalus. Finally, in Prague, my heartfelt thanks to Dad's dear friend Hana, and her late husband, Mirek, for their hospitality and guidance on the first stage to uncover my roots all those years ago in 2002.

I owe a great debt to the late Angela Ladd for translating most of Dieter Sudhoff's exhaustive and exhausting tome on *Hermann Ungar: Life and Works*. Deep thanks also to Miroslav Imbrisevic who patiently translated articles, letters, diaries, poems by and about my grandfather from German into English and my great-uncle Max Ungar's memoir. The late Mike Coles also helped with some of the academic article translations.

In Boskovice I was guided and supported by the late Dr Jaroslav

Bránský, who was my father's playmate as a child and was the last great Ungar expert. He generously shared his research on my family tree, photographs and anecdotes, and showed us the family graves when we visited him. Bránský alerted me to Max Ungar's memoir, and Hans Wellisch kindly forwarded me the first part of it which enabled me to track down the rest. It gives a unique insight into life in the Boskovice ghetto at the end of the nineteenth century. Thanks also to Jaroslav Klenovsky, the Jewish cemetery expert from Brno, who accompanied Bonnie, Julius and me around the graveyard and the town on my last visit.

Thanks also to my cousins Helen Stransky, Kitty Strauss and her son Eran, for providing documents and information which have helped unravel the fate of our families and for entertaining me in Israel. Thanks also to Leorah Kroyanker, Gustav Krojanker's daughter-in-law, who set up my visit to the Jewish National Archive in Jerusalem despite a broken arm, and has provided photographs and information.

None of this would have been possible without the help of the websites JewishGen, myheritage.com and geni.com. Thanks also to Randolph Schoenberg, administrator and resource extraordinaire on matters genealogical, for helping me with various queries during my research. To Shaul Sharoni at Yad Vashem, who provided the link to Kitty and to many of the testimonies on their Holocaust database, another big thank you; and to Arthur Berger who directed me to Steven Vitto of the United States Holocaust Memorial Museum, who sent me their records of Richard Kohn, Pauline Stransky and various other relatives.

I am so grateful to the various professionals and friends who have helped steer me along the way and offered great advice and encouragement: to Joanna Frank, Sarah Helm and Fiona Walford who read early drafts and outlines; to the two Richards, Tomlinson and Collins, respectively my private editor and my Unbound editor, for knocking it all into shape and asking the important questions about chronology and context. Richard T in particular provided enormous constructive and emotional support when the going was tough. Thanks to my in-house editors Imogen Denny and Martha Sprackland who remained calm when dealing with an anxious (must be those genes!) ex-publisher prone to impatience; to Penny Butler who transcribed all my mum's Africa letters; to publishers Alan Samson and Richard Charkin, who urged me on and gave sound advice. And not forgetting Joelle Owusu who commissioned the book when I was beginning to lose heart. Thank you!

I am indebted to each and everyone of my subscribers whose names are included here, as well as those who prefer to remain anonymous. Your generosity has been an inspiration and a comfort.

My biggest supporters have been my family: Ross who has put up with me and this project for so long, and scanned and photo-shopped all the pictures with his unflagging good humour; and our son Tommy for being so cheerful throughout these past difficult years without Louise, whose spirit has inspired and guided me to the finish line. She would have been so thrilled to discover all the things she wanted to know about our past.

But most of all my thanks to my sister, Bonnie, who has encouraged me throughout. The book is my gift to her and her children to make up for the absence of a father, grandfather and great-grandfather for so many decades.

Unbound is the world's first crowdfunding publisher, established in 2011.

We believe that wonderful things can happen when you clear a path for people who share a passion. That's why we've built a platform that brings together readers and authors to crowdfund books they believe in – and give fresh ideas that don't fit the traditional mould the chance they deserve.

This book is in your hands because readers made it possible. Everyone who pledged their support is listed below. Join them by visiting unbound.com and supporting a book today.

Super patron
Ross Cattell

Patron
Bonnie Fogel

Supporters

'Nise

Grant Cameron Anthony

Mark Armour

Linda Aspey

Robert M Atwater

Mackie Bahrami

Jenny Balfour Paul

Jane Barclay

John Barker

Judy Bastyra

Nigel Batchelor

Steve and Helen Batchelor

Shahin Bekhradnia

Lynsey Bell

Meredith Bell

John Benson

Sarah Berger

Simon Berthon

Ann Birrell

Jennie Bonnalie

Lizzie Bowen

Patrick Brooks

Fergus Brownlee

Kate Buckley Weber

Catherine Bunting

Maggie Butcher and Robert Vas Dias

Penny Butler

Cass and Etti

Caroline Cattell

Pat and Bill Cattell

Ross Cattell

Sheila Cattell

Tommy Cattell

Christine Cattell de Oyarzun

Susan & Iain Cheyne

Rita Clifton

Pam Clover

Mary Cooke

Clare Cooper

Eileen Cooper

Mary Corby

Flo Coughlan

Bill Critchley

James Currey

Stephen and Alyson Currid

Sarah Curtis

Anna Davies

Linda Davies

Eira Day

Caroline De La Bedoyere

Nick Denton

Gilpatrick Devlin

Anne Duke

Nancy Durrell McKenna

Jane & Tony Elliot

Sharon Epstein

Tilly Flaux

Rebecca Fleet

Stuart Fletcher

Bonnie Fogel

David Fogel

Adela Forestier-Walker

David Forster

Nick Forster

Sabine Gardener

Liz Gerschel

Jill Geser

Sarah Gilmour

Philippa Gimlette

Janet Gourand

Jean Goutchkoff

Adam Grainger

Susan Grant

Barbara H

Tim Hailstone

Elizabeth Hannaford

Robin Harrison

Amanda Hickey

Jane Hindley

Deborah Hodges Maschietto	James McConnel
Robyn Hollingworth	Cyril Megret
Roger Hooper	Jean-Daniel Mégret
Tim Howarth	Marion Milne
Darren Hutchins	David Mitchell
Tom Hutchon	John Mitchinson
Judy Hyman	James Moon
Miroslav Imbrisevic	Matt Morris
Paul Jackson	Claire Morton
Azmina and Jan Janmohamed	Robin Mulvihill
Sandrine Jensen	Ercan Murat
Annie Jermain	Susheila Nasta
Jo and Peter	Carlo Navato
Kirsty Johnston	Tim & Ann Nettleton
John Paul Jones	Sue Nieland
John Kelly	Alastair and Helen Niven
Olivia Kesner	Ann Marie Nugent
Dan Kieran	Brigid O Connor
Jan King	Louise Olivier
Henrietta Knight	Samira Osman
Joseph Koniak	Joelle Owusu-Sekyere
Katya Krausova	Catherine Paice
Leorah Kroyanker	Midge Palley
Christa Lancaster	Alexandra Palmer
Susan Lawrence	Anthony Palmer
Sandra Lawson	Ashly Payne
B Lerner	Esme Pears
Richard Lewin	Fiona Pearson
Jane & Alastair Macduff	William Pike and Cathy Watson
Lino Mannocci	Dick Playfair
Clare Mansfield	Justin Pollard

Hilary Pooler
Caroline Powell
Neville Purssell
Adarsh Radia
Priti Raja
Radhika Rani
Matt RB
Louise Rice
Jo-Anne Richards
Jane Richardson
Bev Rickett
Simon Rigby
Amanda Roberts
Missy Russell
Lynda Sale
Jeremy Sare
Anne Sebba
Ingrid Selberg
Mary-Ann Sheehy
Erica Shelton
Martin Shenfield
Alastair Short
John Siebert
Smith College London Book
    Club
Zachery Stephenson
Maryon Stewart
Bill Stokoe

Eran Strauss
Tom Streetley
Elizabeth Sturgeon
Sabiha Sultan
Annie Tempest
Cindy Thomas
Natalie Trotter-King
Kim Turzynski
John Unwin
Arabella van Niekerk
Diana Von Rettig
Janet Voute
Victoria Waldock
Eliza Walter
Fiona Walter
Fiona Walter and Richard
    Walford
Daniel Wanek
Natalie Warren-Green
Stephen Warshaw
Anne Webber
James Wellesley Wesley
Melanie West
Caroline Whalley
Francis Wheen
Robert Wilson
Jane Winehouse